Fathers Work for Their Sons

Fathers Work for Their Sons

Accumulation, Mobility, and Class Formation in an Extended Yorùbá Community

Sara Berry

UNIVERSITY OF CALIFORNIA PRESS
Berkeley   Los Angeles   London

University of California Press
Berkeley and Los Angeles, California

University of California Press, Ltd.
London, England

Copyright © 1985 by The Regents of the University of California

Library of Congress Cataloging in Publication Data

Berry, Sara.
    Fathers work for their sons.

    Bibliography: p. 207
    Includes index.
    1. Yorubas—Economic conditions. 2. Yorubas—Social conditions.
3. Cocoa trade—Nigeria. I. Title.
DT515.45.Y67B47 1984   306'.089963   84–122
ISBN 0–520–05164–5

Printed in the United States of America

1 2 3 4 5 6 7 8 9

For my children
Rachel and Jonathan

Formerly, sons worked for their fathers,
but today we have schools and civilization,
and now fathers work for their sons.
                    —A Yorùbá farmer, 1966

Contents

Acknowledgments

Research for this study, supported by grants from the Ford-Rockefeller Research Program on Population and Development Policy and from the National Science Foundation, was made possible by the University of Ifẹ̀ where I was a member of the Economics Department in 1978–79 while undertaking fieldwork. I am particularly grateful to Professor Ọ̀jẹ́túnjí Abóyadé, then vice-chancellor, for arranging my affiliation with the university; to Professor R. O. Ekúndáre and my colleagues in the Economics Department for providing a hospitable environment in which to work; to Dr. Dípèolú and the staff of the University of Ifẹ̀ Library for unfailing and courteous assistance in facilitating my research; and to many other members of staff who contributed to making my stay in Ifẹ̀ pleasant and productive.

In collecting material for this study, I drew on the patience and generosity of literally hundreds of people, who welcomed me into their homes, shared their recollections and knowledge with me, invited me to participate in meetings and ceremonies, and sometimes fed and sheltered me as well. For such kindness and cooperation, I owe a profound debt of gratitude to the chiefs and the people of Ìreé, Ẹripa, and the villages I have called Abàkinní and Abúlékejì; to the officers and members of the Ifẹ̀ Mechanics Association, the Ifẹ̀ branch of the Nigeria Union of Teachers Thrift and Credit Society, the Ìreé Progressive Union, and the Ìreé Youth Movement; and to individuals too numerous to name. I do, however, want to mention several people who went out of their way to facilitate my inquiries and whose friendship gave special meaning to my work. They include Professor and Mrs. A. Afọláyan, J. O. Ògúnránti, Oba M. O. Ọmọ́tọ́sọ, Dr. S. O. Ọmọ́tọ́sọ, S. O. Àlàbí, M. O. Àjàyí, Bálẹ̀ Ògúnwọbí, Mrs. R. Ògùnwọbí, Y. Adébíyi, P. Ìdòwú, and A. Awóyalé. Also it is a special pleasure to acknowledge the untiring efforts of my research assistants, Francis Ìgè, Israel Oyètúnjí, and Michael Ọládèjọ Afọláyan. They cheerfully accompanied me on innumerable, sometimes inconvenient, quests for information, invariably earned the respect and goodwill of our informants, and often assisted me with their own knowledge and insights, as well as with the labor of field research.

In writing this book, I have been supported by Boston University, which granted me leave of absence in 1978/79 and 1979/80, and by the African Studies Center there, which provided generous assistance in preparing the manuscript, as well as an exceptionally stimulating and congenial environment in which to work. Fred Cooper, Bill Freund, Jane Guyer, John Harris, Gill Hart, Jean Hay, Jeanne Henn, Chris Jones, John Peel, Pauline Peters, and two referees for the University of California Press read all or parts of the manuscript and made many acute and helpful suggestions. None of them, of course, bears any responsibility for the final version of the book. I have also learned a lot about many of the issues addressed herein from students and colleagues affiliated with the African Studies Center. I acknowledge them all with affectionate appreciation, especially Jane Guyer and Fred Cooper who, in very different but equally important ways, have done a great deal to sharpen my thinking about social processes in Africa and to encourage me to get on with my research.

Introduction

Issues and Review of Literature

During the 1970s the rapid growth of Nigeria's petroleum industry was accompanied by dramatic changes in the structure of the economy. In less than a decade agriculture's share of gross domestic product (GDP) declined from a half to less than a third, and its role as generator of state revenues and foreign exchange dwindled to insignificance. By the mid-1970s oil accounted for more than 80 percent of federal revenues and more than 90 percent of Nigeria's foreign exchange earnings. Manufacturing accounted for only 6 percent of GDP at the end of the decade, and neither manufacturing nor mining (whose share of GDP rose from 10 to 25 percent) generated meaningful increases in employment opportunities. Aggregate employment data are too conjectural to cite, but sample surveys and local observations suggest that Nigerians were leaving agricultural pursuits in large numbers. Many found jobs in the rapidly expanding civil service, but even more significant was the proliferation of small-scale private enterprise, comprising mostly commercial, transport, and artisanal businesses engaged in distributing and repairing imported commodities purchased with oil revenues by the state and its clients and employees. By the end of the decade Nigeria had clearly ceased to qualify as a predominantly agrarian economy.[1]

If agriculture no longer dominated the Nigerian economy, however, it was rapidly becoming a serious constraint on Nigerian economic development. Not only did agricultural exports decline absolutely as well as relatively, but domestic supplies failed to keep pace with domestic demand, giving rise to an increase in food imports and rapid inflation. When oil revenues declined, in 1978 for example, the country's need for imported foodstuffs forced even deeper cuts in other imports, which further aggravated inflation and led to bottlenecks in domestic supply. The deterioration of agricultural performance evoked widespread expressions of concern among observers and officials alike, but it brought little effective response from either the Nigerian state or foreign governments and agencies.

That agriculture should become an increasingly significant deterrent to economic development at a time when its aggregate economic importance was declining is perhaps less surprising than at first appears. If we look at processes rather than indicators of structural change,[2] the impact of oil on the Nigerian economy has been less dramatic than the figures suggest. Both state and economy remain heavily dependent on foreign markets and foreign capital; domestic accumulation continues to be mainly commercial rather than industrial; and the state continues to play a major role in the regulation of foreign transactions and the absorption of domestic surplus. As in the colonial period, the state occupies a crucial position vis-à-vis Nigerians' access to foreign markets and resources. Although oil has financed the consolidation and extension of the power of the ruling class, it has not changed the basis on which its power rests. Nor has it altered the structure of Nigerian politics: the perennial demand for the creation of new states simply carries on the pattern of regional and ethnic competition for state-controlled resources which was established under colonial rule and which dominated the history of the First Republic. The growth of petroleum exports served less to bring about structural change than to reveal with unprecedented clarity economic, social, and political processes that have been underway for some time. The current agricultural crisis has been long in the making and, since neither the interests nor the processes that shape state policies toward agriculture have changed fundamentally, it is not surprising that those policies have not changed significantly either.

In the present study I develop this argument with reference to one segment of Nigerian agriculture: the cocoa-producing sector of Ọ̀yọ́ State. This book is a study not of the development of cocoa production per se[3] but rather of its consequences for the structure of the regional political economy and for the processes of accumulation, differentiation, and political conflict which shape that structure. My argument is based on a case study of accumulation and social mobility among Yorùbá cocoa farmers and their descendants. I collected information on the life histories of farmers and farmers' children which enables me to trace changes in the uses of agricultural surplus and to explore their implications for the structure of economic and social relations in western Nigeria, for the character and performance of the economy, and for the terms on which farmers and their descendants have participated in it, both before and after the development of the petroleum industry.

On an empirical level I use histories of individuals and of their communities, institutions, and social movements to elucidate aggregate processes of economic, social, and political change. On a theoretical level the case study forms the basis for a reinterpretation of the nature of accumulation arising from the expansion of export crop production, during and after the colonial period, and the historical relationship among accumulation, differentiation, and political action in western Nigeria.

Both in its method and in its focus on the uses of agricultural surplus, this study departs from much of the existing literature on the place of agriculture and agricultural producers in the political and economic history of western Nigeria. Most studies emphasize levels of production and/or political protest and portray the behavior of farmers, traders, or the state as sets of discrete responses to relatively invariant structural parameters. The prevailing view, among Nigerians and expatriates of all ideological persuasions, is that the Yorùbá farmer has been a victim of unfavorable circumstance. Enterprising, hard-working, and perceptive, farmers are held to be capable of meeting the region's growing needs for foodstuffs, raw materials, and export earnings so long as they are provided with adequate incentives and logistical support (Ọlátúnbọ̀sún, 1975; de Wilde, 1980; Oni, 1971; Onitiri and Ọlátúnbọ̀sún, 1974). For various reasons, however, incentives have become increasingly unfavorable since at least the mid-1950s, and support in the form of improved inputs and infrastructure has not been sufficient. After 1955, for example, when the world market price of cocoa fell steadily for fifteen years, the Marketing Board in Nigeria kept the domestic price consistently below the world price, seeking to protect its own revenues rather than to cushion the impact of world market conditions on domestic producers (Onitiri and Ọlátúnbọ̀sún, 1974; see also Helleiner, 1964). State-sponsored agricultural loans or subsidized inputs usually failed to reach the majority of small cocoa growers, serving instead to benefit a minority of wealthy farmer-traders (Essang, 1970). From 1970 on, production stagnated, rural poverty intensified, and, when the government tried to impose additional taxes on rural producers in the late 1960s, hard-pressed farmers rose in open rebellion against the state (Ayọọla Commission, 1969; Beer, 1976; Beer and Williams, 1975).

Although there is widespread agreement concerning the facts of rural decline, inequality, and state exploitation of agricultural producers in western Nigeria (Bienen and Diejomaoh, 1981; Williams, 1976, 1981), observers are divided over the reasons for the government's choice of policies and the nature of farmers' reactions to them. Efforts to explain the western Nigerian situation in terms of standard paradigms of rural commercialization and state intervention in pre-capitalist agrarian societies are not entirely convincing. Arguing, for example, that Yorùbá farmers are as "responsive" to market incentives as any, some economists have criticized the state for failing to raise producer prices in order to promote faster and more balanced economic growth and to forestall growing inequality and political unrest (Qlátúnbọ̀sún, 1975; de Wilde, 1980). In fact, there is little evidence that short-term responsiveness to price is sufficient to explain long-term trends in output, or that rapid agricultural growth is conducive to rural equality.[4] Nor does the neoclassical paradigm explain why, if it is both possible and desirable to improve agricultural performance by restructuring producer prices, the government does not simply get on with it.[5]

Studies that seek to explain farmer-state relations in terms of the structure of peasant society also leave important questions unanswered. It is sometimes argued that the spread of cocoa cultivation created a peasantry in western Nigeria, in the sense of a class of small, relatively undifferentiated farming households, dependent on external agencies for the terms on which they exchange their products for commodities and services and increasingly conscious of their common oppression at the hands of the ruling class. In this view, the Àgbẹ́kọ̀yà uprisings of 1968 and 1969 were a manifestation of peasants' solidarity in the face of state exploitation and of their determination to defend their "way of life" against external oppression (Beer and Williams, 1975). Yorùbá cocoa farming households, however, are anything but self-sufficient, nor are farmers particularly committed to remaining peasants. Even holders of small plots of cocoa normally purchase most of what they consume (Galletti et al., 1956) and, as we shall see in subsequent chapters, most farmers look upon cocoa as a means to upward mobility rather than as a way of life. State exploitation is resented because it constrains farmers' ability to accumulate and to diversify their activities, rather than because it threatens to disrupt the stability and autonomy of village life. Indeed, in the changing economic circumstances of the 1970s peasant militancy virtually disappeared, as farmers channeled their political energies in apparently more promising directions.

If Yorùbá farmers cannot be described as a Chayanovian peasantry, however, neither does their history correspond to the Leninist paradigm of agrarian capitalism (Lenin, 1966; Banaji, 1976), nor to de Janvry's (1982) notion of "functional dualism." Agricultural commercialization has generated increasing inequality among Yorùbá farmers (Galletti et al., 1956; Essang, 1970; van den Driesen, 1971; Williams, 1981), but it has not divided rural society into agrarian bourgeoisie and proletariat. Successful farmers tend to diversify their assets rather than to acquire large farms, whereas most agricultural labor in the cocoa economy is supplied by people with farms or other enterprises of their own (Berry, 1975b). Differentiation within the cocoa-growing sector has more to do with farmers' differential links to the regional political economy as a whole than with differential access to rural land and agricultural capital (Essang, 1970). Many farmers suffered declining incomes during the 1970s because of the impact of oil wealth on the structure of opportunities in the regional economy (see chaps. 3 and 4, below). There is, however, nothing functional about rural poverty or the forms of accumulation out of agricultural surplus in western Nigeria, from the viewpoint either of the Nigerian ruling class or of foreign capitalists. The commercialization of agriculture has been shaped by and has contributed to a developing national division of labor comparable to, but hardly identical with, patterns of capitalist development in other parts of the world.

Finally, neither Marxist nor liberal conceptions of the state suffice to explain the particular relation of state programs and patterns of accumulation to the history of agrarian expansion and decline in western Nigeria. If, as some Marxists have argued, the Nigerian state is essentially an agent of the accumulating classes (foreign and/or indigenous), why has it not acted more consistently in their interests by, for example, expanding agricultural production in order to reduce commodity prices and the socially necessary cost of labor? On the other hand, cliental models of the state—which recognize that many members of the Yorùbá ruling class are children of peasants and workers and that they rely on the loyalty of their kith and kin to achieve and maintain positions of power—remain unclear as to just how patronage affects differentiation or the forms of state intervention in economic activity (Joseph, 1978; Turner, 1978). If powerful patrons need to reward their clients, why has this not led to a more equal distribution of wealth or to larger increases in production and investment by farmers and other small-scale entrepreneurs?

Accumulation, Class Formation, and Sectional Conflict: Argument of the Book

To understand agrarian change and its place in the development of the political economy in western Nigeria, we need to know not only how agricultural production and marketing were organized and how they grew, but also what was done with the surplus generated by rising agricultural output and sales. My argument in this book centers on an analysis of the forms of accumulation out of agricultural surplus and their consequences for the development of the forces and relations of production in the regional economy. I understand accumulation to encompass the use of resources to maintain or alter conditions of production (i.e., techniques, organization of productive activity, and conditions of access to productive resources) as well as to replenish or increase the stock of reproducible capital goods. Because the conditions of production include relations among people—which are shaped, in turn, by legal and political processes, as well as by material conditions and cultural norms and practices—the study of accumulation illuminates interrelations between economic change per se and processes of differentiation, class formation, and political mobilization.

The argument in brief.—In approaching the relationship between economic activity and social organization as a dialectical one, in which material processes shape and are transformed by people's struggles over access to productive resources and control of productive processes, the present study may be said to follow a Marxist approach. Yet my analysis of economic and social change in western Nigeria differs both from Marx's theory of capitalist development and from much of the recent Marxist literature on the articulation of capitalist and precapitalist modes of production in Africa. Because capital accumulation in western Nigeria has taken place in a different political and legal context from the one that obtained in Europe on the eve of the industrial revolution, accumulators in Africa have faced different conditions of access to the means of production which have, in turn, affected the forms of accumulation and the structure of class interests and conflict. Many Marxist writers have attempted to conceptualize the specific process of capitalist development in Africa in terms of the articulation of modes of production (Wolpe, 1980; Rey, 1973; Meillassoux, 1972, 1981; see also Foster-Carter, 1978). In doing so they have treated modes of production as structural entities rather than as historical conjunctures of material conditions and social relations, and they have, accordingly, found it difficult to explain social transformations. In contrast, in the present study I seek to unravel the ways in which people at different levels of social agency have mobilized and organized resources, allies, and ideas in a continuous effort to cope with changing circumstances. The task of analysis is complicated by the fact that the course of social transformation is never determined by the strategies of a single group but arises from struggles among many.

For Marx, capitalism was founded on the historical separation of workers from the means of production, which permitted capitalists to exploit them through voluntary wage employment. Accumulation arose from the profits of exploitation, but it was threatened by its own success: increased investment raised the demand for labor and tended to bid up the wage rate, thus reducing the rate of profit. To escape this dilemma capitalists developed laborsaving methods of production which kept wages down by throwing people out of work, into "the reserve army of the unemployed." The contradictions of capitalist accumulation thus led both to increased productivity and to mounting class tension, struggle, and crisis. In western Nigeria, as in many other parts of Africa, the penetration of foreign capital under the aegis of European imperialism drew Africans irreversibly into production for both world and local markets, and into centralized political systems, but it did not dispossess them. People were exploited through commodities markets and by administrative fiat (e.g., taxation, labor requisitions, penal codes, etc.), but they retained access to land, labor, and some forms of credit.

Access to the means of production was usually mediated through membership in various preexisting social units, which not only were tolerated by colonial officials, as long as their leaders professed loyalty to the colonizers, but often were deliberately incorporated into the colonial administrative apparatus. Indeed, precolonial social units and institutions took on added significance under colonial rule as channels of access to productive resources and opportunities controlled by the colonial state, as well as to local land and labor. Consequently, Africans often invested considerable effort and resources to ensure or advance their status within kin groups or local polities. This pattern of accumulation served, in turn, to divert investable surplus from more directly productive activities and to promote strategies of management and labor control which, as we shall see, favored the proliferation of small-scale enterprise but impeded the growth of labor productivity. The central contradiction of accumulation in western Nigeria was not that expansion led to declining profits through increased demand for labor, but rather that it gave rise to expanded reproduction of certain forms of social relations which inhibited the development of the forces of production (cf. Teríba et al., 1972).

To understand why accumulation has often taken unproductive forms, and how this has affected the structure of class interests and social conflict in western Nigeria, it is necessary to look in more detail at historical interactions among commercialization, colonial policy, and Yorùbá strategies of resource acquisition and use. Most of this book presents evidence from a detailed study of life histories of resource acquisition and use among descendants of a single Yorùbá community. Before turning to the historical material, however, it is useful to spell out more fully the general argument derived from it, both to assist the reader in following the empirical chapters and to place the argument of this study in a broader context. In particular, I wish to show how the argument bears on the larger debate over the relationship between kinship and class in African social change and on the articulation of capitalism with precapitalist economic and social processes.

Kinship, capital accumulation, and colonial rule.—In precolonial times Yorùbás gained access to the means of production through membership in such social units as houses,[6] lineages, towns, or kingdoms, and access was in turn governed by the principles and practices of authority and distribution obtaining within them. As in many African societies, the boundaries and organization of Yorùbá social units were frequently delineated in terms of kinship. Relations so defined were not limited to those of agnatic descent, however, but encompassed individuals or groups of people linked by marriage, adoption, conquest, settlement, patronage, or mutual consent. In Yorùbá parlance, the statement that a person is a "child" of such and such a lineage, house, or community may apply to people of quite varied ancestry and origins (Barber, 1979; Peel, forthcoming).

Just as membership in a Yorùbá kin group or community could be negotiated as well as inherited, so could rights of access to productive resources. Control over cultivable land was usually vested in lineages or lineage segments (Lloyd, 1962) and lineage members were theoretically assured of access to it. Individuals could also obtain rights to cultivate land controlled by other lineages so long as they agreed to respect the rights and the authority of the grantor lineage's head. Similarly, individuals could attach themselves to communities other than their places of origin and, in the process, obtain rights not only to cultivate local land but also to allocate it to others.

In precolonial Yorùbá society relations of authority and subordination were organized in terms of seniority. People of junior status owed service, obedience, and loyalty to their seniors, both within and beyond their immediate household or descent group. Juniors' obligations included labor services, in return for which they could expect both maintenance and protection. Seniority, in turn, was not based solely on age, sex, or demographic status; it could also be achieved, principally by demonstrating one's ability to command the loyalty and service of others. The relationship between seniority and wealth or status was thus a dialectical one: seniority conveyed authority and access to the productive services of others but was also dependent on them. A chief, an elder, or a "big man" who failed to satisfy his subordinates' expectations ran the risk of losing their support and, in consequence, much of his own influence and/or wealth. In short, differential access to the means of production was defined in terms of kinship and seniority, and it also helped to define them.

The colonial order both reinforced and altered preexisting relations of power and production in Yorùbá society. The colonial economy offered people new opportunities for production, trade, and wage employment, many of them geared toward foreign markets. Access to world markets was, in turn, mediated by the colonial state. The imposition of colonial rule not only subordinated formerly independent Yorùbá polities to a new structure of centralized authority but also rendered them dependent on that structure for access to an increasingly important source of economic opportunity. The role of the state in controlling access to the means of production has expanded since independence, both because of the rapid growth of foreign trade and because of increasing efforts by postcolonial regimes to control and manage the domestic economy.

Access to the state may, in turn, be pursued in various ways. The colonial authorities in Nigeria depended on the spread of local commerce and export production to create a taxable surplus. They were anxious to promote local political stability, both to facilitate trade and to minimize the costs of administration. To this end they sought to co-opt local chiefs into the colonial administrative system and to preserve local systems of law and authority, so long as these systems did not conflict with commercial expansion and administrative convenience. In practice, established Yorùbá polities were not simply frozen within an overarching colonial framework. Colonial officials intervened actively in the appointment and deposition of chiefs, created their own institutions for the enforcement of "native law and custom," redefined political jurisdictions, and imposed their own standards of social conduct on chiefs and people alike. Moreover, in western Nigeria the very principle of preserving local structures and practices implied change. Because status and authority rested on achievement as well as on age or ancestry, the emergence of new social and economic opportunities in the colonial period created new means of access to seniority or traditional offices as well as new channels of upward mobility. People who acquired wealth and influence through commerce or education could thereby enhance their positions within kin groups or local polities. Their inclination to do so was strengthened by the fact that Yorùbá chiefs, as local agents of the colonial state, could to some extent mediate their subordinates' access to resources controlled by the state. Thus, access to the state could be pursued by participating directly in trade, government employment, or, after 1952, regional politics, and by investing in traditional forms of power and privilege.

Indeed, it was not only possible but also necessary for Yorùbás to seek wealth and power through both traditional and colonial avenues. Because colonial policy upheld the power of lineage heads and title-holders to regulate access to resources, accumulators were obliged to preserve good relations with traditional authorities, or even to assume such offices themselves. People at all socioeconomic levels have found it advantageous to participate actively in kin-group and community affairs, to compete for traditional titles, and to develop relations of patronage with nonkin patterned on the principle of seniority, both to increase and to defend their access to the means of production. Seniority and patronage have become objects as well as instruments of accumulation in western Nigeria, and a substantial part of the investable surplus created by agricultural and commercial expansion has been directed toward reproducing such social relations (Williams and Turner, 1978). Often this practice required outlays on consumption (for entertainment, ceremonies, or maintaining dependents) or underutilized structures (e.g., a house in one's ancestral town) rather than on productive equipment.

The structure of opportunities and the conditions of access to the means of production which developed in western Nigeria during and after colonial rule have affected not only the allocation of surplus but also the organization of productive activity. Because workers have alternatives to wage employment, including access to the resources of senior kin or other patrons, accumulators must act as patrons in order to recruit and retain laborers. If agricultural laborers feel themselves inadequately rewarded—in kind, in cash, or in prospects of future assistance and patronage—they can and do leave the farm in search of more obliging employers. The same is true of workers outside agriculture: because wage rates are relatively high and cash incomes uncertain, most small-scale traders and artisans rely on apprentices, who are not paid but must be sponsored, and who will also leave if not reasonably satisfied with the conditions of their employment. Under these circumstances it is difficult to force apprentices to work efficiently, and personal supervision by the master is usually necessary to get them to work at all. The expansion of a firm, however, is often directly related to the amount of time and energy the proprietor spends away from the shop, cultivating good relations with potential customers, creditors, and bureaucrats who control access to key resources. Thus the entrepreneur faces a contradiction between developing his enterprise and keeping it running. Expansion of a firm often undermines its performance, both in farming and outside it.

We are now in a position to explain more clearly how the process of accumulation in western Nigeria differs from the standard Marxist paradigm of capitalist accumulation. Because colonial policy and practice tended to protect Africans' access to land and labor, most Yorùbás were not compelled to work for wages in order to subsist. People sought employment as a means to future accumulation rather than survival. The spread of commercial activity and wage employment in the early years of colonial rule provided many ordinary farmers with the means to engage in cocoa production or expanded commercial enterprise (Berry, 1975a; Peel, in press). But many people without financial resources were also able to mobilize labor among their juniors in exchange for future assistance in establishing farms or other enterprises of their own rather than for cash wages. This permitted many people to launch farms or other small businesses without prior access to working capital, but it also placed limits on their ability to control labor and expand their enterprises.

As patrons, employers could expect loyalty and obedience from their workers, but not necessarily efficiency. In addition, entrepreneurs, to be successful, had to devote both money and their own time to cultivating the patronage of customers and creditors and to ensuring the protection of political authorities. These activities diverted profits from the purchase of productive equipment and tended to take proprietors away from their shops, thereby reducing the time they spent personally supervising their workers. Thus the conditions of accumulation favored the proliferation of small-scale enterprise but militated against the development of labor productivity. In a capitalist economy accumulation promotes increased productivity and labor is kept both cheap and manageable through the threat of unemployment, but in western Nigeria accumulation led to the proliferation of patronage relations and small-scale enterprises, which absorb surplus labor but keep levels of productivity low. Workers are recruited, not from a reserve army of the unemployed, but from a pool of would-be accumulators whose contribution to the development of the forces of production is undermined by the strategies of accumulation they seek to emulate, and whose labor is cheap because it is unproductive.

Implications of the argument: class formation and the state.—Marxist writings on Africa have demonstrated that articulation between capitalist and precapitalist modes of production can take many forms (Kitching, 1980; Cowen, 1981; Rey, 1973, 1979), and Rey in particular has moved toward a clearer conceptualization of the underlying process (see also Lonsdale and Berman, 1978; Berman and Lonsdale, 1980). In a recent article Rey (1979) shows how changes in material conditions give rise to struggles over the control of resources and their use, which may lead to a restructuring of social relations within lineages or lineage-based societies. As we have seen, agricultural commercialization created new opportunities in western Nigeria for production and employment which threatened to upset traditional authorities' control over the assets and the loyalty of their subordinates. However, the ensuing struggles to turn these opportunities to advantage were not, as Rey implies, confined within the boundaries of lineages or traditional communities. Yorùbás sought access to economic opportunities and the means of production within and beyond their kin groups ánd communities of origin, while colonial officials were attempting simultaneously to consolidate their financial and political position by co-opting established institutions and authorities. In the process, capitalist penetration and colonial rule neither destroyed nor subsumed intact precolonial Yorùbá social units but operated both to reproduce and to transform them, giving rise to a pattern of class interests and struggles specific to the conditions of resource acquisition and use in the regional political economy.

In the rural sector the growth of agricultural production for export created a mass of small-scale commercial farmers, but not a class of self-reproducing peasant households. Because juniors worked on their senior kinsmen's farms in return for future assistance in establishing independent farms or other enterprises of their own, over time individuals tended to cycle in and out of a given farming enterprise, and often in and out of the farmer's household as well. The same thing was true of capital. Even in colonial times, although the spread of cocoa growing and commercial food-crop production created widespread opportunities for modest increases in income, the best opportunities for accumulation lay not in agriculture but in trade, the professions, and the civil service. Hence, agricultural surplus was often invested in nonagricultural enterprises (or in education), and successful farmers (or their children) tended to leave farming in pursuit of wealth and influence in the wider regional economy. Even hired laborers, who often had farms or other resources, moved in and out of agricultural employment on a casual or seasonal basis, in search of cash rather than subsistence. Thus the commercialization of agriculture created neither a peasantry nor a stable rural structure of agricultural capitalists and proletarians; rather, it facilitated participation by farmers and their descendants in the emerging regional and national division of labor.

The structure of class relations in the regional economy was, however, rooted in specific local conditions of production and accumulation. These were defined not by the predominance of agriculture but rather by the particular history of legal and political struggles over access to power and resources during and after the colonial period. As we have seen, relations of production in the colonial economy were founded on patronage and seniority, rather than superseding them. This did not guarantee, however, that assets and income would be distributed in egalitarian ways or that collective welfare would take precedence over individual aggrandizement in the allocation of productive resources. New sources of wealth were used both to acquire traditional forms of authority and to exploit them. Chiefs have appropriated newly valuable land or the savings of their subordinates in the name of traditional prerogatives; successful merchants and professionals have exploited or expropriated their poor relations in the name of kinship solidarity.

The fact that kinsmen or patrons and clients depend on one another for services and support may mask but does not alleviate the tensions arising from differential access to wealth and power. In a capitalist system tension arises between bourgeoisie and proletariat because labor and capital are both needed for production: each class must have access to the resources of the other in order to survive and prosper. In a society like that of western Nigeria, where access to the means of production and the organization of productive activity operate primarily through relations of seniority and clientage, the differential advantages of patron and client (or seniors and juniors) lead to tension because of their interdependence. Capitalist penetration has not obliterated established principles of solidarity and differentiation, but it has created new contradictions within them. People do not choose between relations of kinship and those of class, depending on immediate circumstance (as pluralist models suggest), but pursue the interests of each in terms of the other.

In this context class relations are based partly, but not exclusively, on differential access to the state. Politicians, senior civil servants, and military officers exercise a great deal of power over access to foreign and domestic capital and markets, and they have used this power both to accumulate large fortunes and to consolidate their control of the economy. Both endeavors have been strengthened by the growth of oil exports, which have brought money into the Nigerian economy at an unprecedented rate and are easily controlled by the government. Exploitation in the Nigerian economy occurs not so much through the labor market (indeed, very little labor is needed to create oil revenues) as through a burgeoning de facto market in government contracts, licenses, and offices. Corruption is not a matter of personal ethics but a central mechanism of resource allocation and control (Turner, 1978; Joseph, 1978).

The mechanisms and the strategies the state class has employed to reproduce itself are often incorporative rather than exclusive in nature. Education, for example, has become increasingly important as a criterion for recruiting people into the ruling class, and the educational qualifications for entry into the senior civil service or political leadership have risen as competition for entry into the ruling class has intensified. This very process has, however, also increased popular pressure for the expansion of educational opportunities, and the government has invested heavily in all levels of education, as much to forestall social unrest as to "modernize" the economy (see Abernethy, 1969). Similarly, sectional political mobilization and conflict serve not so much to redistribute state resources across class lines as to divide the ruling class into warring factions and divert surplus into the proliferation of patronage ties and sectional affiliations rather than into productive forms of investment. A concrete example is the practice of periodically creating new states within Nigeria's federal structure. Each state requires substantial outlays on administrative structures and personnel, while serving only to perpetuate jurisdictional competition for access to the federal government.

To prevent open conflict and organized assaults on its own position, as well as to consolidate control over the development of the economy and over opportunities for accumulation, the federal government has steadily expanded its domain, centralizing control over public revenue, imposing controls and regulations on many aspects of economic and social life, and even absorbing whole sectors of the economy, together with their internal class divisions and tensions (see chap. 5, below). In using the machinery of the state to manage the economy and to reproduce itself, the state class has thus succeeded largely in incorporating social tensions rather than dissipating them. The contradictions of this process are analogous to those pointed out by Albert Hirschman (1958) in an early critique of the theory and practice of development planning. To satisfy their constituents' demands for economic growth and rising standards of living, Third World governments are often obliged to assume responsibility for investment in infrastructure and outlays for public welfare. In the process they have "internalized" many of the social costs of industrialization which, in nineteenth-century Europe or North America, were left to private enterprise or simply ignored. In return, governments of today's underdeveloped economies have faced political pressures and protests which interfere with the implementation of state investment plans (see Lofchie, 1971). In western Nigeria the state has internalized not only the external costs of economic growth but the entire process of class formation. The result has been a kind of explosive paralysis: the state is not free to act either as an untrammeled agent of the accumulating class or as an arbiter of class conflict; instead, it tends to reproduce simultaneous impulses toward class division, unproductive accumulation, and sectional conflict—and is rocked periodically by the resulting upheavals.

Method

In the chapters that follow I illustrate and amplify the processes of accumulation, differentiation, and collective action outlined above by tracing the histories of men and women who have lived through and participated in them. My decision to undertake the fieldwork on which this book is based was made partly out of dissatisfaction with my own previous research which, confined as it was to the cocoa-producing areas per se, was thus based on the presumption that most of the significant determinants and consequences of the development of cocoa production occurred within the rural areas where the crop was grown. The inadequacy of this assumption became clear as I proceeded. Especially in the eastern half of the cocoa belt, the majority of cocoa farmers were immigrants whose continuing relations with their home communities played an important part in the way they allocated resources and organized their family lives and political activities (Berry, 1975a; Olúsànyà et al., 1978). Also, most farmers were extensively engaged in commercial transactions and political activities governed by people and interests external to the farming sector, and many of their children were said to be leaving their parents' farms for urban residence and employment. To understand developments within the cocoa economy, as well as its links to regional processes of economic, social, and political change, I decided that it would be necessary to investigate those links directly.

Thus, in the present study I have extended the scope of my inquiry from the cocoa villages to the regional political economy as a whole. In doing so, however, I did not wish to work only with aggregate data but wanted rather to try to bring the richness and immediacy of individuals' experiences to bear on understanding the historical processes in which they were involved. To this end I set out to collect individual life histories of mobility and accumulation and to observe patterns of social interaction among men and women in different occupational, institutional, and socioeconomic niches within the regional economy.

I began fieldwork in two cocoa-farming villages (which I call Abàkinní and Abúlékejì) about twenty miles southeast of Ifè. One of them was a village I had studied in 1970–71. Most of this area was planted in cocoa between the late 1940s and early 1960s by farmers who migrated after 1945 from Yorùbá communities in the savannah to the forest belt to plant cocoa. In each village I took a census of residents and their emigrant children. (In Abúlékejì, the village I had studied in 1970–71, this procedure enabled me to document patterns of migration and occupational change over most of a decade.) In addition, I collected individual life histories from some sixty men and women, and I also attempted to map out and observe the major institutional networks and linkages in which they regularly participated. These included institutions (households, kinship networks, enterprises, government agencies, and various religious, recreational, and political associations) within the village as well as outside it. In the latter case I focused in particular on farmers' relationships to different markets and marketing institutions, on their continued ties with their hometowns, and on the whereabouts and occupations of their emigrant children.

In the second stage of the research I followed up some of these extravillage connections. Most of the farmers in Abúlékejì came from two neighboring communities on the edge of the savannah, Ẹripa and Ìreé. In December, when many farmers pay annual visits to their hometowns, I accompanied some of my informants and eventually spent quite a bit of time collecting information on the history of community development efforts, especially in Ìreé, and on patterns of emigrants' participation in hometown affairs. This effort meant tracking down a number of prominent and/or knowledgeable "sons" of the town in villages and towns throughout western Nigeria—including a few successful businessmen and professionals living in Lagos—as well as conducting numerous interviews and attending public functions within the town itself. I also selected two occupations common among farmers' emigrant children—schoolteaching and motor repair—and carried out small-scale studies of people practicing these occupations in Ifẹ̀, Òṣogbo, and a few smaller towns. As in the village, I sought to combine individual life histories with observations of networks and institutions in which my informants were involved. In working with motor mechanics, I first gained an introduction to the leaders of the Ifẹ̀ Mechanics' Association, attended a number of meetings, and then approached individual mechanics who had become familiar with me through the association. The teachers interviewed were all employed in schools attended or staffed, in part, by emigrants from the same savannah towns as my rural informants. Thus, in both the design of the field research and the selection of informants, I sought to observe from various angles the "extended" community of emigrants from a single Yorùbá town,[7] as well as to tap into various strata of the regional economy and society.

I made no effort in my research to generate data that would be statistically representative of any particular segments of Yorùbá society. Apart from the formidable logistical problems of designing and managing good sample surveys in Nigeria, I felt that I would learn more about the workings of economic and social change by getting to know some of the people concerned than by trying to construct a random sample of informants and using other people as interviewers. Thus I deliberately limited my research to a small number of informants (ca. 160 in all) and a particular extended community.

Taken together, my informants' histories of spatial and occupational mobility, social relations, resource use, and political activity provide a chronicle of class formation and of the growing influence of class differences and class interests on the daily lives and life chances of Yorùbá men and women. My evidence tends to confirm the well-known points that, while the social origins of many of the Yorùbá elite lie in the agrarian sector, the majority of cocoa farmers' descendants have not risen to elite status or entered the ruling class. Imoagene (1976) and others have shown that many of the politicians, civil servants, and wealthy businessmen of postcolonial western Nigeria were the children of cocoa farmers or of small-scale traders and artisans. Similarly, my evidence includes cases of farmers' sons who hold important positions in the government or operate highly profitable businesses in or near Lagos. The majority of the rural emigrants I studied, however, were not much better off than their parents or any closer to positions of power. A significant minority did earn more than their parents had, but their incomes were still a long way from the highest levels in the region. These people included secondary school teachers, middle-level civil servants, and self-employed professionals. By tracing their histories, comparing their strategies and experiences with those of their parents, and observing relations among parents and children within households, kin groups, and local communities, I have tried to illustrate the implications of class formation for the majority of Yorùbás who are neither very poor nor very rich, but somewhere in between.

Plan of the Book

Although this study is predicated on the belief that social processes are neither weighted sums of individual behaviors nor logical consequences of structural parameters, but that they arise from people's actions, struggles, and alliances, both within and between different levels of social agency, it is impracticable to discuss all the relevant social levels at once. Accordingly, I begin my narrative by sketching developments in the regional political economy of western Nigeria, during and after the colonial period (chap. l); move on in chapter 2 to the history of the particular savannah communities whence most of my informants originated; and then take up the stories of particular occupational groups and individuals within them (chaps. 3–6). In chapter 7 I return to the savannah towns and the history of towns-people's efforts to mobilize and allocate resources on behalf of the community as a whole.

Chapter 1 describes changes in the structure and performance of the regional economy and in political relations and processes that affected the conditions of production and accumulation during and after the colonial period. It shows how colonial and postcolonial patterns of economic development laid the basis both for widespread participation in commercial activity and for the emergence of differential access to economic opportunities. I also discuss the role of education as a source of differentiation, as well as of specialized knowledge and productive skills, and I argue that, in the context of an export-oriented economy, colonial administrative policy served to establish sectional mobilization and conflict as central mechanisms of access to wealth and power. Chapter 2 traces these processes at the local level, showing in particular how the political importance of established communities and descent-based relations and the emergence of new centers of economic opportunity combined to produce a highly mobile population and a distinctive pattern of community relations in western Nigeria. By the middle of the twentieth century, towns such as Ẹripa[8] and Ìreé consisted predominantly of absentee members who lived and worked elsewhere, but who nevertheless maintained lifelong connections with their home communities and participated regularly in their affairs. The method of field research employed in this study was designed to take the geographical dispersion of the community into account, and I argue that this pattern is sufficiently common in contemporary Yorùbá society to raise questions about the interpretation of community studies that are carried out in a single location.

Chapters 3 and 4 deal with the two cocoa-farming villages, Abàkinní and Abúlékejì. In chapter 3 I analyze the process of accumulation associated with cocoa production per se and discuss its implications for the organization of agricultural production, the forms of rural social relations, and the structure of rural households. I also describe the ways in which my informants—both men and women—used surplus derived from cocoa and how their uses of surplus affected their children's careers and the development of the regional economy. Chapter 4 focuses on cocoa farmers' involvement in trade and politics. Both spheres of activity linked cocoa growers to the regional political economy; both also confronted farmers with sources of exploitation and opportunity. To the extent that farmers, merchants, and government compete for the proceeds of the cocoa crop, their interests are mutually antagonistic, and farmers have every reason to combine among themselves to resist exploitation by traders or by the state. At the same time, trade has provided an attractive outlet for farmers' savings and a chance for accumulation and upward mobility to those willing and able to invest in it. Although opportunities for political participation are by no means equally distributed among the general population, farmers have not been entirely excluded from power. Strategies for achieving power or exerting political influence have, in turn, encompassed both producer solidarity and sectional alliances.

Politics, like trade, serves both to unite farmers and to divide them. Chapter 4 shows how the resulting tensions have affected individuals' life experiences and forms of collective action within the village. It also compares trading activities of men and women, arguing that women's opportunities for independent accumulation were circumscribed by their husbands' fortunes. In both chapters 3 and 4, my understanding of the processes at work has benefited from the opportunity to document changes that occurred in a particular village between 1970–71 and 1978–79. People's responses to accelerated change often throw underlying processes into sharp relief, and the experiences of the people of Abúlékejì during the first decade of Nigeria's oil boom are no exception.

In chapters 5 and 6 I turn to the experiences of cocoa farmers' children who have left agriculture. In chapter 5 I describe the life histories of schoolteachers and explore further the importance of education in western Nigeria as a strategy of upward mobility, a target of accumulation, and an instrument of class formation. Chapter 5 also extends the comparison of men's and women's strategies of income use begun in chapters 3 and 4. Chapter 6 presents a case study of the motor repair business in Ifè, to illustrate the experiences of farmers' children who left agriculture for self-employment in the tertiary sector. (In 1978–79 this situation was still the typical one. The majority of farmers' economically active children above the age of 14 were self-employed as traders or artisans.) In chapter 6 I compare the conditions of accumulation in the tertiary sector with those in farming and discuss their implications for economic development and class formation. In both chapters 5 and 6 I show how the forms of political mobilization and conflict outlined above are reflected in the political activities of teachers and mechanics.

Like cocoa farmers and village traders, teachers and mechanics maintained an active interest in the affairs of their descent groups and hometowns, whether or not they happened to live there. In chapter 7 I trace the history of community development efforts and political conflict in Ìreé, one of the savannah towns from which many of my informants were descended. The story of people's efforts to mobilize resources to "develop" their town brings together many of the threads of argument and experience laid out in the previous chapters. In particular, it shows how individual enterprise, communal loyalties, and expanding commercial opportunity have combined to produce a local chronicle of growing inequality, unproductive accumulation, and factional strife, which mirrors the processes at work in the region at large.

1

Structural Change in the Political Economy of Western Nigeria

When the British conquered Ìjẹ̀bu Òde in 1892 and proceeded to establish a protectorate over the rest of Yorùbáland not under French control, they found themselves masters of a productive agrarian economy with a long history of local and long-distance trade. Travelers who visited the Yorùbá interior during the nineteenth century described extensive farming districts and flourishing towns and markets (Clapperton, 1829). Most people were engaged in farming at least part of the time, some on a large scale. In Ìbàdàn, for example, at the time of the British conquest "most of the important chiefs had huge farms wherein were engaged many of their domestics" (Johnson, 1921, p. 643). During the nineteenth-century wars the town was able to feed its substantial population, even under siege (ibid.).

Long before the advent of British rule Yorùbás also engaged in trade with Europeans, other African peoples, and one another. Like other West Africans, Yorùbás participated extensively in the Atlantic slave trade (Morton-Williams, 1964; Law, 1977), and they shifted to trade in agricultural and forest products as the slave trade declined. In the mid-nineteenth century Yorùbá traders were found in Nupe, Hausaland, and Asante, and Yorùbá traditions suggest a much earlier association with these and other savannah peoples (Law, 1977; Clapperton, 1829; Johnson, 1921; Eades, 1980). During the wars Yorùbá armies frequently sought to starve their enemies into submission by cutting off their access to trade with neighboring communities, a strategy suggesting that such trade was substantial and that many Yorùbás depended on it for essential supplies. By the end of the nineteenth century Yorùbá merchants were competing actively with Europeans in and around Lagos, and British firms strongly encouraged imperial conquest in order to protect their position on the coast and gain access to the products and markets of the interior (Hopkins, 1973; Ofonagoro, 1979; Cole, 1975).

For much of the nineteenth century a substantial part of the surplus produced by Yorùbá farmers and traders was absorbed in military activity. After the breakup of the Ọ̀yọ́ empire about 1830, Yorùbá towns and states were plunged into a period of conflict and disruption which continued until forcibly suppressed by the British after 1892. Although the wars generated large numbers of captives, many of whom were sold to slave traders, they reflected a basic upheaval in the whole system of political and hegemonic relations in the area rather than a simple response to the presence of European slavers on the coast. As the nineteenth century wore on, the conflict changed from a pattern of raids by marauding armies (Mábògùnjẹ́ and Omer Cooper, 1971) to campaigns by established states (some of them formed by bands of refugees and adventurers) against one another (Johnson, 1921; Akíntóyè, 1971; Awé, 1964, 1965). In both situations it is clear that military activity absorbed a substantial part of the energies of the adult male population and that agricultural produce was frequently consumed by the belligerent forces. Akíntóyè (1971) says the armies of the Èkìtìparapọ̀ disbanded during the rainy season to go home and till the soil so that they could provision themselves for the next campaign season, and Johnson (1921) makes frequent references to the importance of local agriculture for the strength of the various armies.

The British conquest and pacification of Yorùbáland served, accordingly, to release agricultural surplus previously absorbed in satisfying military demands. Some of it was reabsorbed by the colonial regime, through taxes and fees, and used to finance the costs of colonial administration (Ẹkúndáre, 1973; Forde and Scott, 1946). Part of the surplus may have been appropriated by Yorùbá chiefs seeking to replace the spoils of war with tribute and gifts from their own people, though how large a share of locally produced income and wealth was disposed in this way is difficult to say. The colonial administration outlawed many of the tolls and forms of tribute collected by chiefs in the precolonial era and replaced them with much smaller salaries (Àtàndá, 1973; Okonjo, 1974), but chiefs made up for some of the loss in revenue by demanding alternative forms of tribute in exchange for actually carrying out the duties assigned to them by their colonial overlords (Àtàndá, 1973; Peel, in press). Clearly, however, some of the surplus generated by Yorùbá trade and agriculture was plowed back into these activities, enabling many people to take advantage of expanding colonial markets and overseas trading by specializing in the production of agricultural commodities for export or local sale, or by entering trade directly (Hopkins, 1973; Berry, 1975a; Clarke, 1978; Peel, in press).

Agricultural Growth, Indirect Rule, and Colonial Social Mobility

The growth of Yorùbá trade and agriculture in the early colonial period was hardly the result of deliberate colonial policy, although it was so well suited to British interests in the area that colonial administrators did not try to stop it, as they did, for example, in Kenya or the Rhodesias. An important motive for the establishment of colonial rule in western Nigeria was to reduce the risks and increase the scope of European commercial activity. The profits of European firms depended both on the development of local production for export and on the expansion of the local market for imported goods. Cocoa, whose introduction to Yorùbá farmers owes more to African than to European initiative, proved advantageous to foreign merchants on both counts, and the colonial administration was content to leave cultivation of the crop in African hands. By 1908 the profitability of this arrangement was sufficiently apparent that the administration of southern Nigeria effectively turned down Lever Brothers' request for large concessions of forest land by insisting that the company negotiate concessionary agreements directly with indigenous landowners (Great Britain, Colonial Office, 1914; Hancock, 1942).

Britain's adoption of a policy of laissez-faire toward African commercial agriculture in western Nigeria was a matter of expediency rather than of principle, however. Lugard's philosophy of colonial economic policy—"development of native resources for the natives by the natives, under English supervision" (McPhee, 1926)—was applied retroactively in western Nigeria, more as a rationalization of what had already taken place than as a formative influence. When European firms or the colonial administration itself required cheap labor (e.g., for railway construction or tin mining), the colonial authorities did not hesitate to force it out of the local population (Freund, 1981a; Hopkins, 1966a; Agìrì, 1972; Oyèmákindé, 1970), just as they had used force to open the way for European traders when local people resisted (Ofonagoro, 1979; Àyándélé, 1966). When coercion began to threaten the very commercial expansion it was designed to foster, however, the administrators let up (Hopkins, 1973). If Africans were producing an expanding volume of exportable commodities, there was no need to subsidize Europeans to do it.

Nor, despite their claims to having played a catalytic role in the development of native agriculture (McPhee, 1926), did colonial officials intervene directly in agricultural production. The Department of Agriculture carried out a series of campaigns to improve methods of cultivation which were no less misguided, agronomically or socially,

in western Nigeria than elsewhere in colonial Africa (Green and
Hymer, 1966). As the department's methods of implementation were
limited to exhortation, however, their misconceptions had little effect.
Agricultural growth and specialization were, for the most part, initi-
ated, financed, and executed by Nigerian farmers and European firms
(see Hogendorn, 1975). The colonial state did exert considerable
influence on the uses of agricultural surplus, but this influence arose
more or less fortuitously from colonial legal and administrative practices rather than from deliberate economic policy.

The growth of agricultural production and trade created widespread opportunities for Africans to earn modest gains in income and
led to increasing differentiation. Trade and agriculture were mutually
reinforcing: many farmers financed their first plots of cocoa, in part,
with savings from trade or wage employment (Berry, 1975a). Although
wages were low—workers were paid as little as sixpence a day in
railway construction in the late 1890s (Hopkins, 1966a; Oyèmákindé,
1970) and the minimum government wage was still only a shilling a
day in 1939 (Helleiner, 1966)—unskilled wage earners generated some
of the working capital that financed the growth of cocoa production.
Between 1900 and 1940 many Yorùbás migrated from their hometowns to work for a few seasons on the railway, on road construction
and maintenance, or as porters and so on in centers of colonial commerce and administration (Agìrì, 1972; Berry, 1975a; Oyèmákindé,
1970). Thousands of others emigrated to trade in towns and cities
across West Africa (Eades, 1980). Savings from wage employment
were, in turn, often used either to pay marriage expenses and thus
begin a family (which could later provide agricultural labor) or to
enable men to establish cocoa farms at once.

Similarly cocoa growers expanded their farms, or diversified into
trade or crafts, with the assistance of credit obtained from cocoa buyers
(Bauer, 1963; Essang, 1970; Berry, 1975a). The growth of cocoa production and earnings led to the expansion of the domestic market,
creating additional opportunities for local trade and diversification of
agricultural production, in addition to increased trade in imported
commodities. By the 1920s areas to the north of the main cocoa region
were exporting foodstuffs to the towns and the cocoa belt of the
western provinces. Western Nigeria also provided an expanding market for beef from the north and, about 1920, began to supply locally
grown kola to the markets of northern Nigeria, which had previously
drawn most of their supplies from the Gold Coast (Agìrì, 1972;
Lovejoy, 1980). In addition, as cocoa growers hired more workers,
there were further increases in income, demand, and local exchange.

Commercialization also generated inequality. As we have seen, differentiation did not take the form of dispossession or lead to the creation of an agricultural bourgeoisie and proletariat. Rather, it arose from the unevenness of growth and accumulation in commerce itself, abetted—not always intentionally—by the colonial administration. Some Yorùbás made large fortunes in trade in the nineteenth century, and the expansion of trade in the interior after 1900 was accompanied by the emergence of additional nouveaux riches (Berry, 1975a; Peel, 1980; Williams, 1976; Post and Jenkins, 1973). There were inequalities among cocoa growers too (Galletti et al., 1956; van den Driesen, 1971), but prosperous farmers tended to diversify into trade and transport rather than to amass agricultural capital. By the 1920s a division was emerging between cocoa growers and traders (Peel, 1980) which was clearly reflected in farmers' responses to government initiatives in agriculture. In the late 1920s, for example, the Department of Agriculture set out to organize a series of farmers' cooperatives in order to disseminate improved methods of fermenting and drying cocoa (Adéyeyè, 1967; Hopkins, 1966b). The cooperatives were dominated from the first by local farmer-traders who seized on the promise of a premium for "properly" dried and fermented cocoa to increase their trading margins. The movement declined in 1929 when the officers of the Ìbàdàn society absconded with the year's purchases, and it did not revive until the depression of the 1930s had driven some of the prominent local traders back to their farms to ride out the crisis (Hopkins, 1966b; Òbíṣèsan, Diary).

Nevertheless, the rise of an indigenous commercial bourgeoisie was circumscribed in colonial western Nigeria by the European trading firms, which controlled the actual export of most of the cocoa crop. African traders' efforts to obtain independent shipping facilities, and hence direct access to buying firms based in Europe, were impeded by their own limited capital and contacts and by various forms of official discouragement. After World War I the elimination of competition from German trading firms and the crisis of 1920 precipitated a series of mergers among British firms in West Africa, which were condoned by the colonial authorities (Ofonagoro, 1979; Hopkins, 1973). African traders and large farmers in the Gold Coast organized a holdup of the 1937 cocoa crop to protest monopolistic pricing practices by European firms, and there were signs of similar unrest in Nigeria, though they did not amount to much (Hopkins, 1966b). On the recommendation of the Nowell Commission, which was appointed to investigate the disturbances, the colonial regime took over the marketing of cocoa directly, ostensibly to stabilize producer prices and forestall further disturbances. Once established, however, the marketing boards proved to be a convenient instrument for extracting revenue from the agricultural sector, and they were used primarily for that purpose (Bauer, 1963; Helleiner, 1964; Onitiri and Ọlátúnbọ̀sún, 1974).

In addition, the colonial regime influenced the process of accumulation in western Nigeria through its structuring of the colonial administration. As we have seen, British conquest of western Nigeria was motivated in part by the desire to protect and promote commerce, which the British felt was threatened by the lack of order and stability in nineteenth-century Yorùbáland. To establish a peaceful and orderly administration was therefore one of the first aims of the colonial authorities, and they sought to accomplish it as cheaply as possible, by minimizing the costs of conquest and of colonial administration. Wherever possible, British officials endeavored to rule through existing chiefs, both to avoid disrupting local relations of power and law enforcement and to economize on British personnel. Chiefs who were willing to cooperate with the British were retained in office and often given increased power in the form of British military backing (or the threat thereof); those who resisted were removed from office or reduced to figureheads (Àtàndá, 1973; Crowder and Ikime, 1970; Lloyd, 1971; Okonjo, 1974; Oyèdiran, 1973a; Peel, in press). The British sought to create not only a body of local chiefs but also a stable hierarchy of chiefdoms (redesignated native authorities) which could serve as an effective chain of command as well as a source of reliable colonial agents. In principle, the colonial administrative structure comprised provinces, divisions, and districts which were designed to coincide as far as possible with precolonial polities. In practice, relations of authority among precolonial Yorùbá states were anything but stable; hence, British efforts to build an administrative hierarchy on them served to prolong rather than to relieve interstate rivalries and tensions (see Lonsdale and Berman, 1978).

Sometimes local conflicts were created by British ignorance or neglect of Yorùbá political realities. The British insisted, for example, on treating the Ọ̀ọ̀ni of Ifẹ̀ and the Aláàfin of Ọ̀yọ́ as, in effect, comonarchs of all Yorùbáland, although by the late nineteenth century both Ìbàdàn and the Èkìtìparapọ̀ exercised greater military power than Ọ̀yọ́, and Ifẹ̀ was scattered and disorganized (Johnson, 1921). Yorùbá chiefs also took advantage of British officials' credulity or ambition to advance their own status within the colonial hierarchy, as in Aláàfin Ládùgbòlú's collaboration with Captain Ross to establish and dominate the "new Ọ̀yọ́ empire" (Àtàndá, 1973, chap. 4). But, official misunderstandings and individual maneuverings apart,

competition among towns and titleholders was intrinsic to the administrative and political system created in the name of indirect rule.
For indirect rule not only attached certain levers of power and aggrandizement to traditional titles and jurisdictions, but it also redefined,
often arbitrarily, jurisdictional boundaries or relations among chiefs
and communities. Since spheres of influence and authority had been
a subject of conflict up to the imposition of colonial rule, there
was hardly an administrative boundary established by the colonizers
to which somebody could not object—and many people did. Thus,
Ìbàdàn chafed under its formal subordination to Ọ̀yọ́; Ilá pressed for
divisional status within Ọ̀yọ́ Province to escape taking orders from
Ìlọrin; and even rural settlements no larger than villages complained
of their junior status vis-à-vis towns such as Ifẹ̀, Ilésà, or Òndó (Lloyd,
1962; Peel, 1980; Berry, 1975a). Claims to higher jurisdictional status,
often based on alleged tradition, were advanced in terms of customary
prerogatives of towns or titles, such as an oba's right to wear a beaded
crown. But the anachronistic formulation of such appeals should not
mislead us concerning their social basis. In general, communities
designated as subordinate to district or divisional centers sought to
establish their right to autonomy, less to escape actual oppression
from local capitals than to advance their claims to the resources
controlled by the colonial regime. By establishing sectional identities
as criteria of differential access to the state, colonial administrative
practice fostered sectional competition as a strategy of political mobilization and a focus of political conflict (Post and Vickers, 1973).

The slogan of "native development under British supervision" was
applied to legal and judicial arrangements as well as to administration.
In principle, the colonial regime sought to preserve indigenous systems
of law and law enforcement as long as they were not "repugnant" to
British notions of justice and "civilisation" (Adéwoyè, 1977). In practice, colonial authorities established a set of higher courts in western
Nigeria, where cases were tried according to English law and judicial
procedure (Elias, 1953; Lloyd, 1962; Adéwoyè, 1977). Advocates and
judges received English legal training and court proceedings were
conducted in English. The higher courts had jurisdiction over capital
cases, such as murder, and over cases involving disputes between
"natives" and "strangers." They also served as courts of appeal. Otherwise, civil cases were heard in customary courts, where chiefs approved
by the colonial administration were supposed to decide them according
to "native law and custom." The location of customary courts (like the
demarcation of boundaries) was an issue of intense communal concern
and sometimes of conflict (Francis, 1981).

On the face of it, this system seems to extend direct English law and judicial proceedings only to major criminal cases and disputes between Nigerians and foreigners. The term "stranger," however, was broadly interpreted to include any person not tracing his or her descent from the community in which the dispute occurred, and it was used by litigants, judges, and colonial officials to manipulate access to resources as well as political alliances. For example, strangers were not supposed to acquire property outside their communities of origin (Berry, 1975a; Clarke, 1980; see also chap. 2, n. 2, below). Under these circumstances membership in a given community became a basis for establishing rights to property as well as claims on the patronage of local chiefs and patrons.

As customary court judges, a number of Yorùbá chiefs enjoyed prerogatives that, though circumscribed by British restrictions on scope and procedure, nevertheless enabled them to exercise a good deal of influence over the allocation of locally based resources, to their own advantage and that of their loyal followers and clients. Most of the cases heard in the customary courts had to do with disputes over land, debt, or divorce, all of which concerned people's access to productive resources. Àtàndá (1973) complains that not only the issues subject to adjudication, but also the number of chiefs and chiefs' clients, messengers, and the like involved in the settlement of disputes, were more limited under the native court system than in precolonial Yorùbá society: "In introducing this system, the Government overlooked the fact that in the pre-colonial Yorùbáland, many functionaries—family and compound heads, chiefs of all grades and their messengers and so on—were involved in the judicial process. All these had benefits proportional to their status in the hierarchy. [Under the native court system, however,] the number of . . . judges hardly exceeded eight in any one court. Even for these few, the remuneration could not compensate for the tributes, gifts and so on, which they had been receiving in the precolonial period" (p. 180).

Nevertheless, the chiefs exercised more power through the native courts than through the other functions formally allocated to them by the colonial regime. Since cases brought before the native courts were decided according to unwritten native law and custom, the chiefs had leeway to interpret customary practice in the light of current interests, whether or not they attempted to circumvent the judicial procedures laid down by colonial authorities. In Ilé̩ṣà, divorces were granted as much to enable chiefs and other senior men to extract compensation from their juniors as to exercise control over their wives (Peel, in press). In Ifè̩, while Ọ̀ọ̀ni Adémilúyì (reigned 1910–1930) managed to be regularly consulted by native court judges throughout his district on cases over which he had no formal jurisdiction (Àtàndá,

1973, pp. 181–183), his successor, Ọ̀ọ̀ni Adérẹ̀mí, used customary law itself to enlarge the economic as well as the political scope of his authority (Berry, 1975a; see also Oyèdiran, 1972, 1973a).

In general, Yorùbá chiefs were placed in a contradictory position under British rule, since the colonial authorities both reinforced and circumscribed their authority. Chiefly titles were sought after as a means of exercising local authority and gaining limited access to the state, but they rarely sufficed to ensure successful accumulation or lifelong prestige and power. Chiefly prerogatives were sufficient to encourage continued sectional mobilization and competition for extralocal resources in colonial Yorùbá society, but chiefs did not become a class. To become a chief and to maintain elite status required more than proof of descent from the right ancestors; it was also necessary to command a loyal following. Such leadership depended partly on personal qualities—someone not considered to be "of good character" would not be respected or obeyed—and partly on achievements, especially in the form of wealth (Aronson, 1978; Bascom, 1951). The ability to reward supporters or engage in public displays of generosity (institutionalized, for chiefs, in the title-taking ceremonies, as well as in other ritual observances) was essential to acquiring power and status, as well as to accumulation per se.

In addition to trade and commercial agriculture, some Yorùbás found opportunities to earn above-average incomes or exercise authority through government or professional employment. If unskilled labor is excluded, both these careers required some Western schooling. Since nearly all the primary schools in colonial western Nigeria were operated by missionaries, access to Western education often required at least nominal conversion to Christianity. Thus the lower levels of the colonial administrative apparatus came to be staffed primarily by Christians (a point to which I return in later chapters). Education also proved an avenue to upward mobility outside the colonial service, specifically through professional self-employment and through politics. As several historians have shown, Yorùbá teachers, lawyers, doctors, and journalists produced some of the earliest nationalist propaganda and organizations in western Nigeria. Educated people also became active and influential in local political affairs (Abernethy, 1969; Coleman, 1965; Àyándélé, 1974; Sklar, 1962).

The fact that Nigerians literate in English possessed an advantage in dealing with the colonial regime dovetailed with existing Yorùbá concepts of status and authority. Individuals gain respect and wield influence in Yorùbá society in accordance with their ability to attract a following. That ability, in turn, depends not only on wealth and generosity but also on possessing knowledge that enables one to help

people cope more effectively with the environment and with one
another (Aronson, 1978; Peel, 1978). In the past, persons such as
blacksmiths and diviners (*babaláwo*), whose specialized knowledge
could be used to effect physical well-being and social harmony, were
accorded special status. Similarly, chiefs' effectiveness as leaders depended partly on their mastery of the history (*ìtàn*) of the community
and its constituent quarters and kin groups (Peel, 1978). Value was
placed not on knowledge per se but rather on knowledge that could
be used to accomplish personal and social ends.

As it became clear, under British colonial rule, that knowledge of
English and of Western law and custom enhanced one's ability to deal
with Nigeria's imperial rulers, Yorùbás came to regard Western education as a new form of socially effective knowledge and to accord
prestige to its possessors. John Peel's Ìjèṣà informants often used the
term *ọlàjú* (enlightenment, lit., that which opens the eyes) to refer to
social progress. *Ọlàjú* "is at bottom a technical rather than a moral
notion. It proceeds from a desire to understand the conditions of
individual and communal success" (ibid., p. 159). In the early colonial
period *ọlàjú* was seen to derive from a variety of activities, including
trade, travel, commercial farming, conversion to Christianity, and
Western education, all tending to "open the eyes to the operation of
the wider system" (ibid.). As the colonial order solidified in Nigeria,
and educated Africans began to articulate and then to organize expressions of nationalist opposition to it, education came increasingly to be
seen as a key not only to coping with but eventually to controlling the
colonial state. As Azikiwe proclaimed on the masthead of the *West
African Pilot*, a leading nationalist newspaper in the 1930s, "Show the
light, and the people will find the way" (quoted in ibid., p. 154).

In the Yorùbá states, the Pax Britannica was followed by the spread
of commercial activity and increased agricultural specialization. British
firms, profiting from trade in agricultural exports and imported
commodities, did not seek to enter or control production directly.
The growth of colonial trade created opportunities for thousands of
Yorùbás to engage in commercial agriculture or trade. Accumulation
by Yorùbá farmers and traders was limited, however, by the organization of agricultural production, by the monopoly power of European
trading firms, and by the administrative and legal practices of the
colonial regime. Both in cocoa and in food-crop production, the
development of large farms was restrained by the absence of
economies of scale in agricultural production, by problems of labor
supervision on a large scale, and by land-tenure and inheritance practices which often preserved or extended collective rights to rural
property. Also, because nonagricultural accumulation depended on

access to foreign transactions and to the state, Africans with money and resources to invest were encouraged to direct them toward creating or maintaining channels of access to the state and to foreign capitalists. These channels included relations of clientage with merchant firms, education, government employment, and competition for a better position within the hierarchy of native authorities through which the colonial regime delegated power and distributed revenues. All avenues of upward mobility were limited by the overarching interests of the colonial administration and of foreign capitalists. At the same time, however, all served to promote nonexclusive forms of access to productive resources and opportunities, which permitted differentiation but tended to impede increases in productivity. The implications of colonial patterns of accumulation became clearer after 1945, as the colonial authorities prepared to withdraw from Nigeria.

Decolonization and the Formation of an Indigenous Ruling Class

Under colonial rule some western Nigerians amassed substantial personal fortunes, but they were limited in terms of access to foreign markets and capital by their subordination to the colonial state and the monopoly power of foreign firms. By transferring control of the state and, hence, the power to regulate foreign transactions to Nigerians, Britain's withdrawal opened the way for indigenous accumulation on a larger scale and for consolidation of the indigenous colonial elites into a ruling class. From the early 1950s Nigerian politicians and civil servants worked energetically to strengthen both their political position and their access to wealth by expanding the state apparatus and by increasing the government's role in domestic accumulation. At the same time the indigenization of government intensified the sectional divisions and conflicts of colonial society, both in popular struggles for access to the state and within the state apparatus itself.

The first Nigerians to take office in the newly formed Western Regional government inherited a buoyant economy. Cocoa production stagnated during the depression of the 1930s and World War II, but after 1945 the world market price of cocoa rose steadily for a decade, and the unit value of cocoa exported from Nigeria increased from less than £30 a ton in 1945 to nearly £400 a ton in 1954 (Helleiner, 1966). Rising cocoa prices stimulated extensive new plantings, primarily by farmers who migrated from Yorùbá communities in the savannah to the eastern districts of the cocoa belt (Berry, 1975*a*; Olúsànyà et al., 1978). Output more than doubled and a whole new generation of Yorùbá farmers shared in the resulting gains. Their share of the gains, however, was limited by the exactions of the state. The indigenous leaders to whom the British transferred power during the 1950s reversed the colonial government's policy of conservative portfolio management with respect to Marketing Board surpluses while preserving intact the Marketing Board system and tending to increase the rate of surplus extraction from cocoa producers (Helleiner, 1966). As long as the world cocoa price rose, both growers and the state prospered from the crop, but when prices began to drop after 1955 (table 1–1) the tensions inherent in their mutual dependence became increasingly apparent.

TABLE 1–1
PRODUCER PRICES OF COCOA

Year	Producer price (₦/ton)	Consumer price index, Ìbàdàn (1953 = 100)	Real producer price (1953 = 100)
1954–55	392		
1960–61	296		
1961–62	192	127	46
1962–63	202	137	44
1963–64	212	128	50
1964–65	232	127	55
1965–66	130	131	30
1966–67	180	146	37
1967–68	190	141	40
1968–69	200	136	44
1969–70	300	148	61
1970–71	310	166	56
1971–72	310	203	46
1972–73	310	204	46
1973–74	450	210	65
1974–75	660	232	86
1975–76	660	317	63
1976–77	660	384	52
1977–78	1,030	466	67

SOURCES: Western Nigeria Marketing Board; Federal Office of Statistics.

Confrontation between farmers and the state over allocation of the cocoa surplus has been rightly identified as a central theme in postcolonial politics in western Nigeria (Beer and Williams, 1975; Beer, 1976; Post, 1973). The regional government used the Marketing Board to appropriate as much as 50 percent of the value of the cocoa sold abroad, and the federal government derived substantial revenue from taxes on foreign trade (Helleiner, 1966; Onitiri and Ọlátúnbọ̀sún,

1974). As the proportion of government expenditures devoted to rural amenities or agricultural development programs was relatively small (Helleiner, 1966; Wells, 1974), cocoa growers contributed more to state revenues than they received in infrastructure, services, or rural development programs. When federal military expenses mounted during the civil war and the government tried to impose additional levies on farmers in a period of declining export prices and rural incomes, Yorùbá farmers launched the Àgbékòyà rebellion. As both the Ayoọla Commission, appointed to investigate the disturbances, and subsequent academic studies of the farmers' movement have shown (Ayoọla Commission, 1969; Beer, 1976), the violent attacks on local government functionaries, police officers, and chiefs in 1968 and 1969 bore a striking resemblance to earlier rural protests against state policies, such as the Máiyégùn League's opposition in the 1950s to government efforts to destroy cocoa trees infected with swollen shoot. The fact that the protest subsided and the Àgbékòyà movement collapsed after the Marketing Board raised the price of cocoa by 50 percent in 1970 underscores the extent to which the conflict was focused on the issue of the distribution of cocoa earnings and exacerbated by the steady decline in cocoa prices from 1955 to 1969.

Conflict between farmers and the state was only one form of struggle over the surplus generated by agricultural production and foreign trade. Competition was also intense within the ranks of elected officials and civil servants. Britain's efforts to create a parliamentary government based on the regional divisions of the colonial administration broke down precisely over the issue of who would control the federal government and the disposition of its resources (Post and Vickers, 1973). Control of the state's revenues and of its power to regulate foreign and domestic transactions was the central issue in parliamentary debates over the allocation of tax revenues among various sections of the country, in the census crises of 1962 and 1963, and in the breakdown of the electoral process in 1964 and 1965 (Oyovbaire, 1978; Post and Vickers, 1973; Teríba, 1966). In the west, antagonism between farmers and the state over disposition of the region's agricultural surplus was overshadowed by the growing conflict over strategies for controlling the potentially much larger surplus of the nation as a whole. Eventually the Yorùbá ruling elite split over whether to ally themselves with the politically dominant Northern People's Congress (NPC) or try to construct a coalition against it, and the First Republic collapsed in the resulting confrontation between the two Yorùbá parties, the Action Group (AG), and the Nigerian National Democratic Party (NNDP).

The political parties of the First Republic did not represent the interests of particular classes; they consisted, primarily, of shifting alliances of people from all socioeconomic strata who hoped to use regionally based political organizations to advance their own access to the central levers of power (Mackintosh, 1966; Post, 1963; Post and Vickers, 1973). Even ethnic or community-based loyalties were not consistently related to party alignments. Politicians used any means available to mobilize support, including appeals to ethnic solidarity, but as ethnic boundaries were subject to multiple and conflicting definitions this policy did not give rise to stable political alliances. Leaders of the Action Group, for example, were quite capable of seeking support for the party both by appealing to Pan-Yorùbá sentiment and by arousing jealousies among Yorùbá communities which had been perpetuated or created under indirect rule (Oyèdiran, 1979; Post and Vickers, 1973; Sklar, 1962). Ordinary people were equally ready to switch allegiances if leaders of another party promised immediate assistance in local power struggles. The Máiyégùn League, for example, was supported by cocoa farmers opposed to the government's campaign to destroy cocoa trees infected with swollen shoot, by Muslims opposed to the power of Christian-educated professionals, and by Ìbàdàns opposed to Ẹgbà-Ìjẹ̀bu influence in regional politics (Post and Jenkins, 1973; Beer, 1976; Sklar, 1962). Similar configurations of interests and identities characterized political factionalism in Ìreé, as we shall see.

The sometimes murderous character of sectional conflict in western Nigerian politics does not mean that sectional interests precluded socioeconomic differentiation. To a large extent the mounting tensions and violence between regionally based parties, which brought about the demise of the First Republic and helped plunge Nigeria into civil war, revealed resentment over differential access to wealth and power and over the greed and high-handedness with which those in office sought to enrich themselves and their clients at the public's expense (Gutkind, 1967; Williams, 1976; Post and Jenkins, 1973; Peel, 1980). Because the basis of differential access to wealth and power rested on access to the state rather than on direct ownership of the means of production, however, class interests were often expressed through sectional alliances and conflicts. Indeed, it may be argued that the very instability of sectional alignments reflects the pervasiveness of differentiation. People kept creating new alliances, or reviving old ones, in a ceaseless struggle to advance their positions within a differentiated structure of opportunity. In the process, a substantial part of the surplus available in the regional economy was channeled into bribes, kickbacks, ceremonies, or the construction of political monuments, all of which tended to increase the consumption of the ruling class rather than to expand the productive capacity of the economy (Turner, 1978; see also Coker Commission, 1962).

The unproductiveness of the state's uses of surplus is reflected in the substantial element of waste and elite consumption in many government-sponsored development projects. In western Nigeria alone the regional government spent a great deal of money on farm settlement schemes, loan boards, industrial estates, and so forth, with little discernible effect on output or productive capacity (Helleiner, 1966; Kilby, 1969; Roider, 1968; Schatz, 1977; Wells, 1974). Similarly, plans to improve producers' incentives or upgrade their inputs typically failed to reach any but a few wealthy or well-connected people (Essang, 1970), and state-managed production schemes often achieved lower returns to labor and capital than the unaided efforts of local producers which they were supposed to improve upon.

The interplay among emerging class interests, sectional conflict, and the allocation of state revenues is clearly reflected in the expansion of the educational system after 1952. In the west, the first regional House of Assembly adopted the policy of universal primary education and set about implementing it as quickly as possible. Between 1954 and 1955 primary school enrollment leaped from 451,000 to 811,000, and government outlays on education rose from 34 to 47 percent of the regional budget (Abernethy, 1969, p. 128). As Abernethy has argued, the rapid expansion of education in western Nigeria was a somewhat contradictory undertaking. It was designed to increase popular support for the regional government by broadening opportunities for western Nigerians to attend school and thereby acquire the qualifications for salaried or professional employment. Yet the very process of expansion deflated the value of schooling, both by increasing the supply of educated people seeking jobs and by undermining the quality of schooling provided. Also, because educational development was much more rapid in the southern than in the northern part of the country, it tended to exacerbate regional differences in income and employment and hence to intensify regional competition over resources and opportunities.

Educational expansion was also closely related to changing patterns of political recruitment. During the 1950s secondary schooling became a prerequisite for employment in the middle and upper echelons of the expanding civil service. In addition, numerous graduates of secondary schools, teacher training colleges, and universities campaigned for elective office on the grounds that their schooling rendered them particularly well qualified to step into the shoes of the departing colonialists. The member of parliament who began a speech on the 1956 Western Region Appropriations Bill with the reassuring declaration, "I left St. Andrew's College [Òyọ́] in 1928. I therefore know what I am saying" (quoted in Abernethy, 1969, p. 138), expressed a widely held attitude.

Political ambitions of men with Western schooling were endorsed by many uneducated Yorùbás who, as we have seen, had come to look upon Western education as an effective tool for dealing with the colonial state and economy. The Western Region House of Assembly was dominated by educated members. In 1951 nearly 25 percent of the members were schoolteachers (ibid., p. 136; Ezera, 1964). In a 1969 survey of the Yorùbá elite, Imoagene (1976) found that 80 percent of the civil servants, 55 percent of the former politicians, and a third of the businessmen in his sample had at least a primary school education, and that more than half of the first group and a third of the second held the West African School Certificate or higher qualifications. Educated politicians tended, in turn, to be especially responsive to the needs of educated constituents. Other studies seem to confirm Imoagene's finding that, after independence, education became increasingly important as a condition for access to the state (Beckett and O'Connell, 1978; van den Berghe, 1973; Àyándélé, 1974) and hence for accumulation.

The growing significance of education as a means to power and prosperity in the 1950s and 1960s served not only to intensify popular demand for additional schools but also to incline the ruling class toward educational expansion. Universal primary education proved infeasible when, in the 1950s, it was first tried in the southern regions of Nigeria, but the attempt represented more than the populist sentiments of Nigeria's first indigenous regime. Universal primary education appealed to the governing classes not only for its immediate political popularity but also because it might be expected to produce an electorate sympathetic to the notion that government ought to rest in the hands of educated people. At the same time that the Western Regional government decided to proceed with universal primary education in the 1950s, it also took steps to build secondary schools and universities, not for the masses, but in order to provide advanced training for those who would join or succeed them at the "commanding heights" of the economy (Ashby Report; see also chap. 5, below). With the encouragement of their foreign advisors and creditors, the new Nigerian ruling class embarked on a strategy of educational development which was ultimately designed to secure power to the educated.

But this strategy, too, was not free from contradictions. Just as educational expansion tended to dilute the value of education as a means to upward mobility and hence as a populist political strategy, so it also served to undercut the power of educational differentiation to restrict entry into the ruling class or to legitimate the claims of educated people to rule on the grounds of their superior expertise. Thus, even well-educated politicians needed to create or preserve additional bases for mobilizing popular support. Sectional loyalties and conflicts have been fostered by some of their most highly educated and articulate critics, when the popular appeal of communal sentiment appeared to serve their political ambitions.

The 1970s: Realizing "One Nigeria"

The tendencies toward unproductive accumulation, increasing differentiation, and sectional competition which emerged from colonial society in western Nigeria were heightened and intensified after 1970. The federal government, strengthened by the civil war, moved to consolidate and extend its power (Panter-Brick, 1978; Ọṣọ̀bà, 1977; Joseph, 1978). Wartime restrictions on foreign trade proved a stimulus to import-substituting industrialization and, in the aftermath of the fighting, popular support was readily mobilized in support of the consolidation and further expansion of centralized state power as a means to preserve the peace and promote national unity. The military-bureaucratic coalition that governed Nigeria until 1979, as well as its civilian successors, consolidated federal control over public revenue and foreign trade. Their efforts were facilitated by the rapid growth of petroleum exports, which not only provided the central government with unprecedented levels of revenue and foreign exchange earnings but also reduced its dependence on localized sources of revenue over which state governments could claim exclusive control. Former regional elites were rapidly absorbed into the national ruling class through oil-financed expansion of the state and its control over both public and private accumulation (Panter-Brick, 1978, passim).

The strategies used since 1970 to extend and consolidate the power of the federal government and of the ruling class have intensified and perpetuated the contradictions of previous patterns of state power and accumulation. Three issues in particular, which have dominated public debate over federal policies and expenditures, have become central elements in ruling class strategy. They are the continued expansion and elaboration of the educational system, the creation of additional states, and the periodic revision of the civil service salary scale. All three have absorbed a good deal of the oil wealth that has flowed into Nigeria since the end of the civil war. Between 1970 and 1976, for example, outlays on education increased from 0.6 to 13 percent of the federal budget. In addition, roughly a quarter of federal revenues were transferred to the states, which spent a major part of their total revenues on education (Kirk-Greene and Rimmer, 1981). Education absorbed 37 percent of the Ọ̀yọ́ State budget by 1979 (Ọ̀yọ́ State, *Current Education Statistics*). Although it is not possible to measure directly the costs of state creation or the growth of the bureaucratic wage bill, it is clear that administration absorbed a substantial share of the oil wealth. It has been estimated, for example, that the share of real gross domestic product (GDP) originating in public administration grew at an average annual rate of 25 percent between 1970 and 1977 (Collier, 1981).

The expansion of the educational system was resumed by the military regime after the disruptions of the civil war and accelerated by the return to civilian rule. (In 1980 the proportion of the federal budget devoted to education surpassed that spent on defense for the first time since the military took power in 1966. *West Africa*, May 12, 1980.) Universal primary education was reintroduced in 1976, this time on a nationwide basis. In addition, both secondary schools and institutions of higher education have proliferated at a rapid pace. In Ọ̀yọ́ State alone enrollment increased by almost 40 percent between 1975 and 1977. In the latter year there were three times as many pupils in secondary grammar school as there had been a decade earlier,[1] and on the national level the number of universities rose from six to thirteen, and whole new categories of specialized postsecondary institutions were established.[2] The civil service also moved to formalize the relationship between levels of schooling and levels of pay by attaching specific educational requirements to each grade in the civil service salary scale. The elaboration of the educational and occupational hierarchy within the expanding state apparatus tended to offset the equalizing and devaluing effects of mass education, but only in part. As we shall see in chapter 5, incomes and the social status associated with particular levels of schooling have declined relatively and, in years of rapid inflation, absolutely as well.

Popular and political enthusiasm for mass education as a means to upward mobility is not only inherently contradictory, but it also contributed to sectional antagonism in the 1970s. Regional differences in access to education, which originated in the colonial period, continued to produce differential rates of educational attainment in different parts of the country. When university admissions procedures were centralized in 1976, rates of application and admission were much higher among students from the southern states than among those from the northern ones. Northern leaders demanded regional admission quotas so as to increase the proportion of university entrants coming from northern states, while southerners countered with charges of discrimination and the argument that a policy of university admission based on merit would better serve the national interest than a system of regional quotas.

Contradictions and controversies surrounding educational policy were exacerbated in the 1970s by the growth of the civil service. Government wage and salary scales have tended to set the pace for wage determination in the Nigerian economy as a whole, since the 1950s as well as before.[3] In the 1950s and 1960s the government periodically convened public commissions to review government pay scales. When increases recommended by the commissions were awarded within the civil service, they were followed by demands for comparable increases in the private sector. Such claims were often successful: foreign employers, in particular, often granted raises in order to avoid unfavorable publicity, and indigenous firms usually followed suit in the wake of mounting labor unrest.

In the 1970s government payrolls expanded rapidly, through both administrative growth and the incorporation of new occupations and enterprises into the state. Teachers, for example, were brought into the civil service in the mid-1970s. As larger proportions of wage and salary earners have been drawn into government employment, conflict over wage and salary increases has been further internalized within the state apparatus. Thus the civil service salary scale has become central both to the strategies of the ruling class for consolidating and strengthening its position and to workers' strategies for improving their lot. One of Yakubu Gowon's last efforts to stave off the overthrow of his increasingly corrupt and unmanageable regime was the famous Udoji award of 1974, which granted across-the-board pay raises of up to 100 percent to most upper- and middle-level civil servants. In recent years teachers at all levels of the educational system have been spending more and more time on strike. Efforts by the ruling class to close their ranks tend to break down, partly because they often operate through mechanisms of incorporation.

The integration of sectional loyalties and conflicts into the process of political centralization and ruling class consolidation in Nigeria is nowhere more clearly manifest than in the periodic creation of additional states. Conceived initially by the military regime as a way to defuse regional conflict (Panter-Brick, 1978; Ọdẹ́tọ́lá, 1978; Oyèdiran, 1979), state creation has become a method of forestalling sectional conflict by perpetuating it. Groups who feel themselves at a disadvantage in the struggle for power and access to centrally controlled wealth and opportunities seek to improve their position by forming a new state, with a presumptive claim on federal resources equal to that of every other state. When their efforts are successful, the strategy of agitation for more states tends to be legitimated, and others are encouraged to try it for themselves. The Ọbásànjọ regime increased the number of states from twelve to nineteen in 1976, and pressure for the creation of still more states has emerged as a central issue of public discussion and political campaigns since the return to civilian rule.

As states proliferate, however, the proportion of federal resources accruing to each one declines, and the amount each state receives is likely to be devoted largely to creating and maintaining the administrative infrastructure of state government. Thus sectional conflict over access to wealth and power in a differentiated political and economic system tends to promote unproductive accumulation from the state's own surplus and to create a comparable set of incentives for private enterprise. In these circumstances, the oil revenues have led primarily to the expansion of the tertiary sector rather than to diversified growth in productive capacity. According to recent figures from the Federal Office of Statistics, in 1980–81 the composition of GDP at current factor cost was as follows: agriculture, 19 percent; mining and quarrying, 25 percent; manufacturing, 6 percent; construction, 15 percent; distribution, 22 percent; other services, 13 percent. The demand for commodities has been met largely from increased imports, and Nigerians have profited primarily from the distribution, repair, or outright hoarding of a vast stock of imported goods or from employment in construction which also uses imported materials. Opportunities to make money in distribution have served, in turn, to draw labor away from more onerous forms of employment, especially in agriculture. The result has been a rapid increase in food imports, not only of relatively exotic commodities such as wheat or frozen meat, but also of crops formerly produced in and even exported from Nigeria. Groundnuts, once the country's largest foreign exchange earner, have been imported since the mid-1970s. The inflow of oil wealth has not only aggravated problems of agricultural decline; it has also perpetuated Nigeria's overall dependence on imports, both to maintain the opulent consumption standards of the rich and to provide for the basic needs of the poor. Every glut in international oil supplies provokes a balance-of-payments crisis in Nigeria, which forces the government to cut back on domestic expenditures and leads to increased instability in domestic markets, higher risks for productive investment, and intensified competition for access to the state.

2
Migration and Community in Historical Perspective: Ẹripa and Ìreé

The incorporation of Yorùbá states and communities into a regional and, later, a national economic and political framework set a great many people in motion.[1] Their movements linked precolonial settlements to new commercial and administrative centers and also led to changes in the spatial arrangement of social activities and relationships. Migration to areas of expanding economic opportunity did not necessarily entail a corresponding shift in the locus of all migrants' social relations, however. Many migrant farmers, workers, traders, and professionals continued to maintain close ties with their kin and to participate regularly in the affairs of their communities of origin, as well as to establish new connections in other areas. At the same time, kin- and community-based identities served in part to define and organize social relations in areas of expanding production and employment. Many settlements were established, modified, or destroyed in the course of the economic and political changes described in chapter 1. In the process the relationship between settlement and community was redefined as well.

Most Yorùbá migration in the twentieth century did not give rise to major changes in people's life-styles or social relations. Whether people migrated in order to engage in wage employment, trade, or commercial agriculture, they retained strong ties to their descent groups and communities of origin. Emigrant farmers and traders often brought relatives or neighbors from home to work with or for them, sought marriage partners among the descendants of their hometowns, and returned home in times of need or celebration or when ready to retire from active (self-) employment (Eades, 1980; Adépòjù, 1974; Sudarkasa, 1979; Hündsalz, 1972; Berry, 1975a). Even wage earners retained or recreated associations based on descent in order to cope with the exigencies of urban life and labor (Aronson, 1978;

Lloyd, 1974; Peace, 1979). Economic specialization did not automatically lead to sharper divisions or weaker affinities between rural and urban areas in western Nigeria. Traditions of origin, which are preserved in new areas of employment and residence, may be used to mobilize resources or to manage relations with members of the migrants' host community. Property rights and political strategies are often based on the distinction between "locals" and "strangers," in urban as well as in rural areas[2] (Eades, 1980; Berry, 1975a). Thus the spatial arrangement of Yorùbá social and political relations does not correspond exactly to that of productive activity, nor is location an unambiguous indicator of social differentiation. Because so many people have connections and spend time in both rural and urban areas, efforts to measure and explain rural-urban differentials in income or wealth do not reveal very much about either the extent of economic inequality among people or the sources of differentiation in Yorùbá society.

The changing spatial configuration of economic, social, and political activities and relations in western Nigeria has important methodological and conceptual implications for the study of social change in the region. Yorùbás' complex patterns of movement among places of birth, work, residence, exchange, and other points of rendezvous with kinsmen, friends, or business and political associates make it difficult to study social relations in a single place. A Yorùbá community in the middle of the twentieth century cannot be treated as a territorially based settlement whose inhabitants define their social identity and organize their interactions around the fact that they live and work in the same place. Rather, it is likely to comprise a group of people, scattered or moving across the map of the region and beyond, who maintain a tradition of descent from a common place and who often organize social actions and interpersonal relationships in terms of that tradition. Some students of Yorùbá communities have taken these circumstances into account, even while confining their research to a single location, by playing close attention to extralocal linkages.[3] Too often, however, surveys of migrants which are conducted at one site fail to place informants in either a historical or a wider social context.

Studying people in a single place not only affects the way in which their behavior is described and interpreted; it also determines the kinds of questions addressed in research on social change. Explaining the fact of migration often becomes more important than understanding the processes of social and economic change; migrants' motives become the principal explanatory factor, and altering rates of migration the chief end of public policy. The literature on migration in western Nigeria, for example, states repeatedly that rural-urban migration has increased since the end of World War II and that, since people migrate primarily for economic reasons, raising rural output and incomes will reduce rural-urban migration (Adépòjù, 1974, passim; Caldwell, 1978). In fact, people's movements are so frequent and so complex in contemporary western Nigeria that estimates of net rural-urban migration are likely to vary widely, depending on how a migrant is defined. Moreover, in the past, increases in rural incomes have probably increased overall rates of migration, as people have expanded and diversified their economic activities.[4] In general, the frequency and complexity of populaton movements in Yorùbá society make it difficult, if not thoroughly misleading, to assume that location can be used as a proxy for patterns of economic specialization or social organization.

The fact of Yorùbá mobility also forces us to define carefully the terms with which we speak of social processes other than migration. Urbanization, for example, is not necessarily a force for significant social change. During and after the colonial period many Yorùbás left towns to specialize in growing cocoa or in pursuing other, related forms of rural enterprise. Others sought urban employment as a means to accumulate rural property or to gain prestige in their towns of origin, however remote these may be from contemporary centers of commerce and administration (Peace, 1979; see also Aronson, 1971; Peel, forthcoming). The complex associations of urban residence for many Yorùbás were nicely expressed by Ìjẹbu residents of Ìbàdàn who told one ethnographer that "the city is our farm": "a place of drudgery and deprivation" where people go to create the means to enjoy "the good life of the traditional [home] town" (Aronson, 1978, p. 186).

As subsequent chapters show in detail, Yorùbás' residential histories and social ties are more likely to extend across rural-urban boundaries than to be confined within one or the other. The expansion of non-agricultural employment and the growth of urban populations have not led to the polarization of Yorùbá society into privileged urban dwellers and a "neglected rural majority" (Ọlátúnbọsún, 1975), or even into urban rich and rural and urban poor (Williams, 1976). Instead, these developments have engendered a kind of perpetual restlessness: no one stays anywhere for very long lest he miss an opportunity somewhere else. If the majority realize little at any point in their travels, this only intensifies the urge to keep moving in order to avoid falling behind in the political and economic lottery of accumulating good connections (see Berry, 1983).

Like the movements of individual men and women, kinship and class relations in western Nigeria also cut across rural and urban boundaries. Members of a descent group or a community are likely to be scattered across the region (and beyond), living and working in a variety of communities and occupations. People at all socioeconomic levels maintain relations with kinsmen and home communities; at the same time, differential access to wealth and power divides members of the same community or lineage, just as members of the ruling class or a group of wage earners may seek support from kin or clansmen as they struggle to protect or advance their positions.

This study is certainly not the first to point out the presence of multiple and interacting forms of social cognizance and organization in western Nigeria. Peace (1979) shows, for example, how relationships based or modeled on descent both facilitate and constrain young men's search for urban employment, security, and accumulation, and Peel (1980) chronicles shifting socioeconomic and sectional configurations of conflict and alliance in the political history of Iléṣà. Both studies provide ample evidence of the interplay between communal and class interests and identities in the lives of Yorùbás and the histories of their communities. Both authors conclude, however, by seeking to identify a prevailing trend. Peel finds "a complex interdependence between rivalry of communities for access to the state's resources and the development of inequality between social strata. . . . Within the social system of Nigeria, class and community are coordinated. But community would seem to have priority" (1980, p. 499). Peace, on the other hand, asserts that "a form of class analysis is quite essential" to understanding African social change, and he interprets urban migrants' participation in descent-based networks in the context of their "class situation" as proletarians (1979, p. 14 and passim).

In one sense, each author's conclusion is appropriate for the particular sphere of social activity he chose to study: forms of collective action among factory workers in Lagos, and the social history of an old community, respectively.[5] But it does not follow that class interests and conflicts prevail in the city and that kinship and communal ties dominate rural life. Rather, the ceaseless mobility that pervades the life histories (and even the daily routines) of the people described in this book reflects the degree to which struggles to mobilize kin and community in the pursuit of wealth and power, and vice versa, transcend rural-urban divisions. To study the history of accumulation and conflict in an extended Yorùbá community is to address the question of class formation, not to preclude it.

The extended community portrayed in this study consists of men and women who trace their descent from two neighboring and closely related towns on the edge of the savannah. Both towns are small by Yorùbá standards: according to the 1963 census, Ìreé had 19,514 inhabitants; Ẹripa, 1,459. Both figures are, however, subject to uncertainty.[6] The majority of people interviewed for this study describe themselves as ọmọ (i.e., children of) Ìreé or Ẹripa; that is, they regard these communities as their hometowns or places of origin and trace their descent from one of the compounds (agbo ilé) located therein. Within the towns, however, most compounds maintain traditions of descent from somewhere else, including several compounds in Ẹripa which trace their descent from Ìreé. Indeed, people living in the same compound sometimes trace their descent from different lineages or different towns. Karin Barber (1979) has pointed out that traditions of origin are remembered for long periods of time, even among people settled together in the same compound for several generations. Differences that arise may exacerbate divisions and conflict among neighbors or even kin. Such traditions are just one of many overlapping expressions of Yorùbá social identity which may be used both to pull people together and to divide them, when questions arise concerning access to property, power, or prestige. To appreciate the significance of traditions of origin in the lives of the men and women discussed in this book it is useful to sketch briefly the history of their hometowns before turning to their individual life histories.

Ẹripa and Ìreé: Historical Outline

During the final phase of the nineteenth-century Yorùbá wars, when the struggle centered on the contest between Ìbàdàn and the Èkìtìparapọ̀, Ìreé and Ẹripa occupied a central spot on the frontier between the belligerents. Under colonial rule the locus of political power and activity shifted, leaving the "border towns" of the Kírìjì war on the periphery of the colonial political economy. People from Ẹripa and Ìreé who wished to take advantage of expanding colonial opportunities for wage labor, commercial agriculture, trade, professional employment, or craft and service production for the growing local market have usually had to emigrate to do so. Today the two towns provide, in some respects, a classic example of a dependent economy. Apart from some food crops for local consumption, little is produced there.[7] Traders sell "imported" foodstuffs, fuel, bottled drinks, and sundries in local periodic markets and a few small shops, but the money to buy them comes primarily from remittances sent or brought into Ìreé and Ẹripa by citizens who live and work outside the towns. Full-time residents of Ìreé and Ẹripa are mostly dependents—children, old people, and women—whose trading or agricultural processing activities probably do not provide for their own maintenance.

(Many of the women actually commute between the hometowns and their husbands' places of work.)

Yet Ẹripa and Ìreé are not ghost towns. Their schools (together they boast three primary schools, one secondary modern school, and a secondary grammar school) are well attended; the two maternity clinics in Ìreé do a lively business; and a good deal of construction of both private dwellings and public buildings—notably a new palace for the Areé (traditional ruler) of Ìreé—is underway. Lines are being installed to bring electricity to Ìreé, and there are hopes for piped water from a new storage tank in Ẹripa in the not too distant future. During the first half of 1979 Ẹripa acquired a new town hall and a petrol depot. In short, there is evidence of a considerable inflow of resources to these towns which cannot be explained as a response to the growth of local production or employment opportunities. To understand the reason for these developments and what they portend for the structure of the rural sector in western Nigerian society, we must begin with the historical background.

Early history: aspects of the formation of precolonial communities

I was unable to ascertain the date of founding of either Ìreé or Ẹripa. Informants and one published local history (Taiwo, n.d.) list between thirteen and fifteen obas as having reigned in Ìreé since its establishment, five of them in the twentieth century. The founder of the present ruling house is said to have come from Ìpeé, near Òfà, where his ancestor had settled after leaving Ọ̀yọ́ because of difficulties with the Aláàfin (Johnson, 1921). The reigns of the first few Areé are said to have been peaceful, suggesting that the town was well established before the struggles leading to the breakup of the Ọ̀yọ́ Empire. This is confirmed by Àtàndá (1973, pp. 6–7), who includes Ìreé in a list of towns near the Iléṣà border which were controlled by Ọ̀yọ́.

How long Ìreé had existed before the late eighteenth century is not clear. Local sources differ as to whether the founder of the town was Arólù (the progenitor of the present ruling house) or someone else. Houses in Ìreé trace their descent to various towns, including Òfà, Ogbómọ̀ṣọ́, Ẹsìẹ, Iléṣà, Ìkọ̀lé Èkìtì, Itake, Ìkòyí Ile, Ẹrìnle, Igbája, and Ọ̀yọ́ itself. In Ẹripa, houses were established by immigrants from Èfọ̀n Àláyè, Ọ̀yọ́, Ìlọ́ta, Ìpolé, Ọtan, and Ìkòyí (near Ọ̀yọ́). Local sources disagree, however, over whether the first settlers came from Èfọ̀n Àláyè or from Ìreé. Although none of the local traditions I collected suggest that Ìreé was founded by Ìjẹ̀ṣàs, its population resembles that "mixed population of Ọ̀yọ́s, Ìjẹ̀ṣàs and Èkìtìs and other clans"

(Johnson, 1921, p. 425) found in neighboring towns. Some neighboring towns—Ìgbájọ, Ada, Ọtan, and Ìrèsì—were claimed by the Owá of Ilésà during peace negotiations with Ìbàdàn in 1884 as "having been his originally" (ibid., p. 497). Also, the major chiefs in Ìreé and Ẹripa have Ìjèsà rather than Ọyọ́ titles. Clearly, the Ìjèsà presence in Ìreé is an old one; whether it predates that of Ọyọ́, and by how much, cannot be determined from available evidence.

The "cosmopolitan" makeup of Ìreé and Ẹripa, not unusual in Yorùbá towns, reflects a high degree of mobility in precolonial times (Barber, 1979; Peel, in press). In Ìreé and Ẹripa some houses maintain that their founders settled in Ìreé while traveling to escape personal misfortune[8] or the disruptions of war. More often, a house's tradition of origin suggests that political conflict was a primary reason for the founding ancestor to have left a previous home and settled in Ìreé. In several instances the founder of a house was said to have quarreled with the oba in his previous town of residence, or to have contested unsuccessfully for a title and fled to escape ignominy or indebtedness. For example, Arólù, the founder of the current ruling house, was reported to have been, as a chief at Ọyọ́, so successful in defending his followers against charges of misconduct that he deprived the court of revenue that would otherwise have accrued from their fines and was consequently asked to leave the capital. He first settled with his followers at Ipeé, near Ọ̀fà, but his wives did not conceive there or else bore infants who died soon after birth, so he proceeded to Ìreé, with better results. Such politically motivated movement presumably meant a decisive break with the emigrant's hometown, although separate traditions of origin have clearly been preserved in the orìkì[9] and in traditions of individuals and families, and they may serve as rallying points for conflict within the "host" community long after the original migration (Barber, 1979). Such traditions do not, however, entail the continuing active participation in affairs of the community of origin which is so characteristic of twentieth-century migrants who have left home to seek economic opportunity rather than to escape political conflict.

The breakup of the Ọyọ́ Empire, under the combined pressures of the Fulani jihad and internal dissension, ushered in a long period of turmoil throughout Yorùbáland (Ajayi and Smith, 1964; Johnson, 1921; Law, 1977; Mábògùnjẹ́ and Omer Cooper, 1971). In the early nineteenth century people fled the crumbling empire and moved south, attacking established settlements and founding new ones. In the early 1830s Ọyọ́ Ile, capital of the old empire, was conquered by the Fulani and its inhabitants were scattered. Many towns that had shaken off Ọyọ́'s rule or been freed of it by these events were attacked by neighboring towns or by roving bands of warriors, and their peoples too fled in search of refuge. By the middle of the nineteenth century Abẹ́òkúta and Ìbàdàn, settled about 1830 by groups of Ẹgbá and Ọ̀yọ́ refugees and warriors, had emerged as important towns governed by ruling oligarchies of successful warriors and self-made chiefs. Ìbàdàn, in particular, subsequently extended its control over a number of towns in the southern part of the old Ọ̀yọ́ Empire, including Ìreé and neighboring towns along the escarpment (Akíntóyè, 1971; Àtàndá, 1973; Johnson, 1921; Law, 1977). From there, Ìbàdàn warriors raided or offered protection to various Ìjẹ̀sà and Èkìtì towns, which often found their "protectors" an exacting and oppressive lot (Akíntóyè, 1971; Awẹ́, 1964, 1965). In the late 1870s the Ìjẹ̀sàs, Èkìtìs, and other eastern Yorùbá groups combined forces to resist domination by Ìbàdàn (Akíntóyè, 1971; Johnson, 1921). Aided by simultaneous assaults on Ìbàdàn from Ìlọrin, Ẹgbá, and Ifẹ̀, and an Ìjẹbu blockage of Ìbàdàn's principal supply route to the south, the Èkìtìparapọ̀ (as the Ìjẹ̀sà-Èkìtì confederation was called) managed to stop the Ìbàdàn forces at Kíríjì, a line of battle a few miles northeast of Ìreé where the two armies struggled inconclusively until the negotiated peace settlement of 1886. Many of the towns along this border were subjected to repeated harassment during the war, both by advancing warriors and by the encamped armies, who often despoiled the farms and communities around them for their own sustenance or amusement (ibid.).

To avoid harassment many people fled Ìreé for the comparative safety of Ìkìrun or Ẹ̀rìnle. Those who remained behind harbored refugees from Ẹripa, which was practically deserted during the war. Ìreé appears to have remained under the control of Ìbàdàn throughout the war; Johnson (1921) twice refers to it as a way station for messengers or troops traveling between Ìbàdàn and the battlefront. He does not mention it among the border towns contested by the Èkìtìparapọ̀ during the peace negotiations. Today, most houses in Ẹripa have branches or close kin in Ìreé who remained behind when their relatives returned to Ẹripa after 1893. Residents of both towns often express a sense of common identity: "Ẹripa and Ìreé are sister towns." "Our people are one."[10]

Migration and the colonial economy

During the nineteenth century most of the inhabitants of Ẹripa and Ìreé were engaged in farming. Ìbàdàn's ability to feed its own armies and its substantial population, even under siege (Johnson, 1921), was based partly on its power to extract tribute in foodstuffs and slaves from a large number of subordinate towns such as Ìreé. Even among ọmọ Ìreé (i.e., children or descendants of Ìreé) who fought with the Ìbàdàn army, many were probably farmers as well, taking part in raids or battles during the dry season and returning to their homes when the rains began (Akíntóyè, 1971; Awé, 1964, 1965). Some Ìreé people were undoubtedly also engaged in trade, but during the upheavals of the nineteenth century long-distance trade was a hazardous undertaking, requiring the means and the ability to organize or join large caravans with effective defense capabilities. Local traditions concerning the war years in Ìreé emphasize the disruptiveness of raids and combat rather than the rewards of trade or plunder.

After the British attacked Ìjẹbu Òde in 1892 and, in the following year, extended British protection to most of the Yorùbá-speaking peoples, growing numbers of people from all over Yorùbáland began to travel away from their communities of residence. As in the past, some people may have moved to avert conflict or to settle in a more auspicious or politically congenial place. Some ex-slaves, purchased or taken captive during the war years, returned home, taking with them ideas and contacts acquired while they were away.[11] But primarily, the beginning of the colonial era saw an increasing outflow of young men who emigrated temporarily from their home communities in search of new opportunities and experiences (see Peel, 1978). They gravitated toward areas where the growth of administrative and commercial activity, or the beginnings of commercial agriculture, created jobs and new opportunities for trade: toward coastal towns such as Lagos or Sapele; toward rural areas such as Agége, Ijan, and Òtà, where farmers were beginning to produce foodstuffs for the new urban markets and to experiment with export crops; to the railways, in Nigeria and the Gold Coast; and to the gold mines and growing urban centers of the latter as well. Emigrants from savannah towns established Yorùbá enclaves in Accra and Kumasi in the 1890s (Eades, 1975; Sudarkasa, 1979), which remained active centers of trade until the expulsion of aliens in 1969.

Men from Ìreé and Ẹripa joined the streams of migrants seeking new opportunities to earn cash incomes and to see something of the world. Most of the sons and daughters of Ìreé and Ẹripa whom I interviewed had spent part of their working lives away from home, employed as laborers on the railway, in Lagos, or in areas of early cocoa development, or trading in places as far away as Ejìnrìn, Sapele, Onitsha, and Sokoto. A number of traders from Ìreé and Ẹripa congregated in strategic rural locations, such as Àlàrí near the Dahomey border or in Ghana. (Of my ninety informants, eleven had lived in Ghana for some part of their lives, either as traders themselves or with parents who were trading there; another seven had spent time

in Àlàrí. See Eades, 1980.) Others, like the present chief imam of
Ìreé, became Muslims and traveled to such centers of Islamic learning
as Ìlọrin, Ìwó, and Ìbàdàn to study with a succession of teachers. Often
these men, too, supported themselves as traders or craftsmen while
they were studying. Of those informants who migrated to Ifẹ̀ to grow
cocoa, many did so after a previous period of nonagricultural employment.

In his richly detailed study of the social history of Iléṣà, J. D. Y.
Peel (in press) has chronicled the complex effects of changing
economic opportunities on social relations in Iléṣà during the early
years of the colonial era. He shows how the increasing economic independence of young men (who were able to earn money as emigrant
traders or wage laborers) enabled them to challenge their elders' control of women, marriage, and of political offices represented by the
title system.[12] In this endeavor the young men were aided, somewhat
inadvertently, by the colonial regime, which created conditions that
greatly facilitated trade, travel, and the growth of employment opportunities. They were also helped by British reform of the fiscal system
in most Yorùbá towns, which required chiefs to forgo the tolls, tributes,
and slave raids of the past and to rely instead on a system of fees,
licenses, and direct taxation under the supervision of the colonial
authorities. Ironically, these developments sometimes placed the
young men in opposition to the chiefs' efforts to preserve Ìjẹ̀ṣà independence from British control by resisting colonial schemes for fiscal
reform, road building, or the establishment of local courts. Eventually
the chiefs themselves were forced to encourage trade and to redistribute women through the divorce courts, in order to bolster their own
revenues.

The development of cocoa cultivation, which created new opportunities to earn incomes locally in both agriculture and trade, encouraged young men to return to Iléṣà after a period of trade or wage
employment "abroad." By the 1920s and 1930s a number of returned
emigrants had invested their earnings in wives, children, and cocoa
farms, often acquiring both families and farms at an earlier age than
their fathers had been able to do.[13] Prosperous farmers were, in turn,
sometimes able to transmute their economic and domestic resources
into political influence within the town. Although the largest personal
fortunes were built in trade or transport, cocoa frequently provided
the initial capital for launching such ventures. By the 1930s wealthy
traders held some of the senior titles in Iléṣà, and the Owá had committed himself to the support of programs to advance their interests
by developing the town's commercial and educational resources.

Because the land around Ìreé and Ẹripa is not especially well suited to growing cocoa, farmers in these and other savannah towns took up cocoa cultivation much later than did farmers in Iléṣà, and then only through large-scale emigration to the forest belt. Nonetheless, early emigrants from Ẹripa and Ìreé tended, like those from Iléṣà, to return home after a period of trade or employment "abroad." They usually married at home and often settled down there to farm, build houses, accumulate followers, and compete for titles. Although traders spent most of their economically active lives away from Ẹripa and Ìreé, they too usually married men or women from their hometowns. Like Yorùbá traders throughout West Africa, they also brought kinsmen and -women from home to assist them in expanding their businesses; they built houses at home, organized societies of fellow townsmen abroad to represent their interests to the local authorities in the host community and to facilitate communications with home, and frequently returned to their hometowns in old age to retire or to assume a title or the headship of a house (see Adépòjù, 1974; Agìrì, 1972; Eades, 1975, 1979; Mábògùnjẹ́, 1972; Sudarkasa, 1979).

In the savannah towns, as in Iléṣà, emigrants' continuing involvement in local affairs was motivated by a number of factors. Though far from the centers of colonial administrative and commercial expansion, Yorùbá communities in the savannah enjoyed some growth of local income-earning opportunities in the 1920s and 1930s. The expansion of trade and traffic between northern and southern Nigeria brought increased commercial activity to towns such as Òṣogbo or Ogbómòṣó, located on the railway or on major roads. In addition, the growing demand for foodstuffs in the major towns and the rural cocoa-growing areas created a market for food crops which was supplied in part by Yorùbá farmers in the savannah. In 1924 the resident of Ọ̀yọ́ Province noted in his annual report that, although little cocoa was produced in the northern districts of the province, "large amounts of foodstuffs are grown . . . and are exported to Ìbà-dàn, Abẹòkúta and Lagos." Five years later the resident of Ìlọrin Province complained that local farmers showed little interest in growing groundnuts, since yams and Guinea corn were "more remunerative," and in 1931 he explained that since declining exports of cocoa and palm oil had produced a "shortage of cash" in the southern provinces and had induced farmers there to grow more food crops, southern demand for foodstuffs from Ìlọrin Province had declined sharply (Ìlọrin Province, *Annual Report*, 1933). Thus, from the 1920s at least, Yorùbá farmers in the savannah enjoyed expanded opportunities to earn income from farming at home.

The administrative policies of the colonial regime also fostered emigrants' continued interest in the affairs of their hometowns. Through
the native authority system, local fiscal and judicial matters were
organized, insofar as possible, in terms of precolonial Yorùbá polities.
For Ẹripa and Ìreé, which were too small to qualify for independent
jurisdictional status in the colonial hierarchy, the question was which
neighbor made the best overlord. Under the new Ọ̀yọ́ Empire, created
by Captain Ross with the enthusiastic collaboration of the Aláàfin of
Ọ̀yọ́, Ìreé and Ẹripa were incorporated into the Ìkìrun District of the
Ìbàdàn Division of Ọ̀yọ́ Province. Access to the administrative and
judicial apparatus of the colonial state (represented at the local level
by the native authority councils or, after 1914, by the native courts)
lay, accordingly, through Ìkìrun. When religious disturbances broke
out in Ìreé in 1910 and 1916, for example, police came from Ìkìrun
to quell the violence, and those arrested were taken to Ìkìrun for trial
(see chap. 7, below). One chief from Ìreé sat on the native court there.
In 1941 Ìkìrun District was reconstituted as the Ìfẹ́lódùn Federal
Council, with chiefs from all the towns in the area, and the district
officer in Òṣogbo congratulated himself that "fourteen or fifteen jeal-
ous and unrelated towns now work together in comparative harmony
and unity" (Ọ̀ṣun Division, *Annual Report*, 1941). In subsequent years,
however, the affairs of the council were dominated by the continuing
jealousy of Ìkìrun, where council headquarters were located and which
received most of the government amenities supplied to the district.
When, in 1952, the old native authorities were replaced throughout
western Nigeria by elected local councils, one of the first items of
business undertaken by the representatives of Ìreé and other towns
in the Ìfẹ́lódùn District was to agitate for independence from Ìkìrun.
To forestall trouble, the colonial authorities acceded to their request
and, in 1954, the district was divided into two parts, and the Ìkìrun
District Council and the reconstituted Ìfẹ́lódùn District Council, with
its headquarters at Ìreé, were set up.

Apart from the native authority, the principal institutional source
of access to external amenities and opportunities in Ìreé was the
American Baptist Mission, located in Ogbómọ̀ṣọ́.[14] Baptist missionaries
began touring the Ìfẹ́lódùn District as early as 1898. At first they were
welcomed by the oba of Ìreé as a potential political asset, but later, as
their converts began to question the authority of local chiefs and
religious specialists, they became targets of hostility and suspicion.
Some of the early converts soon left Ìreé to take advantage of the
training offered at various Baptist institutions, such as the teacher
training college at Ìwó, the seminary and hospital at Ogbómọ̀ṣọ́, and,
later, the Baptist Boys High School at Abẹ̀òkúta. During the early

years of the colonial period the numbers of such Baptist students were very small indeed; later, after the mission opened a primary school in Ìreé in 1923, the flow began to increase. Of the ninety individuals from Ẹripa and Ìreé whose histories I collected, twenty-six had had some form of postprimary education. I was not able to ascertain where five of those had studied; nineteen had attended one or more of the Baptist institutions mentioned above.

Baptist converts were therefore more likely than other ọmọ Ìreé to obtain postprimary schooling and thus qualify for clerical or professional employment. In addition, the Baptists were associated with the few amenities available in Ìreé before the end of the colonial period. In addition to the Baptist Day School, a maternity clinic was built in the town in 1944, with financial support and staffing provided by the Baptist Mission in Ogbómòṣọ́. Although the services of the clinic were available to all, regardless of religious preference, the Baptists were clearly associated with the sponsoring institution. In addition to providing medical services, the clinic was a source of prestige for the town among neighboring communities, whose members also used its services. The Baptists of Ìreé were inclined to take credit for the enhanced status of their town. In short, the presence of the clinic, combined with the fact that most educated ọmọ Ìreé were Baptists, meant that, from the mid-1940s at least, Baptists were felt by many of their fellow townspeople to enjoy preferential access to external sources of opportunity and influence.

Cocoa and the development of extended communities

During the international depression of the 1930s Nigerian export earnings fell sharply (cocoa export value declined by 55 percent between 1929 and 1933), with corresponding declines in commercial activity and in government budgets. Layoffs of government employees affected both clerical and manual workers, and many Nigerian traders were forced out of business either by the collapse of the import/export trade or by the accompanying decline in domestic purchasing power and commerce. Town dwellers who had become involved in the nonagricultural sectors of the colonial economy often were forced to take up farming again in order to subsist (Berry, 1975a; Helleiner, 1966).

The precipitous decline in market activity and opportunities caused by the depression affected the farming sector as well as the towns. Demand for agricultural labor did not decrease in an absolute sense, but money to pay hired farm labor did, so that people who wanted to farm had to do so on their own or within the context of an institutional arrangement that provided for remuneration in kind. Thus, not only former traders and government employees but also men who had previously worked as agricultural laborers began to take up farming on their own account. In particular, men from the savannah who had migrated to commercial farming areas in southwestern Yorùbá-land during the early colonial period, where they worked for local tree-crop growers either for a cash wage or for a share of the crop (and often cultivated small plots of food crops for their own consumption), now found that their former employers were unable to pay them or that the market value of their share of the crop was so low as to provide little incentive to remain in their current positions. Relatively speaking, the returns to agricultural labor declined to a point at which some of these immigrants found it worthwhile to incur the risks and difficulties of seeking out land to cultivate for themselves.

Permission to plant tree crops on uncultivated land was not readily available in the established centers of cocoa cultivation, which is partly why northern Yorùbá immigrants had not already planted cocoa and kola for themselves. However, intrepid individuals who ventured farther east, into Ifẹ̀, Iléṣà, or Òndó, reported that uncultivated forest land suitable for cocoa was abundant there. A few of them set about the delicate political task of negotiating permission to farm in these areas; toward the end of the 1930s, encouraged by their initial success, kinsmen and neighbors began to follow them (Berry, 1975a). The planting of tree crops in previously uncultivated areas was encouraged by the temporary recovery of export prices in 1936–37, and it continued during the subsequent depression which lasted through most of World War II (Berry, 1976). The depressed condition of trade and the concomitant scarcity of cash during the 1930s and the early 1940s meant that few men could afford to hire labor to establish new farms; but they could mobilize it through family connections. Men who migrated into the eastern parts of the forest belt to plant cocoa usually relied on the assistance of their wives, children, and/or junior siblings in establishing their farms.

Like their counterparts throughout the southern savannah, men from Ẹ̀ripa and Ìreé began to plant cocoa in the forests of Ifẹ̀ and Iléṣà in the late 1940s. The first man from Ìreé to settle in Abúlékejì came there between 1946 and 1948, after working for a year and a half as a sawyer in the Èkìtì country. (Before that, he had spent a number of years as a trader in Ghana.) One family from Èrìnle were farming as tenants in Abúlékejì when he arrived, as well as two families from Ifẹ̀tẹ̀dó and Ifẹ̀, respectively, who claimed ownership rights over considerable amounts of farmland in the vicinity of the village.[15] In 1949 the first Ìreé settler was joined by his senior brother, a farmer and *babaláwo* who had earlier followed him to Ghana to sell native medicine, and by another older farmer from Ẹripa who had previously farmed near Òtà. This senior man had gone to Òtà about 1920, worked as an agricultural laborer, and then succeeded in getting land to start his own farm. He had planted cocoa, but the trees did not do well. In the late 1940s one of his sons, who was teaching school in a village east of Ifẹ̀, told him about the two brothers from Ìreé who had obtained land at Abúlékejì. The old man decided to go there too. During the next decade a number of people from Ìreé and Ẹripa followed the earlier settlers, often spending a few years in the teacher's village first, where their fellow townsmen had already established farms and built houses in which they could accommodate friends and relatives from home.

During the 1950s kinsmen continued to constitute the principal source of labor in agriculture, as in trade, despite the increased commercialization of both rural and urban labor markets during the colonial period. Among migrants from the savannah, few men now worked for their elders until the latter agreed to "marry for them" (i.e., help them negotiate and finance a marriage agreement), but many worked for their elders in exchange for help in starting their own trades or establishing cocoa farms. They might marry with money earned fairly quickly through wage labor, but starting a farm or a trading business was a longer-term and riskier process, in which a novice might need outside support, advice, and assistance for some time until he got established. Access to credit, insurance, and technical assistance depended on membership in social institutions which served to mediate and control the terms on which people acquired resources from one another. Emigrant farmers and traders often found it convenient not only to recruit kinsmen for help in establishing a business but to settle near a group of people from the same hometown who could assist in mediating contacts and potential conflicts with members of the host community. Thus, like Yorùbá traders in Kumasi or Lagos, Ọ̀yọ́ cocoa farmers in Ifẹ̀ or Òndó have tended to preserve their identity as ọmọ Ìreé, Ìkìrun, Ogbómọ̀ṣọ́, and so on, both in dealings with their "hosts" and in their relationships with one another. Many commute long distances at regular intervals in order to remain part of their home communities (Adépọ̀jù, 1974; Agìrì, 1972; Aronson, 1978; Berry, 1975*a*; Eades, 1979; Sudarkasa, 1979).

As cocoa prices recovered and then soared in the late 1940s and early 1950s, younger men without a ready pool of dependent labor to draw upon went directly from savannah towns to the cocoa belt to work for their elders, in exchange for help later on in establishing tree-crop farms of their own. As cocoa prices rose, established farmers could afford to feed and maintain a larger number of dependents, thus facilitating increased cocoa planting by their junior kinsmen. By the 1960s it was becoming difficult to obtain uncultivated land for planting tree crops around Ifẹ̀, and farmers who wished to expand their cocoa holdings moved farther east into Òndó to obtain more land. As in the earlier migration to Ifẹ̀, they used family connections to maintain distant farms, often placing junior relatives on each farm and then traveling back and forth to supervise their work (see Hill, 1963).

While farmers from the savannah were moving south by the thousands in the 1950s, the simultaneous introduction of electoral politics brought ambitious men back to their hometowns to seek support as they campaigned for elective office or acquired access to politically controlled employment, contracts, or funds. In preparation for self-rule the British organized elected local government councils—to advise the chiefs and to preside over local administrative and financial affairs—and increased the numbers of clerical and administrative personnel employed by them (Mackintosh, 1966). In towns such as Ẹripa and Ìreé, however, the perquisites of local office were not large, and men who ran for office were usually of modest means. The first elected representatives to the Ìfẹ́lódùn Local Government Council were men with a primary school education or perhaps teacher training certificates. They included a farmer, a retired customs clerk, a dispenser, a clergyman, a schoolteacher, and one man who had served as a medical aide in the British army during World War II. For the most part, candidates were selected on the basis of their education: educated men were regarded by their fellow townsmen as more likely than uneducated men to maintain an effective liaison with the regional government. The local government councils, however, were not given much to work with, in terms of revenue or authority. The members of the Ìfẹ́lódùn Council spent most of their time and energy on tax collection (most of the funds were handed over to the regional government) and on questions of jurisdictional status. In the 1950s the Baptists did more than local councillors to bring opportunities and amenities to the town. The Ìreé High School (opened in 1959), as well as the Baptist Welfare Center, was initially staffed by the Baptist Convention. Baptists, accordingly, became leading contenders in local politics (including chieftaincy contests, party politics, and the Ìreé Progressive Union) and a primary target of local jealousies and factional strife (see chap. 7, below).

Conclusion

The consequences of colonial economic development and the formation of extended Yorùbá communities for postcolonial patterns of agricultural growth, political action, and class formation were profound. In chapter 7 I discuss in detail the political and economic repercussions of electoral politics, military rule, and oil in Ẹripa and Ìreé, but a brief indication of these developments here will help to set the stage for the following chapters. After independence, the decline in cocoa prices and associated government revenues, and the growing violence of political conflict in western Nigeria, eventually led to conflict within Ìreé itself. The result was, among other things, the demise of the Baptist Old Guard (although not of religious differences as a focus of political conflict) who had dominated town affairs in the 1950s and the early 1960s. During the civil war the rural economy was depressed in western Nigeria, and local political activity was not only officially banned but also inhibited by the limited availability of state resources for local use. During the late 1960s Yorùbá farmers focused their discontent on state expropriation of declining agricultural surpluses and neglect of rural needs, especially in the older cocoa-growing areas where yields and incomes were low. With the revival of state revenues and the reorganization of local governments in the 1970s, however, emigrants' interest and participation in hometown affairs also revived. As we shall see, Ìreé and Ẹripa became once again a focus for increased investment and political involvement by their emigrant sons and daughters, including a number of those known in Ìreé as "Lagos people." These were full-fledged members of the Nigerian bourgeoisie who, while often educated in the same Baptist institutions as the repatriates of the 1950s, looked to the state rather than to the mission for resources and opportunities and identified culturally with other members of their class rather than primarily with fellow converts. Increasingly, in the 1970s, farmers, petty traders, and members of the Yorùbá ruling class have met face-to-face in family meetings, ceremonies, or gatherings of the Ìreé Progressive Union. Class formation, with all its attendant possibilities for co-optation and conflict, has lately come home to rural communities such as Ẹripa and Ìreé, with consequences to be discussed in subsequent chapters.

3

Accumulation, Family, and Class: The Uses of Agricultural Income in Two Cocoa-Farming Villages

The preceding chapters have described the incorporation of Yorùbá states and towns into a centralized political system during and after the colonial period and have outlined accompanying processes of agricultural growth, commercialization, migration, and social differentiation at regional and local levels. In this chapter and the next I discuss the uses of agricultural surplus and the strategies of personal and collective advancement employed by individual cocoa farmers and show how farmers' strategies both reflected and influenced the particular conjuncture of regional and local changes described above. In this chapter I explain how farmers in two cocoa-growing villages have used income over time; I also consider the consequences of expanding cocoa production for accumulation, domestic organization, and social differentiation within the cocoa-growing sector. Chapter 4 takes up the question of farmers' links to the wider regional economy and society and shows how they have been expressed or developed through collective action.

My central argument in this chapter is that the uses of agricultural surplus, and hence their economic and social consequences, were shaped both by the conditions of agricultural production in western Nigeria and by farmers' understanding of those conditions. In migrating to areas suitable for growing cocoa, acquiring long-term land-use rights, and engaging labor in the cultivation of cocoa trees, Yorùbá farmers shaped their strategies in accordance with prevailing ideas about work, property, and authority, as well as with material conditions of the agricultural economy. Moreover, the very process of expanding cocoa production altered or reinforced the structure of incentives and constraints facing Yorùbá producers and accumulators, as well as their views of how resources could and should be acquired and used. These developments, in turn, influenced the uses of agricultural surplus. In allocating the proceeds of their cocoa farms, among people as well as commodities, farmers were influenced both by what they expected to gain and by what was expected of them by relatives, neighbors, and society at large. In other words, the way farmers used resources depended on how they valued them, and their evaluations were shaped by their own history of resource use. Since my approach is somewhat different from standard paradigms of value and resource allocation, I elaborate it in general terms before turning to the evidence from Abàkinní and Abúlékejì.

Value as Social Process: The Problem of Explaining Resource Allocation

Discussion of the nature and determination of economic value is fundamentally divided on ideological lines. Neoclassical economics explains value in terms of scarcity and preference. Producers, consumers, and accumulators are said to allocate resources in accordance with expected net returns which, in turn, are determined by factor endowments, technology, and people's preferences. If, in a given economic system, one factor of production (say, labor) is abundant relative to others, goods that require relatively large amounts of the abundant factor will tend to be cheaper than those requiring more of the scarce factor(s). If, however, members of the society strongly prefer labor-intensive goods, those goods will command a higher price than they would if all goods were equally preferred. Thus values, or relative prices, are determined by the interplay between preference and scarcity. The theory assumes, often implicitly, that goods and productive resources may be readily exchanged for or transformed into one another. This assumption implies that production and exchange occur smoothly—without friction or social turmoil—or that, in the inelegant phrasing of the literature, most resources are "fungible."

Neoclassical economics does not attempt to explain the origin of preferences; they are treated as exogenous to the economic system and hence beyond the scope of economic analysis. In practice, however, economists are often obliged to assign specific content to preferences or to make assumptions about their consequences for behavior, if only to generate testable hypotheses. Accordingly there has been considerable debate over whether preferences vary across cultures and, if so, whether such variation leads to culturally specific processes of resource allocation and use. The issue lies at the center of the formalist-substantivist debate in economic anthropology, for example,

and has also stimulated a good deal of discussion among economists over the universality or otherwise of various decision-making
algorithms (profit maximization, risk aversion, etc.).[1] On the whole,
this literature is inconclusive primarily because there is no agreement
on an acceptable method of observing preferences independently of
the social conditions in which they obtain or, therefore, of docu-
menting their effects on resource allocation. (The convention, among
microeconomic theorists, of formulating models in terms of utility
maximization does not resolve the issue; it only begs the question.)
To date, it remains to be demonstrated that specific patterns of resource allocation and relative value can be explained without reference
to culturally specific norms and attitudes.

Marxists have been profoundly critical of the subjective element in
the neoclassical theory of value. In their view, value is created in the
process of production which is basically a process of labor: production
occurs when and only when people work. Whether they work and
how they work are matters more of social interaction than of biological
necessity or environmental compulsion. Value cannot be explained in
terms of individuals' subjective reactions to material possibilities; it
must be understood as part of the social process. In expanding this
insight into the labor theory of value, however, Marxist economists
have introduced some assumptions of their own which are nearly as
arbitrary as the "black box" of neoclassical utility. For example, the
argument that the productivity of capital (where capital is defined as
reproducible means of production) is directly proportional to the
amount of labor required to produce it has been questioned, even by
some Marxist writers. Joan Robinson (1966), for example, while en-
dorsing Marx's desire to ground economic theory in the rights of the
working classes, argues nonetheless that capital is productive independently of the labor tied up in it, and that accumulation is an ongoing
social process that cannot be explained merely by exhuming the
graveyard of "dead labor" embodied in capital goods.

Furthermore, the labor theory of value does not dispose of the
possibility that values are culturally determined, at least in part. Accumulation requires the employment of surplus value to expand the
stock of reproducible capital goods. Surplus value, in turn, is the
portion of output which is not needed to reproduce the labor that
produced it in the first place. But the cost of reproducing labor is
socially as well as biologically determined and, further, reflects the
conceptual as well as the material dimensions of social conditions. The
point may be illustrated with an example from one of the basic expo-
sitions of "bourgeois" economics. In the fifth edition of his introduc-
tory textbook, Samuelson quotes a study showing that, in 1945, the

average American adult could obtain a nutritionally adequate diet for
$39 a year if he or she subsisted primarily on soybeans, cabbage, and
kidneys. Does it follow that the socially necessary cost of American
labor time was $39 a year (with or without an allowance for shelter
and health care) even in 1945? In short, the underlying problem
remains. Value is not something that inheres in objects, or even actions,
independently of what people think about them. To understand how
values are determined and how they, in turn, affect production and
accumulation, we must confront the question of ideology and its relationship to changing conditions of production and power.

In thinking about value as an outcome of historical interaction between practices and concepts of production, it may be useful to turn
for a moment to another theme in the Marxist critique of neoclassical
economic theory: the issue of fungibility. Fungibility is not the same
thing as perfect competition, although the two notions are related.
Perfect competition implies that production and exchange take place
in the absence of power, and that no social agent is capable of altering
prices or patterns of resource use to his own advantage. Fungibility
on the other hand implies the absence of resistance: commodities
and/or labor may be exchanged or transformed into one another
without raising objections, creating tension, or provoking opposition.
In principle, fungibility is compatible with imperfect competition: a
producer may convert labor and materials into finished output without
resistance, then hold the resulting product off the market in order to
raise its price. Conversely, in the one major exception neoclassical
theory allows to the assumption of fungibility—the time and effort
required to transform raw materials into finished goods—it is asserted
that this obstacle to instantaneous transformation can be exactly compensated for by the transfer of liquid resources equal in value to the
commodities forgone during the process of production. In other
words, neoclassical theory assumes that production and accumulation
do not themselves create social disharmony; this results only from
"distortions" arising from exogenously determined concentrations of
power.

Marxists have attacked the neoclassical assumption of fungibility
primarily in relation to aggregate processes of production and accumulation, though there are exceptions.[2] According to Marxist theory,
production means the exploitation of labor, in all societies except the
truly socialist or the primitively communist. Production therefore gen-
erates tension and conflict between the exploited and their exploiters.
The power to exploit rests, in turn, on control of the means of production; differential control is thus the foundation of class conflict,
whereas the frictions arising from the process of production are what

brings conflict into actuality. Class struggle gives rise to new forms of consciousness among the exploited which impel and assist them to organize politically against their exploiters. Similarly, the exploiters may get wind of the impending crisis and make deliberate use of consciousness and its expression in ideology to override or redefine workers' perceptions in the hope of forestalling revolutionary action.

In the Marxist paradigm, ideology is presented as a consequence of changing material conditions rather than as a formative influence on them, although it may be used as an instrument by opposing classes in their struggles with each other. But this view seems unnecessarily restrictive. If ideas can be used in the pursuit of material or social advantage, then in principle they constitute a kind of resource— potentially an object as well as a condition or instrument of accumulation. This is acknowledged, by neoclassical and Marxist economists alike, with respect to technological ideas. State and corporate outlays on research and development are recognized as a major source of economic growth in industrialized societies, and international differences in the generation and control of technology are regarded as a prime source of global inequalities in wealth and rates of development. But the argument may be equally well applied to social knowledge and concepts, such as ideas about the acquisition and exercise of authority, for example, or rights to property. Clearly, such ideas constitute a crucial point of reference in the organization of production or in the design of strategies for acquiring productive resources or coping with social tensions and conflict. To the extent that they provide potential answers to people's doubts or disputes about who can obtain resources and on what terms, or how they may be used, ideas become a resource to be employed in coping with one's environment and, hence, to be sought after and struggled and sacrificed for in the course of production and material accumulation. And, as objects of accumulation, modes of understanding enter directly not only into current patterns of production and resource allocation but also into the reproduction of productive capacity. Thus they influence forms of accumulation and struggle as well as being influenced by them.

These points are brought out clearly, though not in quite these terms, in some recent studies of the impact of global economic and political forces on local patterns of production, property rights, and relations of power in particular African societies. Throughout sub-Saharan Africa, capitalist penetration and colonial rule confronted African producers with new economic incentives and new pressures: to pay taxes, produce and/or sell particular commodities, and supply labor to foreign firms or the colonial state, often under harsh or unrewarding conditions. These changes led, in turn, to new levels and forms of demand for land and other productive resources and challenged existing ideas about resource acquisition and use. Two examples of the resulting, interrelated changes in productive practices and people's understandings of them are put forward by David Parkin in his study (1972) of the development of copra production in a Giriama community in eastern Kenya and by Pauline Peters in her analysis (1983) of the effects of deep-well boring on the pastoral economy of the Kgatleng district in Botswana.

In both studies the authors claim that changing practices with respect to the acquisition and use of property (coconut palms in Kenya, water and grazing in Botswana) were shaped by prevailing social norms and concepts and that they, in turn, affected the concepts themselves and their application in other areas of social behavior. In the Giriama community, accumulators of coconut palms sought to assure themselves of the testimony of credible witnesses in order to defend their rights of ownership over recently acquired trees. Accordingly, they took steps to uphold the authority and status of elders whose testimony was likely to command respect in local courts. In the Kgatleng district, cattlemen, standing both to gain and to lose from restrictions on communal rights to water and grazing land, adopted an ambivalent stance toward the question of whether water and grazing rights should be limited to those who had invested in a particular borehole. The introduction of new economic, political, and technological conditions gave rise to conflicting arguments and actions, both with regard to the actual allocation of land and water rights and with respect to people's statements about how such allocations ought to be organized.

In both instances, struggles over property and the definition of property rights also influenced the process of social differentiation. In addition, though neither Parkin nor Peters stresses the point, accumulators tended to invest real resources as well as rhetoric in upholding or modifying principles of ownership and social control which impinged on their own accumulative efforts. For example, successful Giriama farmers sometimes spent sizable sums at funeral ceremonies to demonstrate their own commitment to the principles of seniority and gerontocracy. Thus, not only did accumulation shape people's ideas about social relations, but the development of concepts about rights in resources also influenced the ways in which resources were used and hence the resulting processes of accumulation and class formation.

In western Nigeria, colonial rule and agricultural commercialization also led to new uses of land and labor and to new opportunities for production and accumulation. In seeking to exploit these opportunities to advantage, Yorùbá farmers were influenced by prevailing concepts about social relations, in the way they sought access to the means of production and organized the productive process. Increased production and accumulation served, in turn, further to reinforce or modify the ways in which people mobilized resources and the terms they used to define and evaluate them. To trace the consequences of changing agricultural production for the growth and structure of economic activity and the degree and form of social differentiation, it is important to ask both what people did and what they thought about what they were doing.

The Practice and Concept of Agricultural Accumulation: Abàkinní and Abúlékejì

In the nineteenth century much of the productive activity in Yorùbá communities was carried out under the aegis of large patrilocal compounds (agbo ilé). These compounds constituted the principal residence of most Yorùbás and a primary political unit within Yorùbá towns (Fádípè, 1970; Lloyd, 1954; Schwab, 1955). Within the compound, relations of authority and subordination were based on seniority. Seniority was not, however, determined solely by age: it depended also on other aspects of family status (marriage, childbearing), on order of arrival in the compound,[3] on knowledge, and on demonstrated ability to command the loyalty and resources of other people. Both knowledge and the ability to command a following were matters of personal achievement. Older people always merited respectful behavior from their juniors, but not all elders wielded much influence, even within their own compounds or descent groups. To acquire specialized knowledge, for example, people sometimes invested many years in study and service under an acknowledged master. In addition, whether or not a person possessed specialized knowledge, his or her reputation, and hence seniority, also depended on the size of his or her following (see Barber, 1981).

The accumulation of wealth facilitated the accumulation of followers but did not guarantee it. To gain influence and prestige, a rich man had to use his wealth to create obligations and relations of dependency and to establish a reputation for generosity. A man of modest means could also become influential if he was known to have unusual or specialized skill in solving problems or handling interpersonal relationships (Aronson, 1978; Lloyd, 1974). The rights and obligations associated with seniority might thus obtain among nonkin as well as within descent groups. Conversely, relations of seniority among kin could vary in accordance with individual differences in wealth and reputation.

During the twentieth century patrilocal compounds began to break up under the combined impact of colonial political domination and expanding commercial activity (Clarke, 1978; Peel, in press). As people migrated to areas of expanding economic opportunity they spent more time away from their hometowns and compounds, while men who returned to their hometowns in mid or later life often built separate houses within or outside their fathers' compounds. Nevertheless, just as the hometown remained an important focus of social interaction and political mobilization, even among men and women who spent most of their economically active lives away from home, so did the compound and the descent group (Bender, 1972). The reasons for the enduring significance of place and group of origin in twentieth-century Yorùbá economic and social life lay not only in the administrative and political practices of indirect rule but also in the forms of production and accumulation which developed out of the process of agricultural expansion and commercialization.

The social organization of cocoa production.—In the case of cocoa, both the fact and the form of descent-group relations entered into processes of resource acquisition and use. Access to uncultivated land was linked to membership in a descent group (Lloyd, 1962; Berry, 1975a). Individuals were entitled to use land belonging to their own kin groups, provided no one else was actually cultivating it. If the family had no uncultivated land to spare (or, as often happened in the twentieth century, none suitable for planting cocoa), farmers had to seek land elsewhere. To do so a farmer had to find a sponsor, known to the landholding family, who could "introduce" the would-be cultivator to the landholder(s) and vouch for his behavior. The farmer had also to acknowledge the landholding family's continuing rights over the land, often through an annual gift of produce (ìsákólè). As the demand for uncultivated forest land rose with the spread of cocoa cultivation, gifts given to the landholders, both at the time of the initial allocation of use rights and annually at harvest time thereafter, were commuted into cash payments and tended to rise in value over time.[4] In short, because rights in cultivable land were defined according to kinship, the growth in demand for rights to plant tree crops served to reinforce and perpetuate the importance of kin-group membership as a basis of gaining access to resources.

Most cocoa farmers in Abákinnì and Abúlékejì were immigrants from the savannah who had acquired planting rights from local Ifè families.[5] Abákinnì was founded in 1940 by Bákàrè, a man from Ìkìrun who came to Ifè in search of land to plant cocoa after having worked as a farm laborer near Òtà. He obtained cultivation rights directly from the Òòni of Ifè, on land belonging to the Òòni's lineage,[6] and later acted as an agent for the lineage, recruiting fellow ọmọ Ìkìrun as tenants and collecting ìṣákọ́lẹ̀ from them on the landholders' behalf. Since no one from the landholding lineage lives in the village, Bákàrè also serves as village head (bálẹ̀). In Abúlékejì the bálẹ̀ is a local land-holder who has allocated cultivation rights to a number of immigrant farmers. Many of the present inhabitants of Abúlékejì also obtained farming rights from other Ifẹ̀ families; farmers pay ìṣákọ́lẹ̀ to several different descent groups. A majority of the residents of Abúlékejì come from Ẹripa and Ìreé, but there are also quite a few people from other savannah towns.

The fact that most farmers in Abàkinní and Abúlékejì are strangers (àléjò)—that is, of non-Ifẹ̀ descent—as well as tenants to local landhold-ing families has affected the development of transactions in rural assets. In principle, ownership of land is based strictly on kinship: members of one Ifẹ̀ lineage may be tenants to another. In practice, however, when both landholder and cocoa farmer trace their origin to the same community, rights of ownership may become blurred over time, especially since cocoa trees live for many years and memories of the original transaction between owner and tenant often become confused. Strangers, however, are clearly identifiable and universally acknowledged to have no claim to rights of ownership in local land. Hence it has been easier for strangers than for local tenants to sell cocoa trees (regarded as the property of the person who planted them).

Farmers identifiable as strangers also tend to be treated differentially in terms of access to local political institutions, a fact that has had considerable significance for the process of rural differentiation and for forms of collective action (see chap. 4). It is sufficient here to emphasize that, in an economy where access to resources is closely related to access to the state, political discrimination against strangers tends to reinforce their sense of identity with their communities of origin.

Seniority (as opposed to lineage membership per se) was more im-portant for the recruitment and management of labor in the cocoa economy than for redefining property rights or terms of access to land. Cocoa trees take several years to mature,[7] during which time the farmer must have some means of supporting himself and his dependents or of hiring labor. Many Yorùbá farmers financed the establishment of their first cocoa farms partly out of money earned from wage labor, trade, or a craft, but most of them also relied on the labor of people over whom they could exercise rights of seniority and who did not, therefore, have to be compensated directly for their services. A married man with children old enough to work was, for example, in a better position to establish a cocoa farm than was a single man or a husband whose children were small. Farmers also drew on the labor of junior kinsmen other than their wives and children (a category of classificatory junior brothers designated by the Yorùbá term *àbúrò*) or of clients and other subordinates. Bakare, the founder of Abàkinní, in his capacity as agent for the Ọ̀ọ̀ni's family, enjoyed a certain amount of seniority over other tenants in the village and in consequence received labor services from them. His house had been built for him by his fellow villagers, and one farmer described how, in return for Bakare's help in obtaining cultivation rights to land in Ifè, he and other tenants used to work on Bakare's own farms every Friday. In general, the extent to which labor recruitment and control in the cocoa economy were based on the principle of seniority meant that the expansion of cocoa production reinforced the significance of seniority as a paradigm of labor control in Yorùbá society. Even today "any senior has a right to unquestioned service, deference, and submissiveness from any junior . . . in return for which they have their own obligations to lead, to teach, and to aid their juniors. . . . The uniformity that this code of authority imposes on wives, children, servants and employees alike constrains the common language often used for all these relationships: [Yorùbás] often speak of 'sacking' (firing, divorcing) either a recalcitrant wife or a difficult employee" (Aronson, 1978, p. 94). In addition, the fact that workers expect their employers to act as patrons or senior kinsmen serves as a constraint on labor exploitation, and therefore on productivity, and represents one of the ways in which norms and practices governing access to and management of productive resources have shaped the process of accumulation.

In cocoa production, prevailing Yorùbá concepts of seniority and descent have also influenced farmers' lifetime strategies of resource allocation and accumulation. Even before the advent of cocoa growing and colonial economic expansion, it was expected that the disposition of a person's labor would change over his or her lifetime, from working for others to self-employment and then to eventual retirement from directly productive activity into the role of elder councillor and adjudicator in his or her kin group and community. Since seniority depended on achievement as well as on age, men and women might choose to invest their skills and wealth in ways that would enhance their status as seniors: by acquiring specialized knowledge, accumulating followers and dependents, or developing a reputation for effective exercise of authority. The possibility of allocating surplus to the acquisition of power and status was formally expressed, in Yorùbá political processes, through the taking of titles. Chieftaincy titles conferred prestige and often specific powers and privileges on their holders, and even today they are eagerly contended for by men and women of all classes, often at considerable expense (Eades, 1980). Seniority thus became an object as well as an instrument of accumulation, and the investment of surplus arising from cocoa production reinforced the prevailing tendency to define workers as juniors, with all the rights and obligations that implied.[8]

Cocoa farms and rural households.—Although cocoa farmers made extensive use of family labor, the spread of cocoa production in western Nigeria did not serve either to create a body of self-reproducing peasant households or to recreate the patrilocal compounds of the nineteenth century. Both the expansion of cocoa growing and the investment of farmers' proceeds in additional farms and nonagricultural enterprises drew people away from their natal compounds for much of their economically active lives and often supplied the wherewithal to build separate houses for retirement. In addition, the changing pattern of labor requirements and financial flows over the life cycle of a cocoa farm further accentuated the mobility of rural labor and the diversification of rural enterprise.

When a cocoa farm matured it became self-financing because the income, except in periods of unusually low prices, was more than sufficient to cover the cost of labor needed to maintain the farm and harvest the cocoa. The labor could be mobilized in various ways (Berry, 1975a). Farmers could continue to employ their wives, children, and *àbúròs*, maintaining them out of the proceeds of the farm, or they could release their kin from work on the farm and hire in labor instead. The latter practice was, in fact, the more common. In 1978, of the 107 households in Abàkinní and Abúlékejì, 37 contained a male household head living together with one or more adult sons or junior brothers, but in only nine of these did the junior man work for or with his elder kinsman. In two households, clusters of brothers living in contiguous houses in Abúlékejì practiced a form of group farming, involving cooperative work and income distribution, and in one household in Abàkinní, a father and two sons farmed and did carpentry together.[9] In most instances, however, adult sons or *àbúròs* who lived with senior kinsmen either had their own farms, which they worked independently, or were engaged in occupations completely different from that of the elder relative. Farmers' wives almost invariably had their own enterprises, usually trade or the preparation and sale of cooked food.

Most farmers relied primarily on hired labor to maintain and harvest their farms, once their cocoa trees had reached bearing age. Hired labor was supplied partly by seasonal migrant workers who traveled to the cocoa belt from other parts of Nigeria, but a great deal of it was provided by residents of the cocoa villages (Berry, 1975a). Temporary employment on others' farms was a convenient way for village residents to meet short-term needs for cash, needs that arose from the increasing commercialization of the rural economy and from the social organization of cocoa farms and rural households.

Farmers' wives, children, and àbúròs who were released from labor on their senior kinsmen's mature farms were thereby given the opportunity to become independent farmers or traders if they had the means to do so. In western Nigeria uncultivated land was fairly readily obtained—if not in one's father's village, then elsewhere in the cocoa belt (Berry, 1975a, Lloyd, 1962; Olúsànyà et al., 1978)—so that lack of access to land did not prevent juniors from progressing from economic dependence to independent self-employment. Access to capital (and/or labor) was, however, a significant obstacle. As juniors, farmers' dependents usually lacked accumulated claims to others' labor. They therefore needed some form of income or credit to enable them to establish farms or to purchase a stock of trade goods or raw materials (see Peace, 1979).

Access to such income lay either in the market or in family connections. Many men and women hired themselves out to neighboring cocoa farmers when they were not working on their elders' farms, not because of impoverishment or expropriation but in order to accumulate enough savings to enter self-employment. In addition (or instead), people often sought assistance from their senior kin in the form of either gifts of trading capital or food and lodging to sustain them while they established their own farms. As employment opportunities outside farming and trade proliferate, such assistance has increasingly taken the form of paying the costs of an apprenticeship or of schooling. Most individuals obtained assistance from their own agnatic kin; with rare exceptions, farmers' wives did not receive trading capital from their husbands (see chap. 4).

In general, then, family laborers tended to cycle in and out of a given cocoa-farming enterprise, as the farmer's junior kin were released from the farm over time and often received assistance from the farmer in establishing farms or other enterprises of their own. Hired labor also was supplied primarily by people with some assets of their own who sought wage employment as a means to liquidity or self-employment, rather than as their only means of support. Since many opportunities for establishing new farms or other enterprises lay outside the village of their initial employment, in the long run laborers and junior members of rural households often left the employers' places of residence as well as their farms. These practices resulted in high rates of turnover among residents of any given cocoa village and even within individual rural households, a fact that is strikingly confirmed by my censuses of Abúlékejì.

When I first enumerated the residents of Abúlékejì, in 1971, they numbered about 550 (including Hausas), over three-fifths of whom were said to have come to the village after 1960 (Berry, 1975a). Between 1971 and 1978 the total population of the village remained stable at the same level, but 60 percent of the people I enumerated in 1971 had left and been replaced by others (tables 3–1, 3–2). Most of the arrivals were related to people already established in the village. Of the 308 persons living in Abúlékejì in 1978 who were not there in 1971, 95 were children born in the interim to established residents and 127 were related to people already living there (table 3–3). Of the 75 households enumerated in my 1978 census, only six had undergone a complete change of inhabitants since 1971. In all the rest at least one person was there in 1978 who had been there, or whose spouse had been there, in 1971. In other words, most of the turnover occurred within established households rather than through the disappearance of old households and the formation of new ones.

In Abúlékejì, then, cocoa production did not create a stable population of peasant households producing most of what they consumed or acting as integrated, self-perpetuating productive units. In most households in Abàkinní and Abúlékejì, the members were more likely than not to produce, consume, accumulate, and hold property independently of one another. Households functioned not as homogeneous or unitary agencies of resource allocation but rather as nodal points in a diaspora, as places where individuals came to participate in the operation of a farm or other rural enterprise or to draw on the resources of their kinsmen. An expanding household might betoken a declining enterprise: farmers or their widows may take in tenants to compensate for falling incomes, or may house and feed their children in the village because they lack the means to send them to school or launch them into more lucrative and independent careers outside agriculture. Conversely, accumulation often leads to household partitioning, as sons and *àbúròs* released from labor on an elder's farm establish enterprises and households of their own.

Expansion and diversification of rural enterprise.—Despite the high rates of turnover among rural residents, however, the households and villages of the cocoa belt have remained important focuses of social identity and interaction for emigrant farmers and their descendants, just as the hometowns have done for village residents (Berry, 1975a). Village emigrants have often maintained close ties with friends and relatives remaining in the village, and village households have often sheltered a continuing stream of new arrivals (most of them related

TABLE 3–1
EXTENDED YORÙBÁ POPULATIONS OF TWO VILLAGES[a] IN 1978

Status	Abàkinní			Abúlékejì		
	Male	Female	Total	Male	Female	Total
Resident	108	127	235	239	276	515
Nonresident	36	39	75	107	79	186
Total	144	148	310[b]	346	355	707[c]

[a]One and a half households in Abàkinní and four Yorùbá households in Abúlékejì were not enumerated in the census. If these households are assumed to contain the average number of residents for the village as a whole, the resident populations may be estimated at about 240 for Abàkinní and 525 for Abúlékejì. If extended populations, which include nonresident household members, mostly sons and daughters of the household head, are estimated by the same method, the totals would be 322 for Abàkinní and 725 Yorùbás for Abúlékejì.
[b]Includes 22 unknown.
[c]Includes 6 unknown.

TABLE 3–2
RESIDENT VILLAGE POPULATIONS

Residents	Abàkinní	Abúlékejì		
	1978	1971	1978	Change
Total	231	496	518	+22
Remained in village 1971–1978	–	210	210	–
Departed or arrived 1971–1978	–	286	308	+22
Sex				
Male	105	240	239	–1
Female	115	256	276	+20
Unknown	11	0	3	+3
Age				
0–14	114	251	244	–7
15–29	45	144	94	–50
30–49	38	64	79	+15
50+	23	9	43	+34
Unknown	11	28	58	+17

SOURCE: Village censuses.
NOTE: The increase in the population of Abúlékejì is owing to better coverage in the second census rather than to net immigration. Eight households were omitted from the 1971 census, whereas all but four households were enumerated in 1978. The data refer only to Yorùbá residents. In both years about 25–40 Hausas were also living in Abúlékejì.

TABLE 3–3
ARRIVALS AND DEPARTURES, ABÚLÉKEJÌ, 1971–1978

A. Age and sex distribution

	Departures		Arrivals		Change	
Adult men	62		37		−25	
(household heads)		(44)		(24)		(−20)
Adult women	53		60		+7	
(married to departing or arriving men)		(28)		(35)		(+7)
Children under 15	171		211		+40	
Total	286		308		+22	

B. Relationships to village residents

	Departures	Arrivals
Members of resident families		
Wives	34	25
Agnates	31	9
Children	98	139 (of whom 95 were born after 1970
Emigrant/immigrant families		
Men	15	24 (of whom 49 came to join
Women	31	35 relatives in Abúlékejì)
Children	64	67
Others		
Men	6	8

SOURCE: Village censuses.

to the household head); farmers also continue to draw on the labor or assistance of junior kin and clients in establishing and managing expanded and diversified enterprises. A majority of my informants used part of the proceeds of their first cocoa farms to acquire additional plots of cocoa (by planting or purchase or occasionally as pledges against a loan) or to go into some kind of trade.[10] Such expansion or diversification of a farmer's enterprise typically brought about some geographical dispersion of his economic activities. In 1978, seventeen adult men were absent from their homes in Abúlékejì much of the time because they worked elsewhere; another six frequently traveled in connection with their work. Some of these had planted additional farms south of Òndó—45 to 50 miles by road from Abúlékejì—and had to journey back and forth to oversee both farms. Traders, in the normal course of doing business, also moved about a good deal. Some left the cocoa villages altogether, to trade in a larger village or town, but even those who specialized in buying produce from or selling foodstuffs or manufactured items to their rural neighbors were often on the move, delivering produce from rural collection points to bulking centers on major roads or in town, or buying goods in town to retail in rural markets. Thus the diversification of rural enterprise often required a good deal of travel on the part of the entrepreneur.

As a given plot of cocoa matured, the farmer tended to substitute hired labor on the farm for the labor of his relatives, thus releasing the latter for independent (self-) employment. To cope with the problems of managing geographically dispersed farms or trading enterprises, however, farmers turned once again to their junior kin. In Abàkinní and Abúlékejì, a number of families participated in the management of multiple enterprises. Altogether, twenty adult male members of households in Abúlékejì owned additional farms in Iléṣà or Òndó, which they managed with the help of their wives, sons, or àbúròs. One man who had left home in Èrìnle at the age of fifteen to work as a farm laborer near Lagos later followed a senior brother to Ghana, where, after working for five years in the gold mines, the two men used their savings to go into trade. The younger brother returned to Nigeria about 1960 and joined his sister in Abúlékejì. As no farmland was then available at Abúlékejì he obtained some nearer Iléṣà, and he has since acquired an additional farm south of Òndó. His comparatively young cocoa farm near Iléṣà yields enough income to pay for laborers on both farms; he commutes between them to supervise the work and can also rely on his in-laws to assist with supervision if necessary. Another man who headed a household in Abúlékejì in 1971 has since died; his elder son is now a trader in Òkèigbó and the younger son looks after the father's farm in Abúlékejì, where he also works as a tailor. Besides himself, the family's small house in Abúlékejì shelters his mother, his own wife and two small children, and a wife and four children of his senior brother.

Like others in the village, the senior brother left one wife to look after his older farm in Abúlékejì and took his other wives with him to help in his new enterprise. Several other men had also left most of their wives and children to be fed by their brothers in Abúlékejì, sending contributions from the proceeds of their extravillage enterprises when they could. Among farmers who had taken up trade outside the village, polygyny was the rule. A trader who sold hardware in Òṣogbo also had a small shop in Abúlékejì which his village wife managed in his absence. Another trader, a particularly successful one who had started selling cement in Òṣogbo just a year or so before the construction boom of the mid-seventies, had five children attending secondary school in Òṣogbo; they also helped in the shop in their spare time. He had, he said, employed a shop assistant at first but the man cheated him, so he let him go, preferring to rely on his wife and children as a cheaper and more reliable source of labor. In 1976 he rented the shop next door to his first one and added hardware to his stock in trade. Attracted by his success, two other men from Abúlékejì have also opened shops on the same street in Òṣogbo; with the help of wives and children, they sell hardware and sundries (see chap. 4, pp. 000–000).

A final example of family management of diversified enterprises is provided by a man from Ìreé who is both farmer and trader. Born in Ghana about 1945, he had come to Abúlékejì with his father and senior brother in the early 1950s. The father established two cocoa farms, one in Abúlékejì and the other in an Ijéṣà village, and worked them with the help of his sons. By 1971 he had retired to Ìreé, leaving the farms in care of his sons who worked them jointly. Like their father before he moved into cocoa growing, the sons also went into trade. In the mid-sixties Joseph, the eldest, began to buy beans in Kano and Kaduna for sale to traders in rural markets near Abúlékejì. In 1968 he bought a farm of mature cocoa trees in Òndó and sent a junior brother there to manage it. He also provided Ezekiel, another junior brother, with capital to begin trading in beans and millet. When I interviewed him in 1971, Joseph emphasized that he worked his farms without hired labor, relying solely on the help of his three wives and his brothers. Joseph died in the mid-seventies and the family farms passed to Ezekiel, who continued to import foodstuffs from the north and also began to sell kola and oranges from the vicinity of Ifẹ̀ in Kano, Kaduna, Zaria, and Onitsha. His wife and small children live in Abúlékejì while he travels to trade or to supervise his other farms. In 1977 he bought a cocoa and kola farm of his own in Òndó in addition to those inherited from his brother.

As these examples suggest, rural accumulation—like the life cycle of the cocoa farm—has promoted rural commercialization and mobility and perpetuated the use of dependent or subordinate kin in the organization of rural enterprise. The roles of junior agnates and affines varied over the life cycle of the farm: during the maturation period they provided a substitute for working capital; later, when farmers used profits to expand and diversify their enterprises, they often served as a substitute for paid managerial assistance. Junior kin were not locked into their elders' households or enterprises; on the contrary, they expected and often managed to leave, to become economically independent, and to receive assistance from their elders in doing so. Seniority and descent-group membership tended, in other words, both to offset and to reinforce differentiation among agricultural producers. The widespread use of juniors as workers, both on and off the farm, helped to perpetuate acceptance of the idea that seniority entailed command over others' labor. At the same time, seniors' obligations to assist and protect juniors, together with the possibility of achieving seniority through accumulation, meant that the very success of a farming or trading enterprise built on juniors' labor tended to undermine their junior status. Prosperity served, therefore, to limit both the stability of personnel and the subordination and control of labor within the enterprise. Moreover, to the extent that juniors entered expanding markets as producers or employees, they might well outstrip their seniors in earnings and influence. The chances of their doing so were, in turn, affected by their elders' own strategies of accumulation as well as by the changing structure of opportunities in the regional economy.

Investing in seniority.—In addition to expanding and diversifying their own enterprises and assets, farmers in Abàkinní and Abúlékejì devoted a considerable part of their incomes from cocoa to the maintenance or advancement of their relatives, individually and collectively. Such expenditures by my informants took three main forms: maintaining (i.e., feeding, housing, and sometimes contributing to clothing and medical expenses) agnatic and affinal kin, both junior and senior to themselves; training or equipping their children and other junior agnates for productive employment or self-employment; and investing in their communities of origin by contributing to family ceremonies and to projects earmarked for compound or community improvement and, often, by building houses in their hometowns. All these outlays tended to enhance a farmer's seniority, either by increasing his own wealth (and thus his capacity to reward followers or make public displays of generosity) or by advancing the welfare or prospects of his kin and fellow townspeople. Even the construction of a house in the hometown, by demonstrating a man's lifetime commitment to his community of origin, enhanced his status within it. It thus prepared the ground for his retirement, both literally and by improving his claim to participate in any improvements in the economic or political fortunes of the community as a whole.

Some idea of the importance of farmers' financial commitments to their kin may be derived from my evidence on farmers' life histories of resource use. I was not able to obtain reliable information on changes in the numbers of farmers' economic dependents over time. It is noteworthy, however, that even in the depressed conditions of the late 1970s (see chap. 4), when some farmers were unable to feed the wives and children living under the same roof, let alone support additional people, half of the men and nearly a third of the women I interviewed were contributing to the maintenance of one or more persons in addition to their spouses and children. Altogether, 44 male informants were responsible for feeding a total of 315 people, 81 of whom did not live in the provider's house. The importance of descent-group as opposed to nuclear family responsibilities is suggested by the composition of these dependents. Of the 315, 68 were wives of the providers, 178 were children or grandchildren, 15 were parents, and 4 were other kin, mostly agnates.

In addition, most farmers had invested in training their children for productive employment, and some had contributed to the training of junior siblings as well. In 1971, 62 percent of the children (aged 5–15) who were living in Abúlékejì attended school in neighboring villages; others had been sent to live with relatives in order to attend primary school in town. In 1978, 77 percent of the same age-group in Abàkinní attended school, while in Abúlékejì, where a primary school was established in 1976, the proportion had risen to 90 percent.

For secondary schooling or apprenticeship, however, children had to leave the villages, and by 1978 most farmers' children over fourteen had done so. The nearest secondary schools were several miles away at Ọlọ́dẹ, but most of the children from Abàkinní and Abúlékejì attended school in or near their hometowns, where they could live with relatives. Table 3–4 summarizes my census data on postprimary training of household members. For the two villages with a combined extended population of 1,014 (of whom 55 percent were 15 or older), 99 individuals had received or were receiving schooling beyond the primary level; 13 had spent periods of study with Islamic scholars; and 80 had been apprenticed at some time to a craftsman or trader. Nearly all those with postprimary schooling, and the majority of current and former apprentices, were children of migrant farmers, whose training was financed from the proceeds of cocoa farming and related rural enterprises.

A farmer's outlay on training was often substantial. For children from Abàkinní and Abúlékejì who attended school in 1978–79 the average annual expenditure on fees and books was ₦75 per pupil for secondary modern school and ₦150 for grammar school. If pupils boarded at the school or lived in rented lodgings, the cost of a year's maintenance might be an additional ₦150 to ₦200. To put a child through modern school might therefore cost anywhere from ₦ 225 to ₦675, depending on whether the child lived with relatives or had to pay for food and lodging. Grammar school, normally a five-year

TABLE 3–4
POSTPRIMARY TRAINING IN TWO VILLAGES

Village	Extended population aged 15 and above	Type of current or previous education		
		Secondary schooling	Apprentice training	Islamic study
Abàkinní	148 (170)[a]	11 (6)[b]	26 (6)[b]	3 (2)[b]
Abúlékejì	336 (416)[a]	88 (63)[b]	54 (11)[b]	10 (6)[b]
Total	484 (586)[a]	99 (69)[b]	80 (17)[b]	13 (8)[b]

[a] Figure in parentheses indicates total population aged 15 and above, on the assumption that all persons of unknown age are over 15. Extended population includes village residents plus nonresident household members. Of the latter, 82 percent are sons and daughters of village residents.
[b] Figure in parentheses indicates number of persons receiving training in 1978.

course, could cost from ₦750 to ₦1,500 for one child. Some children attend modern school and then go on to grammar school, a sequence that seems to take seven years for most of the pupils.

Some parents were old enough in 1978 to have sons and daughters who had already graduated from secondary school and were earning enough to help with their àbúròs' school fees or maintenance. One man in his sixties, for example, who had sold cloth in Dahomey for thirty years before coming to Abúlékejì, had put four children through school with profits from his trade. They were all employed in 1978 (as teachers or nurses) and were putting a younger brother through secondary modern school, as well as helping to support their father in his old age. Twelve other informants mentioned receiving help with their children's school fees from their wives, brothers, or grown-up children, but most bore the entire burden themselves. Twenty-eight of the forty-four men whom I interviewed were supporting forty-one children in secondary school at the time of my survey and had put another forty through already. Using the average costs cited above, we can estimate my informants' average cumulated outlay on secondary schooling at ₦1,283 per farmer, exclusive of maintenance costs. In 1971 the average cocoa holding was about four acres. If such a farm yielded 500 pounds of dry cocoa per acre for twenty years—say, from 1955 to 1974—the gross (undiscounted) proceeds would amount to ₦10,630. Thus my informants had, on the average, devoted at least 10 percent of their gross earnings from cocoa to secondary schooling, in addition to outlays on apprentice fees.

Besides securing their children's futures by training them for nonagricultural employment, Yorùbá farmers have attempted to provide for their own retirement by maintaining a stake in their home com-

pounds and communities. To this end they have used their resources
not simply to establish a basis for subsistence in their old age, but
rather to gain a position of substance and influence among their kin
and fellow townspeople from which to exercise the authority and
enjoy the respect associated with advanced seniority. During their
years of residence in the cocoa belt, farmers sought to prepare for
eventual retirement by continued participation in ceremonial and
political affairs at home, by contributions to projects for family or
community development, and by building houses in their hometowns.

Farmers' investment in housing, especially, bears strong testimony
to their commitment to their hometowns. A hometown house was
usually started after the farmer had built a house in the cocoa village.
Among my informants, forty (out of forty-three) men had built houses
in Abákiŋnì or Abúlékjì, at costs ranging from ₦200 to ₦700 each.
In addition, twenty-seven of them had built (or were in the process
of building) houses in their hometowns. These houses were invariably
larger and better built than those in the villages, although the farmer
and his family lived most of the time in the village house. Hometown
houses were sometimes two stories high, with cement-plastered walls
and glass windows. Each of my informants had spent between ₦1,000
and ₦8,000 on his hometown house at the time of my survey; many
planned further outlays when they could afford it. Houses at home
are rarely rented out, as there is little demand for accommodations
in savannah towns, whose inhabitants for the most part live and work
elsewhere. Often such a house stands empty, except when the farmer
or members of his family are home for a visit, until the owner retires.
But provision of a holiday and retirement home is only part of the
reason for building a house at home. The house also serves to demonstrate the owner's continued commitment to his kin group and
home community and thus supports his claim to share in their development. The proliferation of "story houses" in towns such as Ẹripa and
Ìreé offers concrete testimony to the vitality of extended community
networks in contemporary Yorùbá society.

The Social and Economic Consequences of Rural Accumulation

Like much scholarly analysis of social change in twentieth-century
Africa, Yorùbá cocoa farmers' strategies of resource use rest on the
assumption that individual and communal advance are closely and
positively related. Since a Yorùbá's personal status and, to some extent,
his authority were likely to be enhanced by evidence of a large and
prosperous following, men sought to advance their dependents' for-

tunes as well as their own. Prosperous and influential children also increased the potential well-being of the whole descent group, both by enlarging the pool of assets to which descent group members could lay claim on grounds of kinship solidarity and by increasing the wealth and reputation of the family. The same thing held true for a town: successful native sons were an asset to the entire community. The possibility of sharing in the wealth or benefiting from the influence of one's kin group or community also encouraged people to maintain close ties with their hometowns and compounds. Such considerations have contributed to the enduring force of communal and ethnic forms of political mobilization and conflict in postcolonial Nigerian history.

Kin-based strategies for the pursuit of wealth and power also have their pitfalls, however, as my informants' experiences show. As children and other juniors become independent of their elders' support they gain seniority of their own which, because it is based on personal achievement as well as age, can rival or even surpass that of their elders. The chances that juniors will outstrip their elders are better in periods of economic expansion or rapid structural change. In western Nigeria economic expansion and decolonization created new opportunities after 1945, not only in commerce and agriculture, but also in administration, politics, and the professions; the inflow of oil revenues after 1970 further increased opportunities for employment and profiteering. The fact that access to those opportunities was increasingly associated with education encouraged farmers to invest in their children's schooling so as to advance their chances of upward mobility and the fortunes of the family as a whole. But education also served to differentiate children from their parents, in terms of both income and life-style. Educated young men and women believed themselves better qualified than their parents to direct the course of family and community progress, and they were often able to dominate their elders in local affairs.

Some of the consequences of outlays on postprimary training are suggested by the patterns of employment among farmers' children who had already completed their training at the time of my survey. As revealed in tables 3–5 and 3–6, most farmers' sons not attending school or seeking work were employed outside agriculture, typically in some form of small-scale enterprise. This was as true among farmers' sons without post-primary schooling as among those who had received some, though only the latter were employed as clerks or teachers. The majority of employed sons had a primary school education or less and were engaged in some form of small-scale trade or artisanal enterprise. Farmers' daughters were more likely to be working in agriculture or trade, but some were employed as seamstresses,

TABLE 3–5
OCCUPATIONS OF FARMERS' CHILDREN

Occupation	Abàkinní			Abúlékejì		
	Males	Females	M/F ratio	Males	Females	M/F ratio
Farming	3	12	.25	8	22	.36
Trade	2	11	.18	1	20	.05
School	45	29	1.55	120	102	1.18
Clerk, teacher	3	1	3.00	13	7	1.86
Small-scale enterprise	20	2	10.00	36	9	4.00
Unknown	34	29	1.21	53	44	1.18
Total	107	84	1.27	231	204	1.13

SOURCE: Village censuses.

TABLE 3–6
OCCUPATIONS OF NONRESIDENT ADULTS

Occupation	Abàkinní			Abúlékejì		
	Males	Females	Total	Males	Females	Total
Farming	0 ⎫	4 ⎫	4 ⎫	9 ⎫	10 ⎫	19 ⎫
	⎬ 5%	⎬ 90%	⎬ 48%	⎬ 21%	⎬ 51%	⎬ 33%
Trade	1 ⎭	15 ⎭	16 ⎭	6 ⎭	14 ⎭	20 ⎭
School	2 ⎫	0 ⎫	2 ⎫	17 ⎫	9 ⎫	28 ⎫
	⎬	⎬	⎬ 12%	⎬ 43%	⎬ 34%	⎬ 39%
Clerk, teacher	3 ⎱ 90%	0 ⎱ 14%	3 ⎭	13 ⎭	7 ⎭	20 ⎭
Small-scale enterprise	14 ⎭	3 ⎭	17 40%	28 40%	7 15%	35 30%
Unknown and other	1	0	1	5	4	9
Total individuals	21	21[a]	43	70[a]	47[a]	117[a]

SOURCE: Village censuses.
[a] Total of individuals is less than sum of figures in column because some individuals have more than one occupation.

clerks, or teachers, particularly in Abúlékejì, where the rate of investment was somewhat higher than in Abàkinní (see chap. 4, pp. 103–104). Similarly, in interviewing people in nonagricultural occupations, I found that the majority were either children of farmers or had been trained for their present occupations out of savings derived from the rural economy (see chaps. 5 and 6 below).

Tables 3–5 and 3–6 clearly show that the majority of farmers' children were neither well educated nor employed in highly paid jobs. As pointed out in chapter 5, the relative socioeconomic position of teachers has declined in recent years. Similarly, artisans and traders face growing but highly competitive markets; the large majority of them earn no more than their parents on the farm (chap. 6). Nonetheless, for those who do succeed as professionals, civil servants, or entrepreneurs, the rewards are substantial and provide a constant inducement to kinsmen and neighbors to try to emulate their success. Success, in turn, is often associated with, though by no means assured by, education. During the period after 1952, when the state bureaucracy and the educational system were both growing rapidly, educated Yorùbás found themselves virtually assured of a comfortable, secure income and were disposed, by both training and wherewithal, to alter their life-styles considerably from those of their parents. In some respects, holders of degrees constitute an economic and cultural elite in Nigeria: they share not only a preference for a Western bourgeois life-style and the means to support it, but also a strong belief in their own ability and their moral obligation to set economic and social standards for their less educated brethren. To the extent that they also enjoy privileged access to the state, they are part of the ruling class.[11]

Farmers send their children to school to enable them to enter this privileged class. The parents hope that the children, once they have achieved that objective, will use some of the knowledge and wealth to which their education has given them access for the benefit of their families and home communities. Children have not altogether disappointed their parents in this respect; they often contribute liberally to the development of their hometowns, but they are reluctant to relinquish control of the resources they bring home to people whom their education has taught them to consider "unenlightened" (Peel, 1978). Thus a new group is emerging within the compounds and communities of rural Yorùbáland, a group seeking to control the process of development in what they believe to be the best interests of "their people." Since their definition of progress has been molded by the fact as well as by the content of their education, their actions for the good of their relatives and neighbors are not likely to undermine the interests or influence of educated people within their home compounds and communities. Increasingly, farmers who retire to their hometowns find themselves confronted there, and even dominated, by a class they have helped, in part, to create.

Conclusion

The evidence presented in this chapter shows how Yorùbá farmers' uses of productive resources were shaped by the changing structure

of economic opportunities and by prevailing principles of social interaction. During the colonial period farmers reorganized their productive activities to take advantage of expanding market opportunities,
often to the extent of resettling themselves and their families in areas
suitable for growing cocoa and other tree crops. In acquiring land
for planting tree crops and in mobilizing labor to work on their farms,
they followed established social and legal practices. Access to land was
contingent on acknowledging the authority of the lineage or community where a farmer sought to settle and start a farm, while recruitment
and supervision of labor were often organized according to relations
of kinship and seniority. Even when increased demand for land and
labor led to commercialization, relations between buyers and sellers
of cultivation rights and labor services continued to reflect established
principles of authority and obligation.

The same thing was true of the uses of agricultural income. Farmers'
outlays on consumption, education, construction, ceremonies, and
productive investment have been largely devoted to fulfilling obligations to kin and other dependents or to advancing their own seniority.
Since seniority depended, in part, on material success, there was no
conflict between investment in expanded productive capacity and the
pursuit of accepted values. Rather, the forms of accumulation out of
agricultural surplus reflect the fact that Yorùbás drew on past experience and familiar ideas in evaluating and exploiting new opportunities.

Changing patterns of livelihood and accumulation did not cause
Yorùbá farmers to reject or discard established principles of social
interaction, but farmers' strategies of resource use have helped to
alter the social and material bases of seniority and patronage and, in
the process, have transformed their meanings. In training their children for nonagricultural employment, for example, Yorùbá farmers
sought to improve their own status and well-being as well as those of
their kin and communities of origin. The consequences of their efforts
have, however, extended beyond the boundaries of kin groups and
established communities. By channeling substantial portions of the
cocoa surplus into tertiary enterprise and training their children for
employment in the tertiary sector, farmers have contributed to a pattern of economic development in which the growth of transactions
tends to outpace the growth of production, and which favors the
proliferation of small-scale enterprises and low levels of labor productivity. Their uses of income have also reinforced relations of seniority
and patronage which both facilitate access to the means of production
and inhibit effective management of them. In terms of the structure
of the regional economy, farmers' efforts to maximize their children's
chances of success have ultimately helped to limit them.

In the pursuit of income and influence, farmers and their children have also embraced new social standards and practices which have altered relations among them. Educated children not only enjoy access to economic opportunities and political connections from which their parents are excluded, but they also consider themselves better qualified to set standards and exercise authority, within kin groups and communities as well as beyond them. Fathers often work for the future success of their sons, only to be dominated by them, and inequality of income and access to the means of production is as likely to occur among members of the same family as between kin groups or communities. As we have seen, membership in a kin group or community implies mutual obligations, not only to assist other members in times of need but also to tolerate their failings. If a relative treats you generously, well and good, but if he ignores or even cheats you, you have little recourse. It is difficult, morally and practically, to prosecute a kinsman.

Commercialization, political centralization, and the resulting patterns of production and investment have created an economy in western Nigeria in which prosperity is possible but uncertain. Competition for resources, profits, and influence has intensified over time; channels of access to resources and opportunities have multiplied but returns are very unequal; and the probability of success in any single venture has declined. These conditions have not only contributed to the pattern of restless mobility described in chapter 2, but they have also increased pressure to exploit the bonds of kinship and the prerogatives of seniority as well as to uphold them. Kinship is no proof against exploitation, any more than seniority won through a lifetime of hard work and conscientious concern for kin and community precludes domination by one's educated and/or influential juniors.

In short, kin-based relations have failed to prevent differentiation in contemporary Yorùbá society, and they do not provide much security either. People cling to them because trade and politics are risky too (see chap. 4). Most of my informants said that their primary strategy for surviving or getting ahead has been to keep their options open, which implies both supporting one's kin and exploiting them[12] (see Berry, 1980). The multiplication of options served, in turn, to increase uncertainty and inhibit productive investment. Farmer's efforts to maximize their own and their descendants' chances of success have served to limit them, and their determination to fulfill the responsibilities as well as to enjoy the privileges of seniority has widened the distance between themselves and their most successful children. In bringing past experience to bear on the task of coping with changing circumstances, Yorùbá farmers and their descendants have contributed to an emerging social order in which old values hold new meanings and parents are sometimes exploited by their children.

4

The Disappearing Peasantry: Rural Trade and Politics in the 1970s

In earlier chapters I have argued that differentiation in western Nigeria has been based on differential access to the state (and foreign capital and markets) rather than on differential access to local land and labor. In chapter 3 I develop this point with reference to the organization of cocoa production: agricultural accumulation did not entail dispossession, nor did it create a rural proletariat, a middle peasantry, or a class of capitalist farmers. Instead, access to land and the control of labor were organized in terms of descent-group and community relations. Rural commercialization occurred within their rubric and extended their influence into the forms of accumulation arising out of the surplus created by cocoa production. The persistence of descent-based relations did not prevent differentiation from taking place; indeed, it has become one of the most obvious features of contemporary Nigerian society. Both the impetus and the arena for socioeconomic differentiation, however, lay outside agricultural production. In the long run farmers' and their descendants' access to wealth and power depended on the extent to which they were able to use the proceeds of their farms to enter the tertiary sector and on the terms on which they were able to advance within it.

In the rest of this book I focus on the form and extent of farmers' and their descendants' participation in the growth and differentiation of the regional economy, apart from farming per se. The present chapter is mainly concerned with the forms and the results of farmers' efforts to participate personally in opportunities for commercial gains, either by diversifying their own assets or by bringing collective pressure to bear on improving their terms of trade. The following chapters trace the consequences of farmers' efforts to acquire wealth and influence by advancing the fortunes of their "children,"[1] individually and collectively.

Many of the strategies used by farmers in Abàkinní and Abúlékejì to participate in extra-agricultural opportunities for gain were directed toward the price of cocoa. Indeed, the terms of trade for cocoa were a central issue in economic and political struggles of the colonial and postcolonial periods. Under colonial rule, agricultural exports provided the principal source of commercial profits and also the tax base from which the colonial regime supported itself. Accordingly, farmers, traders, and the state were engaged in an ongoing struggle over the distribution of cocoa earnings, and shifts in the domestic terms of trade for cocoa sometimes occasioned open confrontation. Because the postcolonial regime also depended heavily on agricultural exports for both revenues and foreign exchange, the tension between farmers and the state did not diminish with independence. Nor, despite the establishment of the Marketing Board in 1939, did the antagonism between farmers and traders. Selected traders became licensed buying agents (LBAs) of the board, presiding over a vast hierarchy of small and marginal buyers. State patronage and their own guaranteed profit margin enabled the LBAs not only to reap substantial profits from cocoa buying, but often to gain preferential access to other assets and opportunities. Essang (1970) has shown that the largest farmers are often LBAs who have acquired extensive holdings of cocoa with their profits from trade, rather than the other way around (see Williams, 1981). In reaction, ordinary farmers have pursued a variety of approaches, ranging from personal investment in trade to collective protest against the state. In this chapter I describe commercial and political strategies used by the residents of Abàkinní and Abúlékejì and show how they have been altered by the changing economic and political conditions of the 1960s and 1970s.

Farmers, Traders, and the State

The struggles among farmers, traders, and the state over the domestic terms of trade for cocoa have taken various forms. Before 1939 overt conflict occurred primarily among cocoa producers, European trading companies, and African middlemen, although efforts by the state to introduce direct taxation of cocoa farmers' incomes or assets provoked protest against agents of the regime as well (Clarke, 1978; Berry, 1975a; see also Peel, in press). The colonial regime's approach to these conflicts reflected the dilemma that confronts any government or state agency seeking to promote capitalist expansion and accumulation. Production and accumulation usually involve some effort to acquire the assets or to control the labor of others. Such actions frequently create tension and conflict which may threaten the conditions of accumulation. In the cocoa economies of British West Africa, the colonial authorities were of course anxious to promote the expansion of British commercial activity. When falling prices threatened to provoke political disturbances, however, the authorities sometimes intervened to curtail the activities of British and other foreign firms. This tendency culminated in the establishment of the marketing boards after the cocoa holdup of 1938, when African traders and large-scale growers in the Gold Coast withheld supplies of cocoa from foreign trading firms, which they accused of conspiring to force down the cocoa price. Rather than risk a spreading confrontation, the colonial authorities took over the marketing of agricultural exports, not only in the Gold Coast but in Nigeria and Sierra Leone as well.

The government takeover of export marketing was initially welcomed by the farmers, and their enthusiasm was sustained by rising world market prices during the decade after 1945. Eventually, however, the postcolonial state had also to confront the tensions that arose when prices again began to fall. Decolonization brought into power a group of Nigerians even more concerned than their colonial predecessors to accelerate the pace of accumulation and, accordingly, more willing to extract surplus from the agricultural sector in the interests of national development. As the world market price of cocoa fell, therefore, the Marketing Board reduced the price paid to its agents who, in turn, deducted as much as they could from the price actually paid to the farmers.[2] By 1965 the official price had fallen to 31 percent of its peak level in 1954. For a time potential conflict between farmers and the state over the declining cocoa price was submerged in the intense struggles over actual control of the state which engulfed Nigeria in the mid-sixties. During the civil war, however, when the military regime tried to impose additional taxes on a peasantry already suffering from the prolonged price decline, farmers rose in open revolt against the state (Beer, 1976). As the violence threatened not only the stability but also the revenues of the regime, the federal government was forced to make some concessions to farmers' demands. Accordingly, the cocoa price was raised by 50 percent in 1970 and, in the most disturbed rural areas, farmers were permitted to govern themselves for some time thereafter.

If the fiscal importance of cocoa gave cocoa farmers a certain amount of political leverage, the costs of collecting agricultural produce at the farm gate discouraged the state from taking over the entire produce marketing system. The Marketing Board, though it had exclusive control over the purchase of cocoa for export, left the collection and bulking of produce to private traders. Firms above a certain size were issued licenses to procure produce for the board at a fixed commission; the licensed buying agents, in turn, purchased most of their cocoa in towns or major rural collection points from a vast network of middle-men and -women, many of whom were members of cocoa farmers' households. The trade was financed through a series of advances, from the Marketing Board to its agents, and from licensed buying agents to middlemen who, in turn, constituted the principal source of credit available to cocoa growers. Thus the state monopoly of export marketing by no means eliminated private traders from the cocoa economy. During the 1950s and 1960s the terms on which cocoa was bought and sold continued to be a focus of competition, coalition, and conflict among farmers, traders, and the state, and rural politics were closely tied to fluctuations in the cocoa price.

The development of the petroleum industry after 1970 brought striking changes. The value of oil exported from Nigeria grew very rapidly after 1970 (table 4–1) and, as we have seen, the sudden influx

TABLE 4–1
COCOA AND PETROLEUM EXPORTS

Year	Cocoa volume (tons)[a]	Cocoa value (₦ mil.)	Petroleum value (₦ mil.)
1950–1954 (average)	107,840	137.2	
1960	154,176	73.5	
1961	183,912	67.4	
1962	195,000	66.6	
1963	175,000	64.7	
1964	197,000	80.2	
1965	259,400	85.4	
1966	193,300	56.6	183.9
1967	248,200	109.4	144.8
1968	173,600	105.2	261.9
1969	173,600	105.2	261.9
1970	187,141	134.0	509.6
1971	270,576	143.0	953.0
1972	224,546	101.1	1,176.2
1973	214,290	112.4	1,893.5
1974	166,587	159.0	5,365.7
1975	175,169	175.5	4,629.6
1976	231,000	217.8	6,196.2
1977	165,400	293.7	
1978	110,000[b]		

SOURCES: Federal Office of Statistics; Central Bank of Nigeria
[a] Long tons through 1964; metric tons thereafter.
[b] Estimate.

of wealth helped to prolong popular enthusiasm for national unity after the civil war, thus facilitating the military regime's program of centralization of state power and resources. Control of oil revenues—a major bone of interregional contention before 1967—was now firmly vested in the federal government, which redistributed it to the states more on the basis of population and development needs than on consideration of where the oil was extracted (Oyovbaire, 1978; Kirk-Greene and Rimmer, 1981). Thus the fiscal structure of the Nigerian state changed dramatically in the early seventies, in terms of both the relative fiscal power of the federal and state governments and the economic source of government revenues.

The influx of oil revenue enriched the Nigerian state but, paradoxically, impoverished the cocoa farmers even more than had the direct state exploitation of the preceding fifteen years (Bienen and Diejomaoh, 1981; Williams, 1981). With the money generated by petroleum exports the government could afford to let up on the farmers—and it did. The domestic price of cocoa was raised by 50 percent in 1970, after the Àgbẹ́kọ̀yà uprising, and continued to climb thereafter as the world price rose. Between 1970 and 1978 the domestic producer price of cocoa increased by 350 percent. The resulting gains to cocoa farmers were partly offset by inflation and were completely swamped by the rising cost of agricultural labor.[3] During the same period the consumer price index rose by about 300 percent, while agricultural wages reported by my informants in 1978 were from 400 to 600 percent of what they had been in 1971 (see Collier, 1981). By the late 1970s farmers were worse off than they had been ten years earlier.

Despite intensified rural economic decline, however, the growth of peasant militancy predicted by some students of the Àgbẹ́kọ̀yà movement did not materialize. Not only was there no recurrence of the rural uprisings of the late sixties, but farmers abandoned even localized efforts to organize in defense of their common interests as agricultural producers, turning instead to other forms of collective action. Although the particular economic and political strategies adopted by farmers in Abàkinní and Abúlékejì were influenced by local conditions and also by individual experience, in general they were consistent with the structural changes brought about in the regional political economy by the oil boom and the accompanying centralization of political power in Nigeria as a whole. By rendering the Nigerian state financially independent of agricultural exports, the oil wealth undercut one of the principal reasons for farmers to organize politically. Since agricultural export earnings were now financially irrelevant to the state, farmers as a group no longer exercised even limited political leverage. At the same time, the ways in which the state used its new wealth tended to shift the structure of economic opportunity even more decisively away from agriculture than had been true in the past.

As we have seen, the oil money was used to expand the size and wealth of the state apparatus in Nigeria, a change that, in turn, led to rapid expansion of the tertiary sector. The growth of elite consumption and of private and public construction generated opportunities in trade, real estate, and services, which were further enhanced by the rapid inflation that followed, especially after the Udoji salary awards of early 1974. Food prices rose too, of course, but cocoa farmers were inhibited from shifting into production of food crops by the tangible form of their agricultural capital.[4] Neither annual nor other tree crops can be grown successfully among mature cocoa trees because the latter provide too much shade. Uprooting the trees and regenerating the soil are extremely labor-intensive processes. With sharply curtailed earnings and rising labor costs, most farmers cannot finance replanting out of their own resources and have found the state-sponsored Cocoa Replanting Scheme to be of little practical assistance. (The scheme provides loans to hire labor for uprooting and rehabilitating old farms, but farmers complain that neither the money nor the inputs provided by the plan are available when they are needed. Only nine farmers in Abúlékejì and Abàkinní were enrolled in the scheme in 1978–79.) Thus within the villages farmers can neither acquire sufficient labor to rehabilitate their own farms nor hire themselves out to their neighbors, most of whom also lack the means to employ labor. Whenever possible, farmers have attempted to leave the villages in search of better opportunities, and accordingly the principal effect of the oil boom on the cocoa-growing sector has been to accelerate the tendency for people to move out of agriculture in the long run. Farmers' children abandoned agriculture en masse—even those who remained in rural areas tended to pursue nonagricultural occupations there[5]—and, whenever possible, farmers followed their sons.

Changing Commercial Relations in Abàkinní and Abúlékejì

The changing structure of farmer-state relations brought about by the oil boom is reflected in the altered structure of rural trade. Trade, particularly in export crops, represents both an opportunity and a constraint for cocoa growers. As sellers of cocoa they are subject to exploitation by traders through the latter's power to reduce prices, especially for farmers to whom they have loaned money. On the other hand, trade in cocoa has also provided an outlet for farmers' savings and an opportunity to expand their incomes. Trade in foodstuffs and manufactured goods commonly purchased by rural households has also provided an opportunity for further accumulation, but it has posed a threat to farmers' real incomes. The structure of rural markets is, of course, powerfully affected by forces external to cocoa villages, but the ways in which farmers have attempted either to shift the terms of trade or to move around them have also influenced market organization and, hence, the distribution of cocoa earnings.

One of the most marked changes that occurred during the 1970s in the economic profile of the residents of Abúlékejì was the increase in the numbers of men and women engaged in trade (table 4–2). In 1971, 7 men and 50 women were engaged in trade of one sort or another; by 1978 the total had risen to 140, including 19 men and 121 women. The rapid proliferation of traders within the village during a period of declining agricultural incomes seems paradoxical at first, but in fact it reflects a process of marginalization which followed directly from the decline of the cocoa economy. Rural economic decline has affected everyone in the village, male and female alike. Since men's and women's trading activities are organized in rather different ways, however, it is convenient to discuss them separately.

Male traders: from cooperation to competition.—In 1971 most of the men trading in Abúlékejì were selling manufactured items to local consumers; only two were engaged in marketing cocoa.[6] By 1978, twelve men in the village were occupied in buying produce (chiefly cocoa), in addition to seven who dealt in other commodities. Part of the increase reflected a larger volume of trade in other agricultural products—notably oranges—but the principal reason for the increase was a change in the local structure of cocoa marketing.

Although the Marketing Board is the sole buyer of the Nigerian cocoa crop, it does not collect cocoa directly from the producers. Instead, the board issues licenses to private firms, empowering them to purchase cocoa in the rural areas for resale to the board at a fixed commission. The licensed buying agents (LBAs) buy cocoa from "scalers," unlicensed private traders who in turn purchase cocoa from "pan buyers," small-scale rural traders who buy directly from the farmers. Scalers bag and weigh what they buy and resell it to the LBAs, who often provide transport from rural bulking points to a major town. Four men in Abàkinní and seventeen in Abúlékejì had been scalers at some point in their careers; about 20 percent of the adult women engaged in pan buying. Officially, farmers are supposed to receive the posted Marketing Board price for their cocoa, from either an LBA or a local trader, but in practice both LBAs and their agents pay less. They manage to do so chiefly by giving farmers

TABLE 4–2
CURRENT OCCUPATIONS OF ADULT VILLAGE RESIDENTS
OF ABÚLÉKEJÌ, 1971 AND 1978

Occupation	Males		Occupation	Females	
	1971	1978[a]		1971	1978[a]
Farmer	70 (73%)	65 (63%)	Farmer	1 (1%)	—
Laborer (agricultural or domestic)	6 (6%)	2 (2%)	Laborer (agricultural or domestic)	57 (47%)	29 (18%)
Trader			Trader		
Produce	2 (2%)	12 (10%)	Kola, Cocoa	25 (21%)	75 (48%)
Other	5 (5%)	7 (6%)	Cooked and other foods	25 (21%)	46 (29%)
Craftsman	16 (17%)	14 (12%)	Crafts	7 (6%)	5 (3%)
Teacher, etc.	6 (6%)	19 (17%)	Teacher, etc.	2 (2%)	5 (3%)
			Unknown	4	0
Total	96[b]	113[b]		121	158

SOURCE: Village censuses.

[a] Employment data for 1978 are based on the assumption that all persons of unknown age are over 15. Most of the increase in total numbers of occupied persons reflects the omission of persons of unknown age from the figures for 1971.

[b] Total of individuals is less than sum of figures in column because some individuals have more than one occupation.

advances on their crops. In exchange for a cash loan or an advance of pesticides and fertilizer, a farmer agrees to deliver his crop to the buyer-creditor who, as my informants put it, could then "pay what he liked" for the cocoa committed to him in advance.

In an effort to offset the costs imposed on them by this system of credit, Yorùbá cocoa growers often tried to organize cooperative marketing schemes, both to bypass the scalers and to generate their own pool of loanable funds (Beer, 1976; Adéyeyè, 1967). Officially sanctioned cooperatives, which have usually operated to the benefit of small groups of men with commercial or political connections, have a long history in western Nigeria. In Abúlékejì and Abàkinní, a few farmers belonged, in 1971, to the Western State Farmers' Union or to the Cooperative Produce Marketing Union, but the majority had formed small cooperatives of their own. In Abúlékejì there were two such societies. The larger was organized in 1959 or 1960 by farmers from Ẹripa and Ìreé. They chose the "head of the strangers" (baba àléjò) in the village as chairman of the society and named it after their home district (Ìfẹ́lódùn). By pooling their cocoa, the members of the Ìfẹ́lódùn Produce Society were able to earn a bulk premium of ₦1–2 per ton from the LBAs. They also used their profits to make loans to individual members, thus freeing them from the hidden interest charges imposed by individual scalers. The society acquired a scale, built a storehouse, and employed one of its members as secretary to keep the books. Most of my informants who sold to the Ìfẹ́lódùn Produce Society agreed that they received a higher price for their cocoa than they would have from individual buyers; they seemed satisfied with the honesty of their chairman and secretary. In 1971 the society had more than twenty members out of a total of seventy farmers then resident in the village.

The other society was smaller, numbering only thirteen members in 1972, when it was formally constituted as a buying society with officers and its own scale. Informants said that the society had been formed by a group of friends who pooled their cocoa in order to earn a bulk premium and to improve their bargaining position with buyers in Ifẹ̀ and Ọlọ́dẹ. Unlike the Ìfẹ́lódùn Produce Society, this group did not limit its membership to men from the same hometown but accepted people from Ọ̀fà, Ìkìrun, and Ẹ̀rìnle, as well as Ìreé.

The cooperative in Abàkinní was also organized in the late 1950s. According to my informants, before a road was built linking Abàkinní to Abúlékejì and the road to Ọlọ́dẹ, farmers used to headload their produce to a village several kilometers away, where they sold it to scalers. Later the *bálẹ̀* of Abàkinní organized the villagers into work gangs to construct the road to Abúlékejì and the farmers began selling to larger buyers in Ọlọ́dẹ. The farmers complained, however, that neither the village scalers nor the buyers in Ọlọ́dẹ paid them on time, so they decided to pool their cocoa and deal directly with an LBA in Ifẹ̀. In 1960 the members built a storehouse in Abàkinní. The LBA paid them a commission of ₦4 per ton, which they divided into three parts: one for operating expenses (the secretary's salary, bags, petrol for the LBA's truck to carry produce to Ifẹ̀), one to repay members for their contributions to building the store, and one for distribution to members. According to the *bálẹ̀*, at one time there were as many as twenty-six members (more than half the farmers in the village).

Thus all three societies were organized during the late 1950s or the 1960s at the grass-roots level by farmers seeking to improve the terms on which they sold export crops to the agents of the state-controlled Marketing Board. Although ethnic or party influences cannot be ruled out as a factor contributing to the rise and decline of these organizations, there is little direct evidence of factional motivation for establishing the societies. Their class-oriented character, on the other hand, seems clear: cocoa farmers within a given village combined with others to try to increase their share of the government's domestic outlay on export crops. None of the three societies had members outside their respective villages, however, so that their formation cannot be taken as evidence of an emerging peasant movement with large-scale membership or wider aims.

Between 1971 and 1978 all three cooperative societies effectively ceased to operate. In Abàkinní the secretary resigned in 1977, having discovered that he could make more money trading on his own. (He may also have quarreled with other members over the management of the society. Although he claimed, in 1978–79, to have several customers in Abàkinní, none of the farmers I interviewed was selling cocoa to him.) In Abúlékejì, the Ìfẹ́lódùn Produce Society dissolved, not, informants said, because of mismanagement or conflict, but because the volume of cocoa the society handled had fallen so low in the mid-seventies that it could no longer afford to pay the secretary or give crop advances to members. Several farmers said they used to sell cocoa to the society, but that they no longer did so because "it had declined" or because they preferred to buy from traders who could lend them money. Several of the former members are now trading on their own. The other society in Abúlékejì was still nominally in existence, although only five or six members remained active in 1978–79. Their ranks had been depleted by the withdrawal of the Sules, whom one farmer described as "the real backbone of the society," and of other members who had left the village to trade in larger towns.

Ironically, the demise of the marketing societies opened up new opportunities for individuals in produce buying, despite the overall decline in the trade. Most of those who entered produce buying, however, were either young men hoping eventually to move beyond that occupation or older men trying to stave off poverty; they were not middle-aged farmers seeking profitable outlets for their savings. Successful produce buyers of the 1950s had, by 1978, moved into other forms of trade or were in the process of doing so. Of the seven men in Abúlékejì whom I know to have taken up produce buying during the 1960s, only two were still so occupied in 1978. One of these said that the volume of his purchases had declined by over 40 percent since 1974–75; at the time of my survey, he was in the process of moving into the lumber trade.

Traders in nonagricultural commodities also complained of declining sales and shrinking profits, which hampered their ability to seek better opportunities outside the village. Elijah Ogunde had begun his working life as a laborer on the farm of a senior kinsman. When, after ten years, the relative had "done nothing" for him, Ogunde decided to leave. He had learned bricklaying while living with his relative and had come to Abúlékejì in the 1960s to build a house there for a local farmer. At that time most of the cocoa planted in the early fifties had matured, and many farmers were building or expanding their houses. Ogunde managed not only to support himself as a bricklayer and to marry, but also to accumulate enough savings to go into trade. He decided to sell manufactured items—shoes, batteries, cutlasses—and opened a shop in his house. By the time he entered the market, however, decline had set in. Most of the men who had been selling sundries in the village when Ogunde came there had moved to Òṣogbo. Today, "there is no money in this area." Ogunde would like to go to Òṣogbo too, but he has not been able to raise the ₦500 he would need to pay a year's rent on a shop in advance.

Another young man had come to Abúlékejì because a distant kinsman lived there. He sold patent medicines, traveling to nearby villages on a bicycle—a sign of relative poverty in 1978, when passenger vehicles passed through the village every hour and some young men owned motorcycles. He lived in a rented room with his wife and three small children, who showed obvious signs of malnourishment. His predecessor had given up selling medicine in 1977 because it did not pay; he had managed to pass the secondary modern school leaving exams after a period of private study. In 1978 he was applying for a position as a schoolteacher while supporting himself meagerly from the cocoa farm he had inherited from his father. One of his two children had been sent to live with a grandmother, in order to reduce the number of people he had to feed while he looked for a better job.

A third man who was trading in the village in 1978 was in his seventies. He sold bottled drinks to maintain himself and his elderly wife. He estimated his monthly turnover at six cases of beer during the slack season, though at cocoa harvest time he might sell two or three cases for a single ceremony. At the time of my survey his profit averaged about ₦1 per case.

In sum, the proliferation of male traders in Abúlékejì in the 1970s cannot be taken as a sign of rural prosperity. The number of individuals engaged in buying cocoa had increased, primarily because the volume of trade had declined, forcing the village-level cooperative societies to disband. Men who could afford to do so had left the village to trade in more promising locations or were in the process of doing so. For most, trade within the village (and adjacent rural areas) provided meager earnings at best and represented an occupation taken up for lack of better alternatives, rather than a sign of upward mobility.

Female traders: the limits of independence.—The literature on Yorùbá women has emphasized their economic independence (Sudarkasa, 1973, 1979; see also Eades, 1980). Unlike women in many African societies, most Yorùbá wives do not farm; instead, they pursue various trades independently of their husbands. As we have seen (chap. 3), wives of cocoa farmers often did work for their husbands when the latter were establishing plots of cocoa, but they were subsequently released from farm work to take up employment on their own. It might therefore be argued that the growth in the number of women traders in Abúlékejì is a sign of rural prosperity, reflecting the successful realization of women's lifetime aspirations to independent self-employment. Evidence from Abàkinní and Abúlékejì indicates, however, that most of the women who described themselves in 1978 as traders were buying kola from local farmers for resale to male Hausa traders, an undertaking that yielded very low returns, as we shall see. More frequently the poverty of my informants not only reflects the decline of the cocoa economy in the 1970s but also suggests that previous studies have somewhat exaggerated the socioeconomic independence of Yorùbá women, at least of those based in the agricultural sector.

As I have pointed out (chap. 3), a married woman, once her husband was self-supporting, was free to earn an independent income and spend it as she pleased. She was, however, obliged to mobilize by herself trading capital or any other resources needed to start an enterprise, either by appealing to her agnatic relatives or by working for wages. Even after they were engaged in independent occupations, wives in Abàkinní and Abúlékejì continued to be hampered by their husbands' economic circumstances, in at least two ways. A wife could still be called upon "at any time" to help with her husband's work. As we have seen, a man who earned enough from his initial cocoa farm to expand or diversify his productive activities often acquired a second farm or began to trade; his wife was expected to assist in these new enterprises too, especially if the husband's expanded activities required him to travel. Two of my female informants, for example, said that they helped with their husbands' trades in addition to carrying on their own. In both instances the husband had opened a shop in Abúlékejì, which was left in charge of the wife when he went to his farm or, in one case, to another shop in Òṣogbo. Similarly, twenty-four of the married women living in Abúlékejì looked after their husbands' local farms, while the husbands spent much of their time farming or trading somewhere else.

Second, unless farmers' wives managed to become completely self-supporting and to leave their villages, the economic opportunities open to them were those of the rural economy. As Yorùbá women rarely farm on their own, rural wives are limited to trade, food processing, or craft production for the rural market, and their incomes depend essentially on the prosperity of the agricultural sector. The proliferation of women traders in Abúlékejì between 1971 and 1978 reflects in part the long-term consequences of the growth of cocoa production, which has enabled most farmers' wives to establish their own enterprises over time. To the extent that they have done so during a period of declining rural incomes, however, entrepreneurial independence has not necessarily made rural women economically independent of their husbands.

Although three-quarters of the adult women in Abàkinní and Abúlékejì were engaged in trade in 1978, the large majority of them (76 percent in Abúlékejì and 90 percent in Abàkinní) were buying kola from local farmers and reselling it to Hausa traders in Abúlékejì or in nearby rural markets. Because of the sheer number of competing kola buyers, it is unlikely that any one of them earns significant profits, and the structure and operation of the kola market make it even less likely. Unlike buyers of cocoa and palm kernels, whose prices have been somewhat stabilized by the marketing boards, kola buyers face a volatile market. Most of the crop is ready to harvest between July and September, so that women make most of their purchases during this period. They soak the nuts to loosen the hulls, peel them, and store them in baskets lined with green leaves to keep them fresh. Kola may be stored in this way for several months, so that women are not obliged to dispose of their stocks immediately. Demand, however, is extremely variable. Both Hausa and Yorùbá male buyers prefer to shift the trouble and expense of storage onto the women, so the women buy only when they expect to sell again quickly. Hausa traders, who ship kola hundreds of miles to dealers in the north, maintain extensive intelligence networks to keep informed of changing prices for different varieties in different market centers; they try to profit from this information by rapid delivery of supplies to the right place at the right time (Berry, 1975a; Cohen, 1966; Lovejoy, 1980; Agìrì, 1972). At the same time, in order to buy as cheaply as possible, the Hausa traders avoid bidding up the purchase price by placing sudden large orders for local supplies. The women, on the other hand, try to store their kola until they hear that someone is buying at a good price; then they hurry to sell before their neighbors do. Obviously this strategy does not pay off for everyone. Many women also take kola to rural periodic markets to sell. This practice too involves risk: if the price turns out to be low on a given market day, a trader has either to sell at a loss or to take her kola home again to wait for a better opportunity.

The result of all these factors is that the prices paid and received by individual women kola traders vary widely. Informants said that they had paid anywhere from N5 to N16 for a basket during the 1978 harvest season and sold at profits ranging from negative to as much as N7 a basket, though average gains were no more than N1 to N2 a basket. The fact that so many women have turned to kola trade as a substitute for farm work, cracking palm kernels, and pan buying of cocoa means that average returns are kept low through competition, and the risks of the trade further reduce the gains. None of the four women kola buyers whom I interviewed could be described as prosperous, and two said specifically that they had turned to buying kola after having unsuccessfully attempted other forms of trade (e.g., in cloth) which required more capital than they could raise.

Women in other trades experienced varying degrees of success. Two elderly women made so little money selling provisions (i.e., soap, matches, candy, tomato paste, sugar, etc.) that they could afford nothing beyond small contributions to the household food supply; another, who had given up buying cocoa because of ill health and now sold ògì (maize gruel), said that she could no longer afford to buy new clothes for her children or send money home to her old father. More successful was Ruth, the wife of one of the most prosperous men in the village. Before her marriage Ruth had helped her mother make and sell èkọ (maize porridge). She continued to sell èkọ and gàrí (cassava meal) after she moved to her husband's house in Abúlékejì, starting out with a gift of money from her mother. She later used the proceeds of her trade to help support her aging mother and also to move into a more profitable business. In 1960 she began to buy raw cowskins in Òfà, which she cooked and sold in small pieces (as a snack or an ingredient for stew) in Abúlékejì and neighboring villages, with the help of her daughters. In 1978 she bought three bags of skins a month, making about N6 (or 8 percent) profit on each bag.

The most prosperous woman in Abúlékejì was in her late fifties. She had been married three times and had six sons, four of whom were employed (a carpenter, a teacher, and two drivers) in 1978. The fifth son was an unemployed ex-soldier whose Ibo wife had left him after the civil war and whose daughter lived with her grandmother in Abúlékejì; the youngest son was in secondary school. Mrs. Oyè had begun married life selling beans in Ìkàrę̀, where her first husband was employed as a clerk, with money her husband gave her. (The amount was not large: "In those days," she said, "beans were so cheap! A bowl like this," cupping her two hands, "cost ten kọbọ.") After her husband died she returned to their hometown, where she lived with her in-laws and sold maize. After her second marriage, her mother helped her to begin selling provisions. In the early 1960s she moved to Abúlékejì with her third husband, and by the end of the decade she had saved enough money (through membership in several *èsúsú* or rotating credit societies) to begin trading in cloth. During the 1970s the cloth trade dwindled, owing to declining demand in the villages around Abúlékejì; Mrs. Oyè said that she now relies on her sons to "take care of her" since her husband "does not." She was not devoid of resources of her own, however. In addition to various trades, she had as a girl learned a good deal about traditional medicine from her father and had inherited his place in a society of herbalists. At the time I interviewed her, in 1978, she had given up selling cloth and was confining herself to "medical practice," which included trading in traditional medicines. Early in 1979 she traveled to Lagos with a shipment of medicinal ingredients, which she sold for a profit of ₦400.

The proliferation of women traders in villages such as Abúlékejì is in part a long-run consequence of the growth of cocoa production and rural commercialization. Rural households' demand for purchased foodstuffs, manufactured items, and so on has been reinforced in recent years by shortages of local food staples and by the expansion of transport services through Abúlékejì, which makes it easier for women to hawk foodstuffs in neighboring villages and markets. In Abàkinní, which is less readily accessible and where trucks travel only when there are likely to be large groups of passengers or sizable amounts of produce to be evacuated, only 7 percent of the women trade in anything other than cocoa or kola. Even in Abúlékejì, demand for luxury consumption goods has decreased in recent years; goldsmiths complained, for example, that business had been poor, and several of my informants had given up cloth selling because of falling demand. Similarly, the increased number of women buying kola is a symptom of the decline in cocoa production rather than a sign of agricultural growth and diversification. As long as rural women remain in their husbands' households, their opportunities are restricted to those of the rural market. With the decline in the cocoa economy since 1970, self-employment has not led to economic independence for the majority of farmers' wives.

Agricultural Decline and Rural Mobility

The deterioration of the cocoa economy during the 1970s not only reduced rural incomes and investment opportunities but also undermined farmers' ability to improve their economic position through combined action. Rural trade in produce, foodstuffs, and manufactured goods—once an attractive outlet for farmers' savings—has increasingly become the province of men and women who lack the means to leave the village and seek better opportunities elsewhere. At the same time the demise of the village cooperatives signaled the futility of continued efforts to improve the terms of trade through collective pressure on produce buyers. Agricultural incomes have fallen too low to sustain the limited organizational costs of such efforts, and in any event there is little to be gained by them even if they could be sustained. Cocoa prices were, after all, rising during the 1970s. Farmers' problems stemmed from declining yields from old cocoa trees, inflation, and the shortage of labor, problems that cannot easily be overcome through local cooperative action. Combination in restraint of trade is no protection against the redundance of what is being traded.

Faced with the decline of local agricultural production, men and women in villages like Abàkinní and Abúlékejì have turned away from the local economy to seek better opportunities elsewhere. In the long run, in one respect, the oil boom simply accelerated the ongoing tendency for farmers, and their children, to move into nonagricultural sectors. Successful farmers who wished to enter trade now left the village to do so, instead of engaging in produce buying or other rural trades, and farmers also intensified their efforts to train their children for nonagricultural occupations. The growth of the petroleum economy, however, has done more than accelerate the flow of labor and capital through an unchanging economic and political structure; it has also altered the conditions for access to power and wealth. Cocoa production has ceased to offer either an opportunity for modest prosperity to men of small means or a source of political leverage for its producers. The demise of the village cooperative societies was paralleled in the 1970s by the collapse of peasant political mobilization. Farmers have turned away from the cocoa sector in search of better channels of access, both to the market and to the state.

The exodus of economically active men from the cocoa-farming sector is reflected in the changing demographic structure of Abúlékejì (table 4–3). Although the total population of the village remained unchanged during the seventies, the turnover was extremely high— about 60 percent—and the proportions of women and older people have increased. The number of children under fifteen declined slightly (from 251 to 244); that of young adults fell sharply (from 146 to 94); while the number of men and women over thirty rose from 73 to 122. The average age of men over thirty increased, however, as those in their thirties and forties left in search of better economic opportunities and were not replaced by new arrivals. These changes in the age structure of the resident population, combined with almost universal primary school attendance by children aged five to fifteen,

TABLE 4–3
Age and Sex Distribution of Extended Village Populations

A. Residents

Age	Abàkinní M	Abàkinní F	Abúlékejì, 1971 M	Abúlékejì, 1971 F	Abúlékejì, 1978 M	Abúlékejì, 1978 F
0–4	22 ⎫	25 ⎫	65 ⎫	53 ⎫	42 ⎫	35 ⎫
5–9	25 ⎬ 55.5%	23 ⎬ 44%	50 ⎬ 55%	43 ⎬ 47%	50 ⎬ 53%	49 ⎬ 43%
10–14	13 ⎭	10 ⎭	17 ⎭	23 ⎭	34 ⎭	34 ⎭
15–19	6 ⎫	9 ⎫	8 ⎫	35 ⎫	11 ⎫	25 ⎫
20–29	10 ⎬ 15%	20 ⎬ 24%	37 ⎬ 19%	64 ⎬ 39%	23 ⎬ 14%	35 ⎬ 22%
30–39	3 ⎫	17 ⎫	24 ⎫	11 ⎫	18 ⎫	26 ⎫
40–49	10 ⎬ 12%	8 ⎬ 20%	21 ⎬ 19%	8 ⎬ 7%	21 ⎬ 16%	14 ⎬ 14%
50–59	9 ⎫	5 ⎫	3 ⎫	2 ⎫	17 ⎫	7 ⎫
60+	7 ⎬ 15%	2 ⎬ 6%	3 ⎬ 2.5%	1 ⎬ 1%	13 ⎬ 12%	6 ⎬ 5%
Unknown	3 2.5%	8 6%	12 5%	16 6%	10 4%	45 16%
Total	108	127	240	256	239	276
F/M ratio	1.18		1.07		1.15	

B. Nonresidents

Age	Abàkinní M	Abàkinní F	Abúlékejì M	Abúlékejì F
0–9	7 ⎫	9 ⎫	5 ⎫	9 ⎫
10–14	4 ⎬ 31%	3 ⎬ 31%	17 ⎬ 20.5%	15 ⎬ 31%
15–19	6 ⎫	8 ⎫	25 ⎫	18 ⎫
20–29	14 ⎬ 55%	10 ⎬ 46%	33 ⎬ 54%	24 ⎬ 54%
30–39	1 ⎫	3 ⎫	4 ⎫	4 ⎫
40+	0 ⎬ 3%	0 ⎬ 8%	8 ⎬ 11%	1 ⎬ 6%
Unknown	4 11%	6 15%	15 14.5%	7 9%
Total	36	39	107	78

help to explain the increasing scarcity of labor for local agricultural production.

The histories of individual migrants shed further light on patterns of emigration during the seventies. Of the 63 adult men who left the village after 1971, seven had died or retired to their hometowns; nine were spending most of their time on newer farms in Òndó; five were farm laborers who had left to find work elsewhere; and eight were trading in larger towns. Except for the laborers, most of the emigrants still owned cocoa farms near Abúlékejì and relied on wives or junior brothers to look after them. The Awóyẹlé family is a good example. In 1971 Alhaji Sànúsí Awóyẹlé headed a household in Abúlékejì consisting of his mother, his two wives, and three small children, all of whom he supported with income from his deceased father's cocoa farm. His junior brother, Yésúfù, was at that time a tailor's apprentice in Ìlọ̀rin. By 1978 Yésúfù was married with two children and had come to live in Abúlékejì. He practiced tailoring there and had also taken over the management of his father's farm, Alhaji Sànúsí having moved to Òkèigbó to trade. Alhaji Sànúsí had taken a third wife. In 1978, two of his wives were living with him in Òkèigbó; the third wife and four children remained with Yésúfù in Abúlékejì. The output from their cocoa farm had declined from six to eight bags a year to only one bag in 1977–78, and Yésúfù's earnings from tailoring were minimal. The members of the household in Abúlékejì depended on remittances from Alhaji Sànúsí to meet basic consumption needs.

Several of the emigrants had taken their families with them and rented out to new arrivals the houses they had built in Abúlékejì. One-fourth of the houses in the village contained tenants: ten were completely rented out and in nine others tenants occupied one or more of the rooms. Very few of the emigrants had made enough money, however, to invest in urban real estate. An exception was Alhaji Tìjání Ọlọ́runsọlá, who was among the migrants from Ẹripa who planted cocoa in Abúlékejì at the height of the cocoa boom in the mid-fifties. He invested part of the proceeds of his first farm in produce buying and also purchased a second farm of mature cocoa trees in 1962. By 1970 he had given up produce buying because the profits "weren't sufficient" and opened a shop in Òṣogbo to sell cloth. Deciding that the cloth trade was overcrowded with competitors, he switched to cement in 1972, shortly before the oil-fed construction boom of the mid-seventies. By 1975 he was able to open a second shop, next door to the first, where he sold hardware and steel rods. In 1978 his turnover in cement alone ranged from ₦2,000 to ₦8,000 a month; after transport and loading costs, he cleared anywhere from ₦400 to ₦1,600 a month. He spent about ₦150–₦200 a month on rent and on the salaries of two assistants who bought cement for him in Lagos; the rest was profit. At the time of our interviews he was supporting seven children in grammar school and had spent ₦80,000 "so far" on a building in Òṣogbo. In early 1979 he was already renting out the first floor for ₦78 a month, and he planned to rent out the rest when it was finished.

Alhaji Tìjání was probably the most successful trader in Abúlékejì. Others who left the village to trade in town were less fortunate. One of the least successful, a man who had been selling farm implements in Abúlékejì in 1971, had for many years spent much of his savings trying to help his first wife conceive, and he had finally taken a second wife in order to produce children. In the mid-seventies he moved his trade to Ọdẹòmu where he sold his wares in a small shop in front of his lodging place, and also in the marketplace every fourth day. His turnover ranged from less than ₦50 to ₦250 a month, depending on the season, and he estimated his average profit margin at about 8 percent. Two others tried to emulate Alhaji Tìjání, opening shops on the same street in Òṣogbo, but with less favorable results. One, who also sold hardware, estimated that he had made about ₦150 profit in 1977, but the rent on his shop had risen to ₦500 a year in 1979, and it was not clear whether or not his sales would be large enough to cover it.

As I was unable to trace many of the emigrants from Abúlékejì, I cannot say whether the experiences of the Ọdẹòmu trader or of Alhaji Tìjání were the more typical. The changing socioeconomic profile of the village residents lends support to the view that men of means were leaving the village, whereas those who arrived or stayed there were increasingly dependent on extravillage sources of income. Most of those who migrated into Abúlékejì after 1971 were either kinsmen of established cocoa farmers or employees of extravillage institutions. The former group included several older men who had spent most of their economically active lives as traders or craftsmen in Nigerian or Ghanaian towns. Most of them traded or farmed in Abúlékejì, but they derived little income from these activities and subsisted on remittances from their adult children who were living and working outside the village.

Other recent immigrants included several young men who were staying with relatives in Abúlékejì because they had at the moment no better prospects elsewhere. Some were doing better than others. Isaiah Ọládélé, for example, after attending four years of primary school, came to the village to work on his senior brother's farm. He later acquired a farm of his own and also worked as an agent for one of the most successful produce buyers in the village. (John Ayé, the produce buyer, employed several young men, to whom he advanced money to make crop advances to farmers in Abúlékejì and nearby villages. The agents were responsible for collecting and storing cocoa until they had enough to warrant summoning a truck from an LBA in Ifẹ̀. Mr. Ayé also advanced his agents money for their own use, thereby ensuring that they would turn over what they bought to him. Most of the motorcycles in the village belonged to Mr. Ayé's agents.) In 1978 Isaiah was married, had two small children, and lived with his brother in a newly built house. His wife sold rice and beans, which she bought in bulk through her mother in Ìreé and resold in rural markets or to individuals in Abúlékejì; she was also doing well in her trade. Isaiah planned eventually to leave the village to trade in a larger town; in the meantime, he appeared to be off to a good start in Abúlékejì. Other young men, such as Yésúfù Awóyẹlé, who had moved to the village during the seventies, were less well off. The medicine seller described above is a case in point; another is a young man in Abàkinní who had done casual labor in Lagos and came to stay on his father's farm when he could no longer find work in the capital.

Finally, there were several young men living in the villages in 1978 who neither farmed nor traded in rural markets. Among them were five primary school teachers, an agricultural extension agent, a miller, and a man who operated an unlicensed clinic with two assistants. Their ties to the village were, in most instances, even more tenuous than those of other recent immigrants. None had agnatic kin in the villages and only the clinician and the extension agent had brought their wives and children. The teachers in particular regarded their rural assignments as an unpleasant necessity, to be borne only until they managed to arrange a transfer or to save enough money for further schooling. They spent all their free time away from the village, often leaving for the weekend on Thursday afternoon or Friday morning and returning on Monday or even Tuesday to resume their classes. The others, though less openly scornful of village life, were no less anxious to leave should the opportunity arise.

Many young men and women had, of course, left the villages during the 1970s, usually with their parents' assistance. Table 3–6 summarizes my information on the occupations of nonresident adult members of village households.[7] The majority of the adult sons of village residents were either away at school or employed in the tertiary sector of the economy, primarily as teachers, clerks, tailors, drivers, or mechanics. Farmers' absentee wives and daughters were more likely than the sons to be engaged in farming or trade, but several daughters were also attending secondary school or working as teachers or clerks.

As noted in chapter 3, farmers' children were usually trained for nonagricultural occupations at their parents' expense, as part of the parents' long-term strategies for upward mobility. The principal change that took place in the 1970s was an increase in the proportion of farmers' children attending secondary school, as compared with those in apprenticeships or other forms of vocational training. As table 3–4 indicates, 70 percent of the persons ever receiving secondary schooling were attending school in 1978, whereas 80 percent of those with vocational training had completed their apprenticeships in the past. Investment in secondary schooling was also noticeably higher in

Abúlékejì, where half of the households had sponsored someone in secondary school, compared with only 25 percent in Abàkinní. Conversely, among farmers' teenage children, pupils outnumbered apprentices by six to one in Abúlékejì, whereas in Abàkinní the two groups were about equal in number. The extended population of Abúlékejì included 88 pupils and secondary school graduates, 54 apprentices, and 10 Arabic students; in Abàkinní, the numbers were 11, 26, and 3, respectively. In short, farmers in Abàkinní had trained a smaller proportion of household members than had those in Abúlékejì (13 percent compared with 22 percent) and had put stronger emphasis on vocational training relative to secondary schooling.

Farmers in Abúlékejì may have invested more in schooling in part because their incomes are somewhat higher. I do not have data on individual or household incomes, but several characteristics of the two villages suggest that residents of Abúlékejì have been somewhat more prosperous than those of Abàkinní. The wider occupational diversity of the former suggests that, over time, village residents may either have had larger resources to invest in additional productive activities or have invested more of what they had in expanding and diversifying productive activities. Abúlékejì is situated on a more heavily traveled road, so that farmers and traders there have easier access to markets. That advantage would tend to increase both their incentive to expand production and exchange and their gains from doing so.

In addition, 90 percent of the population of Abàkinní are Muslims, whereas the residents of Abúlékejì are about evenly divided between Muslims and Christians, and Christians have invested more heavily in secondary schooling. In both villages the proportion of Christian households with one or more secondary-educated members (61 percent) was more than twice the proportion of Muslim households (27 percent). Among my informants, Christians had invested considerably more in secondary schooling, both for their own children and for other relatives, than had Muslims, who tend to have sponsored more apprentices (table 4–4).

During the colonial period most secondary schools were established and run by Christian missionaries or converts. They included mandatory study of Christian doctrine in the curriculum and expected their pupils to follow Christian religious observances. Even Muslims who wanted their children to receive a Western education were discouraged from sending them to explicitly Christian schools, and therefore children of Muslim farmers usually received less education, especially at the secondary level, than their Christian counterparts. The preponderance of Muslim households in Abàkinní seems likely to be a major

TABLE 4–4
MALE INFORMANTS' INVESTMENT IN POSTPRIMARY TRAINING

Religious affiliation	Number of informants sponsoring		Number of apprentices sponsored (avg.)	Number of pupils sponsored (avg.)
	Apprentices	Secondary school pupils		
Christians (19)	4 (21%)	15 (79%)	9 (.47)	47 (3.2)
Muslims (25)	10 (40%)	12 (48%)	17 (.67)	34 (2.6)

factor explaining the lower rate of investment in secondary schooling there.

Postprimary schooling increased farmers' children's chances of obtaining bureaucratic or professional employment outside the cocoa sector (see chap. 3). The accelerated rate of farmers' investment in their children's education during the 1970s not only reflected but also reinforced the growth of state and salaried employment in western Nigeria as a whole; and it accentuated the educational differences between farmers and their children. This, in turn, enhanced the possibility of differentiation and tension within descent groups or among people of common origin. During the 1970s this possibility was realized, in part as a result of farmers' efforts to cope with their changing position in the regional political order. As the fiscal basis of their political leverage dwindled with the growth of the petroleum industry, farmers turned away from the cocoa sector politically as well as economically. Rather than pursue the now fruitless strategy of joint action with other agricultural producers, the residents of Abàkinní and Abúlékejì turned toward their hometowns in search of more effective channels of access to state-controlled resources.

This shift in cocoa farmers' political strategies was not reflected in any measurable increase in the frequency of visits home. In 1978 most farmers traveled to their hometowns at least once a year, but the same had been true in 1971. Indeed, for farmers whose incomes had declined during the 1970s the cost of transport to their hometowns was becoming prohibitive so that home visits were an increasingly unattainable luxury. Instead, the most noticeable change in migrant farmers' activities "at home" occurred in the organization of descent-group activities rather than in the frequency of participation in them. In 1971 migrant farmers whom I interviewed in Abúlékejì and elsewhere emphasized the ceremonial purpose of their hometown visits. They returned home for major religious holidays—Abúlékejì was virtually deserted in March 1971, for example, because farmers had gone home for the Muslim festival of Iléyá—and to celebrate life-cycle events, such as weddings, funerals, and naming ceremonies. Farmers were also active in their hometown progressive unions, to which they sometimes made substantial contributions. In 1978 the influence of cocoa farmers in the Ìreé Progressive Union was minimal (see chap. 7). At the same time, my informants in Abúlékejì laid much greater stress than they had in 1971 on the efforts made by the members of their compounds at home to improve the fortunes of the descent group, individually and collectively.

During the 1970s a number of compounds in Ìreé and Ẹripa made more or less self-conscious efforts to organize themselves as agencies of progress. In twelve of the fifteen compounds for which I obtained such information, annual family gatherings had been reconstituted, to some extent, as formal "meetings." (Called "family meetings"— *ipàdé ilé*—these gatherings were organized by the house or compound. Individuals usually attended meetings in the houses of their agnatic kin—"father's side"—but some attended meetings on their "mother's side" as well. Peel, personal communication.) Such a meeting often chose a secretary and/or treasurer, kept records of attendance and contributions, and opened a bank account where members' contributions, were deposited. Sometimes reorganization was undertaken in response to external pressure—for example, warnings from a sanitary inspector to clean up the compound—but usually informants cited a growing awareness of the need to find more effective ways to gain access to resources and opportunities for upward mobility. Ceremonies continued to absorb a major part of the time people spent in their home compounds, but new activities were added to them.

In discussing the purpose of family meetings, informants stressed solidarity ("we want to know ourselves") and progress ("we want to do something tangible"). In actuality, much of the time spent on such meetings was devoted to urging people to attend and to collecting money from those who did. Compound secretaries compiled lists of emigrant members; meetings were often announced in advance over the radio or in printed circulars; and active members sometimes visited their less enthusiastic kin to urge them to attend meetings. Those who did go to a meeting were expected to make a contribution—often a token amount, although financially successful members were expected to give more. One informant said that in her house "graduates" were automatically assessed an amount several times larger than that collected from other family members.

How to use the resources (human and financial) of the family for its collective benefit was a subject of much discussion. Individual members were advised on how to improve their fortunes; contributions were sometimes used to help pay school fees for younger family members, to repair the compound itself, or just to provide refreshments for the meeting. Whether or not the family meeting served as a source of significant collective investment, however, individuals who attended could always hope to arrange a loan or profitable contact through a prosperous or influential relative. In short, as the cocoa economy offered fewer possibilities for either individual accumulation or collective action, farmers were increasingly inclined to explore the uses of home-based kinship relations as an alternative channel of individual and collective access to resources and opportunities of the state.

The way they went about using kinship relations, however, reflects the inherent limitations of the strategy. The reconstitution of family gatherings into formal meetings was, in part, predicated on the belief in formal education as a key to progress which also informed farmers' strategies of investment in their children's futures. Compound secretaries obviously had to be literate. More fundamentally, insofar as educated members of the descent group enjoyed an advantage in access either to economic opportunities or to state functionaries, they were crucial to the realization of the family's goals. Consequently, farmers found themselves increasingly powerless, vis-à-vis their educated (and often junior) relatives, even within the descent group itself. Not only the compound secretaryships, but chieftaincy titles as well, were increasingly likely to pass to the educated. In Ẹripa and Ìreé, as we shall see, the seventies were dominated by struggles for control of local offices and institutions between groups with differential access to education and the state. By reinforcing both the power of the central government over resources and opportunities, and the importance of education as a necessary (if not sufficient) condition of access to the state, the growth of the oil economy in the 1970s furthered the emergence of class differences within kinship and community systems, a process that had been set in motion by the growth of the cocoa economy during the colonial era.

Conclusion

The transitional role of cocoa cultivation in the socioeconomic transformation of western Nigeria is reflected not only in forms of rural accumulation but also in farmers' strategies of political mobilization and action. As producers of a crop destined entirely for export, cocoa growers could, in principle, increase their incomes either by expanding output or by raising the domestic price of cocoa. The latter required collective action so as to strengthen farmers' bargaining power vis-à-vis private traders or to exert political pressure on the state. With respect

to the marketing, if not the production, of cocoa, farmers have therefore had a strong incentive to act collectively as peasants. And yet
Yorùbá cocoa growers have not behaved consistently as a class for
themselves. Certainly there have been numerous instances of con-
certed action among cocoa farmers to improve their terms of trade
or to resist what they considered to be intolerable state intervention
into the conditions of agricultural production. But there has never
been a farmers' party in western Nigeria at the regional level, nor
have studies of local political history revealed any consistent tendency
for cocoa growers to operate as a cohesive faction in chieftaincy disputes or other local political affairs. Observing that in the 1950s and
1960s "NCNC [National Council of Nigeria and Cameroon] membership in Ilesha was identical in class terms with the AG's [Action
Group's]," Peel (1980) concludes that "even the cocoa economy fell
short of realizing its potential for class-conflict" (p. 500).

Peel attributes the absence of an ongoing peasant-based political
movement in Iléṣà to the enduring importance of community structures as channels of access to economic resources and state power in
colonial and postcolonial Nigeria, and to the dominant economic position of petroleum exports, which served to undercut the fiscal basis
of peasant political leverage after 1970. Both factors undoubtedly
served to blunt the force of farmers' common interest in the domestic
terms of trade for cocoa as a motive for collective action and a focus
for political mobilization. But the presence of alternative channels of
collective action is not sufficient to explain why farmers' protests were
only sporadic, as they were long before the predominance of oil. To
the extent that collective action in the pursuit of socioeconomic advance springs from the conditions of production itself, we may expect
farmers' political strategies to resemble their strategies of accumulation
and social mobility.

In this vein, the preceding discussion suggests that Yorùbá farmers'
political solidarity has not proved any more lasting than their specialization in agricultural production. The demise of farmer protest in
the 1970s was not only a reflection of the growth of petroleum exports
and the persistence of "communal identities" in Nigerian politics but
also an outcome of farmers' own strategies of resource allocation.
These strategies were (as seen in chap. 3) directed toward advancing
farmers' claims to seniority, but the presence of a common theme
underlying the various uses of agricultural income does not imply
that they worked to a common effect. Commercialization of the rural
economy multiplied alternatives confronting rural producers but did
not necessarily reconcile them. Using increased agricultural income
to engender and educate more children could, for example, serve

both to enhance a man's position, by proving him a prolific and provident parent whose children's prosperity augments his own seniority, and to undermine it by reducing the surplus available in the short run for expanding his own enterprises and by enabling his juniors to rival his wealth and power in the long run. Similarly, continued investment in kin group and hometown provided farmers with an alternative framework of political mobilization and access to the state and also committed them to an arena of social action within which their upwardly mobile descendants could effectively pursue their own aspirations for power and privilege, sometimes at their parents' expense.

5

Schoolteachers: The Social and Economic Effects of Occupational Mobility

The rapid expansion of the educational system in Nigeria since the early 1950s has absorbed a sizable share of government expenditures, but it has also provided opportunities for farmers' children to advance and served to differentiate them from their parents. Moreover, the system has employed a substantial number of its own graduates. Among the sons and daughters of Abàkinní and Abúlékejì, those who had gone beyond the primary level were more likely to be employed in teaching than in any other single occupation. The number of teachers in western Nigeria as a whole had also risen rapidly, especially during the 1950s, when the Western Regional government attempted to institute universal primary education, and again in the 1970s, when the states of the old Western Region largely succeeded in reaching that goal (table 5–1). Openings for secondary school teachers have also risen steadily so that, by 1977–78, Ọ̀yọ́ State alone was employing nearly as many teachers as had been employed in the whole Western Region in 1971.

The history of teachers in the economy and society of western Nigeria is germane to the present study in two ways. On the one hand, since a significant number of peasants' children have found employment as teachers, the socioeconomic behavior and position of teachers are relevant for understanding patterns of socioeconomic mobility among farmers' descendants. On the other hand, as providers of educational services, teachers are a central element in the generation of structural change and social differentiation in contemporary western Nigeria. By examining the changing position of schoolteachers in general and the life histories of resource allocation, social relationships and political behavior of some individual teachers in particular, in this chapter I extend the previous discussion of the effects of agricul-

TABLE 5–1
TEACHERS EMPLOYED IN WESTERN NIGERIA

Year	Primary	Secondary modern	Secondary grammar[a]	Total
Western Region (including Midwest)				
1952				11,000
1955				27,000
1961	40,277	4,105	1,641	31,885
1962	40,149	4,726	1,865	32,341
1963	38,856	5,114	2,157	29,923
Western Region (excluding Midwest)				
1964	23,056	2,721	1,936	28,183
1965	23,480	2,076	2,181	28,041
1966	24,110	1,567	2,534	28,458
1967	24,801	1,263	2,863	29,333
Western State				
1968	23,253	1,129	3,080	27,827
1969	22,497	1,116	3,374	27,351
1970	24,055	1,263	3,725	29,431
1971	27,016	1,548	3,824	32,822
1972	29,583	1,789	4,075	36,104
1973	31,640	2,086	4,309	38,658
1974–75	35,837	2,528	4,631	43,375
Ọ̀yọ́ State				
1975–76	19,332	1,663	2,395	23,906
1976–77	23,235	1,670	2,816	28,279
1977–78	25,353	1,433	3,653	31,047

SOURCES: Federal Ministry of Education; Western State; Ọ̀yọ́ State.
[a] This classification includes commercial secondary schools from 1970 on.

tural accumulation on the structure of the western Nigerian economy
and the process of differentiation.

Teachers in the Political Economy
of Western Nigeria

As educated men and women, teachers share professional interests
and attitudes that are distinct from those of other Nigerians with
similar educational backgrounds. During the colonial period teachers
constituted a kind of labor aristocracy in the Nigerian economy. As

employees of foreign missions or of the colonial regime,[1] their incomes and conditions of service were determined by foreign employers against whom the teachers had, ultimately, little real power. Salaries were often very low, particularly those of mission teachers, who were encouraged to think of themselves as evangelists rather than employees and whose mission was to create their own demand, as it were, through proselytization. Though poorly paid, they considered themselves privileged and enlightened, compared with the heathen and/or illiterate mass of their countrymen, by virtue of their training and identification with Western customs and Christian values (Àyándélé, 1974). The encouragement they received from foreign missionaries was reinforced to the extent that other Nigerians looked up to them as possessors of socially effective knowledge, which they could pass on in church and in the classroom or could use to help kinsmen and neighbors cope with colonial officials.

In these circumstances schoolteachers, like privileged subordinates anywhere, sought to improve their own conditions of service while upholding the institutions on which their privileges depended. The Nigeria Union of Teachers (NUT), founded in 1931, was the first union in Nigeria, but it did not officially register as a trade union until 1941 (Fájánà, 1973). Indeed, from the first, the union tended to identify itself as an organization of professionals rather than workers. Union leaders tried to dissociate themselves from the nationalist movement in the 1930s and 1940s and to affect educational policy (as well as their own terms of service) through carefully cultivated contacts with senior British officials rather than through collective bargaining or industrial action (Abernethy, 1969; Fájánà, 1973; Smyke, 1972). Many teachers also identified closely with the missions, using the union and their government contacts, not to oust the missions, but to try to effect changes in mission policy. As Abernethy has pointed out, mission affiliation also gave the teachers a desired measure of independence from government control: they preferred government regulation to outright government takeover of the schools (pp. 115–116).

As already noted, educated Nigerians had a potential role as popular spokesmen in colonial society. Especially in rural communities, teachers were influential figures, often enabling traditional community leaders to communicate with or gain access to external sources of wealth and power. As the British began to transfer power to local and regional authorities in the 1950s, teachers often found themselves favorably situated to run for elective office. Many were elected to local councils in the early 1950s, and teachers constituted the largest occupational group in the Western Region House of Assembly (Abernethy,

1969, p. 121). Because of their professional training and experience, teachers believed themselves (and were so considered by their
compatriots) to be particularly well qualified for political activism and
influence as Nigeria moved toward self-government. It is interesting
in this context to note that, of the three elite occupational groups
studied by Imoagene, politicians were more likely than either civil
servants or businessmen to have begun their careers as teachers[2]
(Imoagene, 1976, pp. 85, 93, 101).

Ironically, universal primary education (UPE), which teachers
helped to establish in the 1950s, ultimately served to undermine their
political influence (see Roberts, 1975). Initially the system created
thousands of new positions for primary school teachers, forcing the
missions to hire large numbers of untrained teachers who from the
first constituted a threat to the professionalism of trained teachers.
The latter, who controlled the NUT, did not hesitate to sacrifice the
interests of their new colleagues in order to safeguard professional
standards, and they did nothing to halt the dismissal of untrained
teachers as trained teachers became available (Abernethy, 1969). In
1968 the Western State Committee, appointed to review the primary
education system, recommended that more promotions be given for
demonstrated teaching skills and that "the listless and the bird of
passage should be weeded out" (Western State, 1968).

This policy, however, created a new dilemma for teachers committed
to the values of professionalism. If trained teachers were more deserv-
ing of jobs and political influence than untrained teachers, then it
might be argued that graduates were even better qualified in both
respects. Both within the NUT, some of whose members formed a
breakaway organization of their own in the late 1950s, and in the state
as a whole graduates began to demand, and to obtain, increasing
influence. Thus the old corps of trained primary teachers found their
position being eroded both from above and from below: the influx
of untrained teachers discredited the status of their occupation, while
their claims to power based on education were weakened by the growing supply of even better-educated Nigerians eager to supersede them.

As political chaos and civil war absorbed a larger and larger portion
of the fiscal resources of the Nigerian state in the 1960s, universal
primary education was shelved. With the growth of oil revenues in
the 1970s, however, development planning could once again take an
ambitious turn. In 1976 the government formally announced a revival
of UPE—this time on a nationwide basis—together with plans to
expand substantially Nigeria's facilities for secondary and higher education. To ensure competent instruction throughout the primary

schools, training for a Grade II teaching certificate was also to be offered free of charge to candidates with the necessary qualifications to enter the program. The Grade II certificate represents five years of postprimary training, although persons with some secondary schooling can qualify for it in less time. Holders of the West Africa Examinations Council (WAEC) School Certificate or the General Certificate Examination (GCE) (O-level) equivalent can do so in a year (Margolis, 1977). In addition, the state governments in the former Western Region assumed full control of all primary and secondary schools, which means that education is now completely secularized in western Nigeria and that teachers have been fully absorbed into the civil service, with salaries determined by its grading scale. As civil service employees teachers were also given the opportunity to seek job assignments in their states of origin, thus facilitating close contacts with their home communities.

The secularization of education and the absorption of teachers into the civil service expanded the power of the state relative to that of other participants in the educational system of western Nigeria. For one thing, control of educational policy and school administration has been removed from the influence of foreign missionaries and of religious or proprietary interests within Nigeria.[3] Second, the full absorption of teachers into the civil service completed the transformation of the political position of teachers which began with the graduates' rise to power. Not only have teachers lost much of their former privileged status as professional advisers to the colonial administration or to elected representatives of the people, but the state now has power to employ or dismiss them and to determine their salaries, as well as to set policies for the entire educational system. These conditions affect teachers at all levels of the system: while secondary school teachers, for example, receive higher pay than primary school teachers, the salaries and working conditions of both are subject to state control. Politically, as well as economically, the position of teachers vis-à-vis the state has been proletarianized: virtually the only way they can exercise power or influence state policy is through union activity, such as strikes.

The changing socioeconomic and political position of teachers as a group means that being employed as a schoolteacher has had different implications for different generations or age-groups of Yorùbá men and women. Young school leavers or graduates who obtained employment as teachers in the 1970s entered an occupation that, economically and politically, was distinctly more proletarianized than it had been for those who entered it in the 1950s. On the other hand, the significance of declining status for the socioeconomic aspirations of young people who entered primary school teaching in the 1970s was considerably attenuated by the rapid expansion of opportunities for higher education during this period. As we shall see, many of the young men and women who were teaching school in the late 1970s regarded their occupation as temporary. It gave them an opportunity to earn money so that they could return to secondary school or even attend a university in a few years' time. For these young people teaching was somewhat like cocoa growing for their parents: it was an immediate source of income and a stepping-stone to better opportunities. The generational difference was that most cocoa farmers were content to use the proceeds of their farms to launch their children into more attractive occupations, whereas young primary school teachers in the 1970s expected to return to school and later move into more lucrative and influential positions themselves. As we shall see in more detail below, it was the older teachers—especially married men with numerous dependents—whose life chances were largely defined by the limitations of the teaching profession and who were most affected by the proletarianization of that occupation.

The Schoolteachers

To show how education and professional employment affected the economic and social lives of farmers' children, I collected information on income use and institutional affiliations for a small sample of primary and secondary school teachers in several communities in Ọ̀yọ́ State. In selecting informants I chose schools through my contacts in Ẹripa and Ìreé. Someone from one of these towns was employed in each of the schools where I interviewed teachers, and I made arrangements to conduct interviews through that person. In selecting individual informants, however, I sought to interview a cross section of teachers in each school instead of limiting myself to people from Ìreé and Ẹripa. I also interviewed a few primary school teachers in Abúlékejì. Altogether, I collected occupational histories for 42 primary school teachers in Ifẹ̀ and in Abúlékejì and for 23 secondary school teachers in Ọ̀sogbo and Ọ̀tan Aiyégbajú; I have information on uses of income for 60 of them (39 primary and 21 secondary school teachers).

Information about the composition of my sample, in terms of age, sex, and marital status, is given in table 5–2. More than half the primary school teachers in my sample were women, compared with one-fourth of the secondary school teachers. In Ọ̀yọ́ State, in 1971, women constituted 32 percent of the primary and 17 percent of the secondary teachers (Western State, *Current Education Statistics*). Accord-

TABLE 5–2
TEACHERS INTERVIEWED

Classification	Primary	Secondary	All
Sex			
Male	43%	74%	54%
Female	57%	26%	46%
Age			
20–29	48%	39%	45%
30–39	26%	35%	29%
40–49	26%	26%	26%
Marital status			
Single	33⅓%	39%	36%
Married: monogamous	59⅔%	61%	60%
polygynous	7%	—	5%

ing to the secretary of the Ifẹ Division Schools Board, married women were given preference in school assignments and usually asked to be placed in urban schools, a request that may account for the relatively high proportion of women in my sample.

Of my informants, 45 percent were in their twenties, 29 percent, in their thirties, and 26 percent, in their forties; on average, primary school teachers were somewhat younger. Just over a third of my informants were single, and most of the rest were monogamously married. Only three men had two wives each. Marital status was closely related to age: all but one of the unmarried teachers and less than 20 percent of the married ones were in their twenties. Most of the married teachers under thirty were women. Unfortunately, I do not have evidence as to age distribution or marital status of teachers in the region as a whole, and I cannot judge the representativeness of my sample in these respects.

The large majority of teachers I interviewed were children of farmers or traders, although the proportion was lower among secondary teachers than in any of the other occupational groups I studied (table 5–3). This evidence is consistent with other studies which have found a correlation between fathers' and children's educational achievements, although it does not directly confirm such a relationship. Occupational categories may, of course, cut across significant differences in income. Traders, for example, range from petty traders selling small amounts of such minor items as soap and matches to international diamond dealers. Indeed, Aronson (1978) has argued that occupational stratification of the sort found in contemporary industrialized societies does not really exist in western Nigeria. His

TABLE 5–3
OCCUPATIONS OF INFORMANTS' PARENTS[a]

Occupation	Villagers	Primary teachers	Secondary teachers	Mechanics and traders
Fathers				
Farmer	42 ⎫ 86%	22 ⎫ 83%	13 ⎫ 70%	22 ⎫ 84%
Trader[b]	8 ⎭	13 ⎭	6 ⎭	4 ⎭
Artisan	6	4	–	1
Teacher	– ⎫	2 ⎫	2 ⎫	– ⎫
Clerk	1 ⎬ 2%	1 ⎬ 12%	2 ⎬ 26%	1 ⎬ 3%
Minister	– ⎭	2 ⎭	2 ⎭	– ⎭
Other	12[c]	–	2[d]	3[e]
Mothers				
Farm work	8 ⎫ 83%	3 ⎫ 93%	5 ⎫ 83%	7 ⎫ 89%
Trader	40 ⎭	36 ⎭	14 ⎭	18 ⎭
Artisan	1	2	1	1
Teacher	–	2	–	–
Other[f]	7	2	4	2

[a] Occupations outnumber informants because some persons had more than one occupation. Percentages indicate proportion of informants practicing designated occupations.
[b] Includes one building contractor and one transporter.
[c] Includes four *babaláwos* (diviners), 1 hunter, 1 drummer, and 6 unknown.
[d] One banker and one nurse.
[e] Includes two drivers.
[f] Housewives and unknown.

informants (mostly Ìjẹ̀bus living in Ìbàdàn) distinguished between people who make a living by buying and selling (*oníṣòwò*) and those whose work requires writing things down (*akòwé*), but, as Aronson points out, each of these groups contains a wide range of occupations and income levels. *Oníṣòwò* include petty traders and self-employed craftsmen as well as wealthy businessmen; *akòwé* range from clerk-typists to lawyers and professors. In Yorùbá parlance, each occupational category includes rich men (*olówó*) and poor (*talaka*).

The breadth of these occupational categories does not, however, necessarily imply that occupational stratification is nonexistent in western Nigeria. What Aronson does not discuss is the importance of education, both in determining who gains access to the upper segments of each occupational category and in effecting ease of movement between them. Uneducated men and women often do quite well as traders, but even a clerk-typist must have some secondary schooling and, while an *akòwé* can always use his savings to go into business, it is difficult for an *oníṣòwò* to earn a salary unless he has attended school.

As one of my informants put it, in commenting on the success of
Alhaji Tíjánì Qlórunṣọlá, the farmer from Abúlékejì who had become
a prosperous cement dealer in Òṣogbo: "Alhaji Tìjání is a brave man;
he knows so many people. If he had been an educated somebody . . .
Ah!" The humble social origins of many Yorùbá teachers (and other
akòwé) testify to the recent emergence of educationally defined classes
in western Nigeria rather than to their absence.[4]

The emergence of a new socioeconomic mechanism for defining or
limiting access to wealth and power need not signal the decline of
existing social forms and relationships, though it is likely to affect
them. Teachers, like cocoa farmers, often acquired the skills and
capital needed to enter their respective occupations with the material or financial assistance of kinsmen and neighbors, and kin and
community-based relationships have continued to influence their allocation of income and patterns of collective action. At the same time,
however, teachers' perceptions of what types of expenditure, investment, and political activity will best serve the interests of their families
and home communities are influenced by their own experience with
the changing structure of opportunities and access to them in their
society. Thus, as we shall see, teachers' roles in their families and
home communities reflect their training and work experience and
serve, in turn, to influence their place in the emerging class structure.

Getting Educated: The Importance of Agnates

Cocoa farmers in Abàkinní and Abúlékejì established their first tree-
crop farms with savings from previous employment or with the assistance of their relatives. Most of the teachers I interviewed owed their
teaching careers to the financial support of their kin. In most instances
my informants' parents or senior siblings had financed their education
at least up to the minimum level required for a primary teaching job:
typically, a secondary modern school leaving certificate or, until its
issuance was discontinued, a Grade III teaching certificate. Only four
of the forty-two primary teachers had received no help from their
kinsmen in meeting the costs of postprimary training; nine others
had partly financed themselves. Of the secondary teachers I interviewed, all but one had been supported by parents and other relatives
through secondary school (i.e., up to the WAEC school certificate
or equivalent GCE (O)-level exams) or, in a few instances, a Grade II
teacher training course. In other words, teachers had relied even
more heavily on parents and senior siblings than had cocoa farmers
in acquiring the skills and resources necessary to enter their chosen
occupation.

Teachers' occupational histories were, accordingly, less diversified than those of cocoa farmers. As we have seen, many cocoa farmers had earned the right to claim assistance from parents or senior kinsmen in establishing a farm by first working on their elders' farms for a period of time. Others had worked as wage laborers or self-employed traders and craftsmen in their youth and had used their savings to help establish their farms (sometimes by acquiring the labor services of a wife). None of the teachers I interviewed had ever performed agricultural or other productive labor for a kinsman, although a few had spent a year or two doing housework for a relative after finishing primary school. Indeed, more than three-fourths of them had never done any kind of work except teaching. Most of those with some variety of occupational experience had held clerical, administrative, or professional jobs before becoming teachers. Only four men had entered teaching after practicing a trade or craft.[5]

Many men and women who had helped to finance their own education did so by teaching. Older teachers, in particular, often began as Grade III or even pupil teachers (with only a primary school education) and then acquired further training when they had saved enough money to do so. Thirty-two of the primary school teachers I interviewed held Grade II teaching certificates and eleven had obtained O-level or associateship qualifications.[6] Two teachers had financed themselves entirely; nine others had combined savings with assistance from relatives or government sponsorship to upgrade their qualifications beyond the minimal level. All but five of the secondary (or higher-level) teachers I interviewed had received government support or had financed themselves. A particularly striking example was a man from Ìreé. He passed the secondary school entrance exam on leaving primary school in 1948, but his father refused to provide school fees and board for one of his nineteen children when he could not afford to educate all of them. The youth went to work as a pupil teacher: at the age of fifteen he was sent by the CMS to open a primary school in a village some miles southeast of Ifè. In order to receive a salary he had also to establish a church in the village. When the parishioners failed to pay him, he lived for a year on donations brought to a harvest service which he had organized in the church; a generous local farmer also helped him. During the next sixteen years he worked his way through the three grades of teacher training then available, studied on his own and passed the GCE O- and A-level exams, and finally obtained a bachelor of arts degree from the University of Ìbàdàn. To finance his teacher training courses he indentured himself to the Nigerian Baptist Convention, promising to teach two years for each year of study sponsored by the mission. He later attended the university under a similar arrangement with the government. After receiving his bachelor's degree he taught for six years at a teacher training college (to "pay" for his university education) and wrote a manual on teaching methods. From the sale of this book he was able to save enough money to finance a year of postgraduate study in the United States. In 1976 he received a PhD in education from an American university and has since been made vice-principal of a new college of education in his home state in Nigeria. Such self-made men and women are not uncommon among Nigeria's graduate class.

Most of my informants had not, of course, gone that far, although several of the unmarried teachers were saving to further their own education. Teachers' job levels and salaries were directly tied to their educational attainments. Primary school teachers with a Grade II certificate received higher salaries than those with only WAEC School Certificate or GCE (O-level) qualifications; similarly, secondary teachers with some form of higher education (GCE (A-level), National Certificate of Education (NCE), or bachelor's degree) were usually paid at or above civil service grade level 08, which carried a minimum salary at least ₦1,800 above that for Grade II certificate holders. Thus, men and women whose families were able and willing to support them through secondary school or beyond possessed a clear economic advantage over those who could not afford to study further or who had had to work and save for years at low salary levels in order to do so.

Uses of Income

Most of my informants devoted the major part of their salaries to the maintenance and/or education of their children, their parents, and other relatives, usually junior agnatic kin. Table 5–4 indicates the numbers of people being supported by my informants, by sex and marital status of the latter. Men tended to support more people than women, but marital status was much more important than gender as a source of additional dependents. Married teachers supported more agnates, on the average, than did single teachers, in addition to their own spouses and children. Teachers also fed and educated more people than did the villagers discussed in chapter 3, partly owing to the fact that teachers' incomes were probably higher and certainly more predictable, seasonally and annually. The median annual salary for primary school teachers in my sample was ₦1,640; most secondary teachers earned more than that. A few teachers practiced subsistence farming on a small scale, and four reported income in addition to their salaries from trade, commercial farming, or rental of a building. Most of them, however, received only their salaries.

TABLE 5–4
NUMBER OF PERSONS FOR WHOM TEACHERS PROVIDED

Informants				Maintenance		Education			
						Currently		Formerly	
Sex and marital status	Number	Total	Per informant	Total	Per informant	Total	Per informant		
Male	31						
Single	11	26	2.1	21	1.8	—	—
Married	20	167	8.3	45	2.2	25	1.2
Female	29						
Single	10	12	1.2	10	1.0	—	—
Married	19	126	6.6	47	2.5	4	0.3

NOTE: Married men were usually fully responsible for dependents' maintenance and school fees. Women, and single men, paid only part of the cost of maintenance and/or education for most of their dependents.

It is difficult to estimate farmers' annual incomes (see chap. 3), although it is clear that most farmers in Abàkinní and Abúlékejì had suffered declining incomes from cocoa, their principal cash crop, during the 1970s. According to my previous research, the average cocoa farm in Abúlékejì was about four acres. Normally, a mature cocoa farm might be expected to yield about 500 pounds of dry beans per acre each year, under peasant methods of cultivation (Berry, 1975a). Most farmers in Abúlékejì and Abàkinní, however, reported that yields had decreased sharply in recent years, to perhaps no more than 100 or 200 pounds per acre. At the 1978 price of ₦1,030, the average farmer in my sample villages might therefore have earned between ₦200 and ₦400 from sales of cocoa. It is not likely that the value of other crops or income from rural trade would have been enough to cover the gap between cocoa sales and a teacher's salary, except for a few of the most prosperous villagers. (Indeed, several older farmers were at least partly supported by their children, rather than the other way around.) In short, teachers were supporting more dependents in 1978–79 than farmers, partly because they could afford to.

I would also argue—though the evidence is admittedly sketchy—that teachers, in comparison with farmers, had probably invested a higher proportion of their lifetime incomes in education. A number of teachers had financed at least part of their own training, and the men had helped to provide secondary schooling for three other people, on the average, compared with 1.8 for farmers. In addition, female teachers had helped to educate an average of two persons each, whereas only a few farmers' wives had made even token contributions to their children's or other relatives' school expenses. A few teachers were spending more than half of their current salaries on education in 1979, and the majority devoted between a tenth and a third of their earnings to educational expenses.

Whether or not teachers had invested more in education, relatively as well as absolutely, over their lifetimes, it is clear that their children were more likely to attend secondary school than were the children of villagers (see table 5–5). Nearly all my informants' children attended primary school, in Abàkinní and Abúlékejì as well as in Ifẹ̀ and Òṣogbo. Among those not in primary school, however, 90 percent of the children of teachers were either in secondary school, at a university, or teaching, whereas only 47 percent of the children of farmers were receiving postprimary schooling or working as clerks or teachers. On the other hand, 42 percent of the children of farmers were farmers, traders, drivers, or craftsmen, whereas only one out of fifty-eight children of teachers not in primary school was engaged in what could be called a manual occupation. These data suggest not only that teachers were contributing to the growth of the educational sector in western Nigeria—through their consumption of educational services and their children's employment as well as their own—but also that, although the children of farmers are not excluded from secondary schooling, they are less likely to get it than are the children of schoolteachers. Thus, teachers' investments in schooling tend to further not only educational expansion but also the consolidation of a class structure based on differential access to education.

Farmers frequently used some of their agricultural income to diversify their income-earning activities, typically by going into trade. In contrast, very few of the teachers in my sample had taken up a second occupation, although several married men grew food crops for home consumption in their spare time.[7] I met only one teacher who was contemplating going into business himself. He had been a watch repairer in the past, and as he had made more money in that trade than he was now earning as a teacher he was thinking of going back to it. Otherwise, teachers had contributed money to their relatives' enterprises rather than engaged in trade or manual work themselves. As table 5–6 shows, informants had given money to their relatives for various types of enterprise. In all, just over a third of my informants had made such contributions. (Some individuals contributed to more than one venture.) Like their investments in education, teachers' contributions to small-scale service enterprises have promoted the growth of the tertiary sector in western Nigeria as a whole. In addition, to the extent that teachers and their own children leave such enterprises

TABLE 5–5

EDUCATIONAL STATUS OF INFORMANTS' CHILDREN AGED FIVE OR MORE

Status	Number of teachers' children[a]	Number of farmers' children[a]
Attending primary school	74	101
Attending Arabic school	–	4
Attending secondary school	41	36
Attending university	3	2
Not in school	14	80
Employed as teachers, clerks, etc.	8	18
Employed as farmers, traders, craftsmen	1	50
Unemployed	5	12
Total	132	223

[a] Includes adults.

TABLE 5–6

INFORMANTS' INVESTMENTS[a] IN SMALL-SCALE ENTERPRISES

Proprietor	Type of enterprise				
	Trade	Tailoring	Mechanic	Farm	Other[b]
Informant	2			2	
Informant's spouse	10	2			
Informant's agnate	15	4	3	2	6
Informant's friend	1				

[a] Money was used for trading capital, apprentice fees, or purchase of tools and equipment.
[b] Photography, plumbing, electrical work.

to their agnates, rather than participating in them themselves, they are helping to create those patterns of educational and occupational stratification within descent groups which, as noted in chapter 3, have increasingly confronted farmers in their hometowns and compounds in recent years.

A final item in teachers' expenditures which also tends to differentiate them from farmers is outlays on durable goods, particularly houses and motor vehicles. Fourteen (23 percent) of the teachers I interviewed owned motorcycles or cars, acquisitions that were beyond the reach of most farmers in my sample.[8] Only a fourth of the teachers, however, had built houses (three of these were women who had built jointly with their husbands), whereas nearly all but the youngest married men in the villages had built houses there, and three-fifths of them had at least started a second house at home. This difference, in turn, raises the question of whether people's relations with their home compounds and communities also change as they move from farming into teaching (a question considered in more detail below).

Investing in the wife's business: marriage, occupational mobility, and income management.—The economic implications of marriage were somewhat different for the schoolteachers I interviewed than they were for the farmers. On a farm a wife is a source of labor and therefore an economic asset to her husband from the time of marriage. Once she establishes her own trade, however, the farmer does not necessarily gain anything from his wife's labor, unless her trade prospers and she contributes more to the children's support or to other household expenses than it costs to replace her labor on the farm by hiring workers. Most cocoa farmers released their wives from regular labor on the farm when the trees were mature and they could afford to hire labor instead, but the women had to find their own trading capital, by working on neighbors' farms for wages if they could not get it from their relatives. In other words, marriage provides a farmer with extra labor as well as additional dependents, and a farmer's attitude toward his wife's economic independence is likely to be somewhat ambivalent.

For a schoolteacher, however, marriage brings increased expenses but no automatic contribution to real income. As we have seen, married male teachers supported more dependents than did any other group of informants. As they employ no labor (other than their own) in the course of earning their salaries, the only way in which their wives can contribute to household expenses is to earn independent incomes. Thus it is in a male teacher's interest to help his wife set up a business or acquire the training needed for a salaried job.

Because marriage has different economic implications for them, teachers may marry later than farmers and invest more in their wives' income-earning capacity.[9] Only one of the male teachers under 30 whom I interviewed was married—compared with 64 percent of the men aged 15–29 in Abàkinní and Abúlékejì—and half of the married male teachers had been 25 or over at the time of their first marriages. (In the villages, among my male informants who knew how old they were when they first married, 70 percent had been under 25.)[10] Moreover, teachers were more actively concerned with their wives' income-earning abilities. One man had gone so far as to divorce his first wife "because she was illiterate, did not trade, and could not contribute to the children's support." When he married again in 1975, he spent N280 on a sewing machine for his new wife and, the following year, gave her N120 to start a trade. At the time of my interview she was practicing tailoring in Òṣogbo and was also trading, in foodstuffs and cloth, between Lagos and Accra. In addition, her parents supported two of the husband's four children. In all, this man's second marriage seemed to be proving a better investment than the first.

Other informants were less explicitly calculating about their marriages, but quite a few had invested in their wives' productivity. Seven of the married men had given[11] their wives money for trade (usually amounts ranging from N100 to N300 at a time) or purchased equipment for them, and three others had helped their wives go back to school. Women, too, sometimes contributed to their husbands' educational expenses: three of those I interviewed were supporting their children and sending money regularly to their husbands who were students at the University of Ifẹ̀, and a fourth helped to support her fiancé at the University of Nsukka. Here again was a contrast with Abàkinní and Abúlékejì, where husbands and wives rarely reported having contributed to their spouses' capital.

On the whole, differences in the economic implications of marriage for farmers and schoolteachers were even more marked for women than for men. Yorùbá husbands and wives commonly manage their individual earnings separately. In principle, a husband provides food and shelter for his wife (or wives), children, and other members of the immediate household (Sudarkasa, 1973; Guyer, 1972). Husbands are also responsible for the children's school fees and, often, medical expenses. Wives sometimes supplement the food their husbands provide for the children and usually supply them with clothing, books for school, and pocket money. In Abàkinní and Abúlékejì, all my married informants adhered to this pattern in general, although some wives contributed regularly to the family food supply and also to the children's school fees.

Most of the teachers I interviewed also kept their incomes separate from their spouses'. As their husbands bore the major burden of maintaining and educating the children, it might be expected that married women would have more income to dispose of in other ways and, in fact, many of my informants did. Most married women spent more on their agnates than did married men, and several women also mentioned having money to spend "on themselves," either for personal consumption or for further education. Two of the older women owned cars and four had built houses, individually or together with their husbands.

In addition to the customary division of family expenses between Yorùbá husbands and wives, however, there was another reason that

married female teachers often had more money to spend on themselves and their agnates than did married men. On the whole, the
occupational status of my female informants' husbands was markedly
higher than that of my male informants' wives. Of my informants'
husbands, 85 percent were teachers (several at postsecondary levels),
civil servants, or university students—in a word, *akòwé*.[12] In contrast,
the majority of teachers' wives were *oníṣòwò*: self-employed traders
(52 percent) or craftswomen (16 percent). Of the others, two held
low-paying clerical jobs, five were teachers, and one was a midwife.
The six professional women (midwife and teachers) were all married
to secondary school teachers. In short, among my informants there
was a strong positive correlation between husbands' and wives' occupational status, and it is very likely that the combined income of husband and wife was higher for most of the married women than for
most of the married men in my sample of teachers.

In contrast with the women in Abàkinní and Abúlékejì, whose
economic opportunities were limited to those of the rural communities
in which their husbands farmed or traded, female teachers found that
marriage often provided a means to upward mobility. Some married
female teachers had even abandoned the practice of keeping their
incomes separate from their husbands'. In addition to the women
(mentioned above) who were supporting their husbands and children
while their husbands studied, three others said that they and their
husbands pooled their incomes and shared all family expenses, including the children's educational expenses and the cost of building a
house. Although these few examples do not constitute a trend, they
do at least illustrate the possibility that, if both spouses are educated,
occupational mobility may be associated with changing methods of
conjugal income management.

Investing in agnates: education, class, and descent-group relations.—
The fact that most teachers had received at least their basic education
at their parents' or other agnates' expense clearly influenced the way
they allocated their own incomes after they began to teach. More than
90 percent of my informants made regular contributions to the maintenance or educational expenses, or to both, of one or more agnates,
and sometimes their contributions were substantial. Teachers who
had not yet married invariably helped pay for their brothers' and
sisters' schooling and often sent money to their parents and siblings
for maintenance as well. Three-fourths of the single teachers I interviewed contributed 20 percent or more of their salaries to their
parents, siblings, or other agnates, and some of them spent more than
half of their earnings in this way. (Eldest children especially often
assumed major responsibility for supporting and training a sibling.)

Married teachers also usually managed to help their agnatic kin, in addition to supporting their own children. Only two married women and two men contributed nothing to their agnates; half of the women spent 20 percent or more of their incomes on agnates. Married men tended to contribute less than married women to their siblings' education, especially if they had children of their own in secondary school, but most of them supported one or more junior kinsmen in their own households and several had spent more on siblings' school fees in the past. At the time of my survey, single teachers (male and female) and married women were educating an average of two agnates each, compared with 1.5 for married men. In short, teachers, like farmers, had relied on kinsmen to help them acquire the resources necessary to enter their present occupation, and they subsequently allocated some of their own earnings to increasing the productive skills of relatives.

Unlike farmers, however, teachers rarely called upon their relatives for managerial (as opposed to financial) assistance. Cocoa farmers often relied on the labor of their wives, children, and agnates, especially while establishing their tree-crop farms. Although today most farmers' children attend school or become apprentices in nonfarming enterprises, farmers in Abàkinní and Abúlékejì often continue to rely on the assistance of their wives or agnates to help them manage diversified and dispersed farming or trading enterprises. Teachers, in contrast, do not need to employ labor in order to earn their salaries, and they rarely diversify their income-earning activities in such a way as to require managerial assistance. (Forty percent of the married men did some subsistence farming in their spare time to help feed their dependents, but they neither asked nor received help from family members on these farms.) For teachers, agnates, like wives, are primarily a source of financial assistance rather than of labor. In addition to help in financing their own schooling, several teachers reported than they had received gifts or loans from agnates to help with their own children's school fees or other major family expenses.

As I argue in chapter 3, many cocoa farmers have sought to maintain their right to draw on kinsmen for financial assistance, help in finding jobs for their children, and other kinds of aid, not only by participating regularly in family meetings and ceremonies but also by building houses in or near their natal compounds. Teachers also take part in family gatherings, but they rarely build houses at home unless they work in their hometowns and can therefore use such a house as a residence. Of the male teachers, 80 percent attended family meetings regularly, and many took an active part in conducting the meetings and organizing projects. Several teachers said that their family meetings had been organized (i.e., more or less formally constituted, with officers, minutes, bank accounts, etc.) in the late 1960s "because of [i.e., to take part in] the development of the country." Teachers often led the way in soliciting contributions from the more prosperous members of their descent groups to be used for scholarships, loans, commercial farming, or contributions to community projects. (One woman said that her family levied individual members in a roughly progressive fashion: people with jobs were expected to contribute N20 at the annual meetings, and graduates were assessed N60.) But only one man had, like the farmers, built a house in his hometown which he visited occasionally but which was otherwise occupied, rent free, by his relatives. The other teachers who had built houses either lived in them or rented them out.

To some extent, teachers may have invested less in housing than farmers because they were at different stages in their life cycles. For example, more than a third of the male teachers were under thirty and had not yet married, whereas about 10 percent of the men I interviewed in Abàkinní and Abúlékejì were under thirty and only one of them was unmarried. Younger, single men do not often invest in housing, so that the high proportion of such men among my sample of teachers relative to my sample of villagers partly accounts for the teachers' lower rate of investment in housing. Further, none of the married teachers in my sample was over fifty, and most of their children were still in school. Consequently, they faced heavy expenditures for dependents and might not be able to afford to build houses until at least some of their children were older and more likely to have completed school. Farmers in my sample included a higher proportion of older men, whose children were self-supporting and, in some instances, were even contributing to the school fees of their junior siblings, so that farmers might be more likely to have money to invest in housing. As we have seen, however, many of the farmers had begun constructing houses at home—or at least acquiring materials for them—when they were in their thirties or forties. In both groups men who have built houses also tend to be those who have supported the largest number of pupils. Consequently, life-cycle differences do not seem to account fully for observed differences in teachers' and farmers' investments in housing. Rather, my evidence suggests that teachers have spent a higher proportion of their lifetime incomes on education and correspondingly less on housing than have farmers.

Taken together with their often active participation in descent-group affairs (especially those seeking the economic and social progress of the family), the propensity of male teachers to send their relatives to school rather than to build houses of their own in their home compounds suggests that education and occupational mobility have affected the form rather than the fact of teachers' affiliation with their agnatic kin. Both teachers and farmers perceive the overwhelming importance of education for personal success in contemporary Nigeria, but teachers owe their incomes and occupational status directly to their educational credentials. Hence they attach even more importance to education as a strategy for personal and family success than do farmers, and they tend to view a house in the hometown as a comparative, or at least a postponable, luxury. This attitude is further reinforced by the fact that, as civil servants, teachers enjoy a security of income unknown to self-employed people; they can thus afford to postpone investment in assuring themselves a place at home.[13]

The effects of education and occupational mobility on patterns of individual investment and participation in descent-group affairs is particularly striking in the case of women. Farmers' wives maintain close ties with their own agnates, primarily through regular visits home and contributions (usually in the form of food and food preparation) to family ceremonies. They do not build houses in their fathers' compounds or contribute much to agnates' school fees or family development projects. Female teachers, on the other hand, are less likely to attend family meetings than either farmers' wives or male teachers; less than half of my female informants attended family meetings at all, more than one saying that to do so "would be a waste of money." Yet, as we have seen, female teachers contributed generously to their siblings' and other agnates' maintenance or educational expenses, even when they were married and helping to support several children of their own.

As noted earlier, female teachers tend to marry men whose education and occupational status is higher than their own, whereas male teachers' wives are generally less well educated than their husbands and usually work as traders or craftswomen rather than as akòwé. In addition, female teachers are more likely than the men to have akòwé for fathers: 31 percent of the women were daughters of clerks, teachers, or clergymen, compared with 13 percent of the men.[14] The fact that the women came from higher-status families, or had experienced greater upward mobility, than their male counterparts, both through education and employment and through marriage, may help to explain why they seem to attach even more importance to education than to other forms of investment or social action, as a strategy for individual and family advance.

Forms of Political Action

Schoolteachers' commitment to the vitality and welfare of their extended families does not of course preclude them from identifying and interacting with their colleagues. Indeed, since their own ability to provide for their children and other kinfolk depends on what they earn, there is every reason to expect that concern for their relatives will reinforce rather than dilute their interest in promoting the welfare of teachers. The possibilities for teachers to improve their economic position through class action have increased in recent years, whereas for farmers class action is no longer a very effective way of raising incomes. As Nigeria's graduate has class moved to consolidate its position by (1) lengthening the chain of educational qualifications required for high-level government jobs and (2) taking over the schools and absorbing teachers into the civil service, it has devalued teachers' claims to elite status and a share of political power and clarified their economic dependence on the state. Thus, the state has acted to promote both teachers' class consciousness and their inclination to class action.

In my interviews, few teachers mentioned the Nigeria Union of Teachers among the organizations to which they belong, probably because they took it for granted. The NUT collects members' dues through a checkoff system and, since the government takeover of the schools in 1976, all teachers are automatically members. As in many organizations whose primary function is to protect members' economic interests, NUT members do not participate actively in union affairs until those interests are threatened. The NUT-sponsored Cooperative Thrift and Credit Society in Ifẹ̀, whose meetings I attended for a while in 1979, was a classic example of an organization foundering for want of a purpose. The society was established in 1978 by fifteen primary school teachers in Ifẹ̀, several of whom were also active in the executive of the Ifẹ̀ chapter of NUT. Members could purchase shares in the society (at ₦50 each), each of which entitled the holder to borrow up to ₦100, repayable in equal installments over periods of three to six months. The nominal interest charge was ₦2.50 a month on ₦100, or an annual rate of 30 percent. If the borrower failed to make payments on time the monthly interest charge was doubled. Also, in transactions I observed, the same amount of interest was collected on loans of less than ₦100. If, therefore, a member borrowed ₦50 and fell behind on the repayment schedule, he or she could end up paying an effective rate of 100 percent a year.

Meetings were held irregularly and attendance was usually limited to officers, executive members, and loan applicants. One executive member complained that people often failed to attend meetings to make payments, sending the money by a messenger (usually a child) instead. He remarked wistfully that "those people should be told, 'We don't want your money; we want your presence.'" Officers sometimes visited delinquent borrowers to exhort them to repay their loans.

Beyond that, it was not clear that anything could be done to bring pressure on defaulters. Those who did attend the meetings spent much of the time bemoaning other members' inactivity and comparing their society unfavorably with similar societies organized by market-women and other "illiterates": "They know how to organize themselves."

When, however, the NUT called a strike in December 1978 to protest the government's failure to pay promised salary increases, so many teachers stayed away from their jobs that the Ọ̀yọ́ State government closed all schools throughout the state (*West Africa*, Jan. 1, 1979). Teachers' aspirations toward elite status and life-styles (reflected in the Thrift and Credit Society members' unease with the thought that illiterate traders excelled them in organizational ability) only increased their willingness to take militant action against their employer. A son of the *bálẹ̀* in Abúlékejì, who taught in Ifẹ̀, but returned to his father's house in the village to eat during the strike,[15] complained that teachers do not enjoy the same perquisites and opportunities for promotion as civil servants with equivalent qualifications. "In the ministries," he said, people with school certificates "have Volvo cars after ten years. My headmaster has been teaching for twenty-three years with nothing to show for it."

In a study of Yorùbá workers, traders, and artisans living in Ìbàdàn, P. C. Lloyd (1974) was struck by his informants' repeated assertions that individual thrift and hard work were the keys to upward mobility in contemporary Nigerian society; he concluded that economic inequality had not yet engendered class consciousness among the urban-dwelling poor. Instead, he argues, rich and poor alike lay greater stress on individual initiative and ethnic solidarity as the means to success: ". . . the political leader . . . may be a lawyer, . . . yet come from a peasant, rather than an urban professional, home. Though occupationally mobile he strives for the interests of his natal group rather than escaping from it into the ranks of middle class society" (ibid., p. 218). The behavior of Yorùbá schoolteachers shows, however, that belief in individual initiative is not incompatible with strikes or other forms of class action when the situation warrants them.

Strikes and participation in union-affiliated organizations, such as the NUT Thrift and Credit Society, often bring teachers specific economic gains, but such action has not restored the political influence they enjoyed in the early days of internal self-government and electoral politics. In this sphere of social action, teachers not only lost out to graduates when the military regime took over government at the state and federal levels in 1966, but their influence has also waned on the local level. Local government all but collapsed in the Western State during the civil war. In some areas, rebellious farmers participating in the Àgbẹ̀kòyà movement actually drove out local officials and administered their districts themselves for a few years. Elsewhere, funds allocated for local services declined and local government activity was, accordingly, minimal. In the 1970s the state moved to reestablish control over local government. Districts were reorganized into local government areas and, in 1976, local council elections were held for the first time since 1965. Accordingly, members of Nigeria's ruling elite became increasingly interested in cultivating ties with their hometowns; they stepped up their participation and often increased their investments in their home communities (see chap. 7, below). Teachers found themselves eclipsed at the local level by graduates from the military or the civil service, whose connections with the government were more useful to their rural relatives than those of ordinary schoolteachers and who could afford to invest more in hometown development and even houses. In the 1970s teachers, like farmers, found their political position weakening within their home communities as a result of processes of educational growth and stratification to which they had personally contributed. Among my informants, nearly all the teachers who played an active role in hometown organizations or projects were relatively well educated secondary school teachers, whose neighbors considered them qualified to promote communal interests effectively and who consequently exerted considerable influence in hometown affairs.

Conclusion

In retrospect, David Abernethy's (1969) suggestion that popular education created a political dilemma in southern Nigeria seems something of an understatement. Educational expansion has not only provided Nigeria's indigenous rulers with a politically popular form of development strategy, but it has also shaped the channels of access to power and the means whereby the ruling class has come to define and reproduce itself. Accordingly, education has served as a powerful agent of class formation as well as of economic development and social mobility. The state's commitment to universal primary education, as well as the development of secondary and higher educational institutions, even at the expense of job creation, for example, is not simply the result of irresistible public pressure on administrators who know better; it has become a central factor in the growth of state power.

Most schoolteachers in Nigeria are children of uneducated parents. By attending school and becoming teachers they have moved out of their parents' socioeconomic sphere. Often their incomes, though modest in comparison with those of graduates, are higher and more stable than their parents' incomes, enabling them to enjoy a somewhat higher standard of living and to do more, financially, for their siblings and cousins. Moreover, they and many of their countrymen believe that education enlightens as well as enriches those who receive it and that teachers, as educated people, can and ought to function as leaders of thought and agents of progress within their own society.

At the same time, the logic of educational expansion has tended to limit the incomes and the influence of ordinary schoolteachers relative to those of their more highly educated countrymen; it has also reinforced their commitment to education as a means to individual mobility and a source of social progress. Accordingly, they have devoted a substantial portion of their own resources to educating themselves, their children, and other junior kinsmen, rather than investing in other types of productive activity, though they have made contributions to relatives' trade and other small-scale enterprises. From an economic point of view, teachers have contributed to the rapid growth of the tertiary sector, both through their own occupational choice and through their investment in the capital and occupational qualifications of their kin.

Socially, teachers' investment in education has also reinforced processes of educational stratification and class formation in western Nigeria. As many of them have invested in the education of their children and other agnatic kin, teachers cannot be said to have ignored or weakened kinship ties by their method of allocating resources. Their strategies of income use, however, like those of farmers and rural traders, have also contributed to simultaneous processes of sectional and socioeconomic differentiation, which in turn have hindered productive accumulation and exacerbated political conflict, especially in the postcolonial era.

For farmers who, in the 1970s, turned to descent-based ties to escape declining agricultural incomes and opportunities, the contradictions of western Nigerian development confront them within their compounds and communities of origin, threatening their enjoyment of the seniority they have worked so long to achieve. For teachers, education has provided not only the means to invest but also the returns on investment in their income-earning capacity. Farmers' children who acquired enough schooling to become teachers have reinforced educational stratification in western Nigeria, but at the same time the elaboration of the educational hierarchy has debased the coin of specific levels of schooling. In recent years teachers have also been absorbed into the bureaucracy; in following the experiences of farmers' children who have become teachers we have been led into the state apparatus itself. Absorption into the civil service has also completed the proletarianization of teachers, who have shown a correspondingly ready disposition to use strikes and other forms of industrial action to protect or improve their salaries and working conditions. In the process they have hampered the state's own efforts to stabilize its power through the populist strategy of expanding educational opportunity. The changing position of schoolteachers in recent years offers a striking and, given the size of the educational establishment in Nigeria, substantial illustration of the way the Nigerian state has internalized the process of class formation and been frustrated by its contradictions.

6

From Peasant to Artisan: Motor Mechanics in Ile-Ifẹ̀

In this chapter I look further at the social and economic implications of farmers' investment in their children's futures by tracing the experiences of farmers' sons who have left agriculture for self-employment in small-scale secondary or tertiary enterprises. Aggregate data on output and employment in the "informal" sector are notoriously hard to come by, but it seems clear that this sector of the Nigerian economy has grown rapidly in recent years. As noted in chapter 1, recent increases in the share of gross domestic product (GDP) originating in extractive industries—principally petroleum—have not been accompanied by substantial increases in employment in that sector of the economy. Most of the people who have left agriculture in recent years have been absorbed in the tertiary sector, many of them in small-scale trade or other service enterprises.

Similarly, most of the children of farmers in Abàkinní and Abúlékejì who were not attending school in 1978–79 were self-employed: 25 percent as farmers, 20 percent as traders, and 40 percent as artisans or drivers (table 6–1). Of the latter group, nearly three-fifths were working as drivers or mechanics; the rest pursued a variety of trades, including tailoring, carpentry, bricklaying, baking, barbering, and goldsmithing. In this chapter I present evidence from the life histories of a small group of motor mechanics in Ifẹ̀ which illustrates the experiences of farmers' sons in small-scale nonagricultural self-employment and examines some of the implications of tertiary-sector growth for the development of the regional economy as a whole. I chose mechanics partly because this occupation was followed by a number of young men from Abàkinní and Abúlékejì, and also because I was able to develop a good relationship with the Mechanics' Association in Ifẹ̀, which permitted me to observe mechanics' efforts to act in concert and facilitated my interviews and observations in individual firms.[1]

TABLE 6–1
FARMERS' EMPLOYED CHILDREN

A. From village censuses

Occupation	Abàkinní			Abúlékejì		
	Males	Females	Total	Males	Females	Total
Farmer	3	12	15 (28%)	8	22	30 (25%)
Trader	2	11	13 (24%)	1	20	21 (18%)
Artisan	20	2	22 (41%)	36	9	45 (39%)
Teacher, clerk	3	1	4 (7%)	13	7	20 (17%)
Total	28	26	54	58	58	116

B. From life histories of sixty informants

Occupation	Abàkinní			Abúlékejì		
	Males	Females	Total	Males	Females	Total
Farmer	2	2	4 (20%)	4	2	6 (12%)
Trader	–	4	4 (20%)	–	5	5 (10%)
Mechanic, driver	5	–	5 (25%)	11	–	11 (23%)
Other artisans	5	–	5 (25%)	4	2	6 (12%)
Teacher, clerk	2	–	2 (10%)	6	5	11 (23%)
Other (nurse, army, housewife)	–	–	–	5	4	9 (19%)
Total	14	6	20	30	18	48

Artisans in the Nigerian Economy

Small-scale nonagricultural enterprise has been the subject of an extensive literature, with reference both to western Nigeria and to Africa in general.[2] Several studies have argued that small firms, using labor-intensive techniques, local or recycled materials, and penny-pinching methods of management, often achieve lower unit costs than larger enterprises, thus demonstrating their ability to use available resources efficiently. In addition, because markets are competitive and production is labor-intensive, increases in income in the informal sector[3] tend to be widely distributed (International Labor Organization, 1972; Liedholm and Chuta, 1976; Steel, 1977; Nafziger, 1977). Like the "optimising peasant" (Lipton, 1968), whose economic acumen and appropriate techniques are often cited in support of populist interpretations of Third World agrarian change, the optimizing artisan has come to occupy a prominent place in the literature on nonagricultural development. On the basis of such studies, economists frequently advocate populist strategies for nonagricultural development. If small firms are economically efficient, then programs of technical and financial assistance ought to be geared specifically to help them overcome limitations on their capacity to expand. Aid to the artisan tends to promote growth and greater equality at the same time.

Actually, the evidence that small firms are comparatively efficient is not unambiguous. Most studies offer cross-sectional comparisons of large and small firms at a given point in time. As the firms compared often produce different qualities or combinations of goods, the common finding that smaller enterprises use relatively labor-intensive methods of production does not necessarily indicate that their unit costs are lower than those of larger, more capital-intensive firms, even in the short run (Page, 1979). And even if their costs are lower, it does not follow that small businesses have been technologically innovative or dynamically oriented. Indeed, even in an expanding economy such as Nigeria's, where demand for the output of the informal sector is increasing at a rapid rate, it is not clear that entrepreneurs who are efficient while they are poor are likely to remain so if and when their businesses start to expand. A number of studies suggest that the African artisan's managerial performance deteriorates as his or her firm grows (Kilby, 1969; Harris, 1968, 1971; Harris and Rowe, 1966; Nafziger, 1977). Small-scale entrepreneurs often find it difficult to delegate financial and managerial responsibility or to devise effective methods of accounting. These deficiencies, in turn, make it hard for them to manage more business than they can supervise personally. Once a firm grows too large for the proprietor to oversee all its operations, workers' efficiency declines; losses from waste, theft, or spoilage increase; and financial affairs may become increasingly disorganized. Partly to avoid such managerial diseconomies of scale, successful entrepreneurs often use excess profits to diversify their activities, thus further reducing the amount and the quality of managerial input into the original enterprise. Also, as some observers argue, the African proprietor does not always draw a clear distinction between the interests and resources of the firm and those of his (extended) family, so that revenues from the former may be diverted to the latter rather than reinvested in the firm. In short, when market or political conditions favor expansion of small-scale enterprise, the optimizing artisan begins to look like a sort of target accumulator, who increasingly diverts scarce capital and managerial resources into wasteful or nonproductive uses.

How do we explain the apparently negative relationship between entrepreneurial success and managerial performance? The answer given by most of the studies cited above is that it is due to noneconomic

factors. Some maintain that African artisans have not had adequate
opportunity to learn managerial techniques, through formal study or
on the job, either because training facilities are not available (Harris,
1968; Nafziger, 1977) or because indigenous entrepreneurs are dis-
criminated against by foreigners who control most large-scale enterprises (Marris and Somerset, 1971; Akérédolú-Àlé, 1975). Kilby (1969)
goes so far as to conclude that African cultures and culturally determined socialization processes inhibit Africans from mastering skills
needed to manage complex organizations and technical processes.
Alternatively, it has been suggested that the motives of African entrepreneurs are different from those of their European counterparts
and that their behavior varies accordingly. As Callaway (1973, p. 37)
expresses it,

Many businessmen, particularly those at the lower economic levels, do not
perceive this conflict between using money for family expenses or as capital
for expanding their businesses because their priorities are family first and
business second. They might well, in fact, turn the idea around and say that
the low income from their business keeps their family from getting ahead
(particularly in education).[4]

In chapter 3 I argue that farmers' ideas about resource acquisition
and use have both influenced and been influenced by the social and
material conditions under which farmers work and accumulate. The
same argument may be put forward about agricultural firms and their
role in regional economic change. If the motives of Nigerian artisans
for accumulation appear different from those of Europeans, for example, we cannot assume that the differences in attitude are independent
of differences in circumstance. African artisans' strategies of labor
management, marketing, investment, and so on are shaped by the
conditions under which they gain access to productive resources or
to customers or markets. For example, Page's (1979) conclusion that
small-scale African entrepreneurs, because they depend primarily on
personal contact in selling their output, have no real marketing strategy simply misconstrues their situation. In western Nigeria, anyway,
it is often necessary for an artisan or trader to spend a good deal of
time and money greeting, visiting, and entertaining potential customers in order to secure their business. Such outlays are, accordingly,
part of the firm's marketing strategy and not evidence of conspicuous
consumption, inattention to marketing problems, or a confusion of
personal and business expenses. Similarly, outlays on children's school
fees may be seen either as evidence that Yorùbás put family ahead of
firm or as part of a strategy of long-run accumulation.

In general, it is unlikely that the difficulties often faced by Yorùbá and other African entrepreneurs in managing expanding firms can be attributed simply to cultural peculiarities or inadequate education. In the case study presented here, artisans' strategies for gaining access to markets and resources seem to come into conflict with their ability to manage the production process, especially as their firms prosper and expand. Thus the potential for small firms to contribute to aggregate growth through reinvestment of their own profits is determined, not only by their efficiency in using available resources, but also by the conditions under which they obtain them.

Motor Mechanics in Ile-Ifè

Like cocoa growing and schoolteaching, the motor vehicle repair industry is a product of the colonial economy in Nigeria, whose growth has been closely related to that of foreign trade and the state. Motor vehicles were introduced into Nigeria by the British and their use was expanded, pari passu, with the development of colonial administration and commerce. Road haulage competed successfully with the railway and with waterborne transport for both freight and passenger traffic in the colonial period (Hawkins, 1958). Some of the earliest opportunities for Nigerians to engage in successful business expansion lay in road transport, and the rapid growth of the industry generated demand for complementary services, such as motor repair, typically provided by small-scale self-employed artisans.

After 1950 the growth of the indigenous professional, bureaucratic, and business classes further stimulated demand for vehicles and for mechanics' services, and the trend was naturally accelerated by the inflow of oil revenues. By the mid-1970s the demand for motor vehicles was sufficient to warrant the construction of a domestic source of supply, and the first Volkswagen assembly plant was opened near Lagos. Since 1970, especially, the increasing volume of vehicular traffic, combined with the poor conditions of even major roads, has created a burgeoning demand for vehicle repair services. Such services require specialized skills, and men who wish to become mechanics usually have to spend several years in training. As the initial capital required to enter the market is fairly small, the number of motor mechanics has grown very rapidly indeed (see p. 143, below). The rate of growth has, in turn, limited the scope for individual accumulation by flooding the market with competitors and reducing surplus available for expansion. Nonetheless, mechanics' incomes were higher than those of cocoa farmers at the time of my survey. Among my informants, the median monthly income for mechanics was ₦200;

the mean, slightly over ₦300 (table 6–2). Although I have no comparable data on cocoa farmers' incomes in 1979, the difference may be
roughly estimated from other information. In 1971 the average-size
cocoa farm in Abúlékejì was estimated to yield one ton of cocoa annually (see chap. 3). At the official 1979 price one ton of cocoa was worth
₦1,070, or just under ₦90 a month. But as yields declined sharply
during the 1970s, the actual monthly income from such a farm in
Abúlékejì would have been considerably lower. Farmers' sons who
had become mechanics were thus earning significantly more, in 1979,
than their fathers, though in comparison with the ruling elite their
incomes were modest indeed (see Williams, 1981; Bienen and
Diejomaoh, 1981).

TABLE 6–2
MECHANICS INTERVIEWED

Year established	Number of partners	Number of journeymen	Number of apprentices	Gross monthly income
Ca. 1950	–	–	3	Low[a]
1955	–	5	4	₦200–500 (plus ₦3,000–8,000 from transport)
1962	–	–	3	₦100–800
1967	–	–	29	₦1,800–2,500[b]
1968	1	–	10	₦200–800[b]
1969	–	1	2	₦100–400
1969	1	2	15	Up to ₦2,000
1969	?	14	16	₦800–1,200
1970	(1)[c]	–	2	₦120–200
1972	(1)[c]	–	1	Up to ₦250
1972	1	1	2	Low[d]
1973	–	–	–	Up to ₦400
1974	1	–	Shared partner's	Up to ₦250
1974	1	–	–	₦50–150
1974	1	1	2	₦40–400
1976	–	–	2	₦150
1976	–	–	–	₦40[b]
1977	–	–	7	₦300 or more
1977	–	2	–	₦50–250[a]

NOTE: Data on employees and incomes are for 1979.
[a] Semiretired and partly supported by their children.
[b] Net income.
[c] Had split up with partner before my interview.
[d] Had recently taken a new partner and reorganized the shop.

Getting established.—The mechanics I interviewed in Ifẹ̀ were mostly married men in their thirties, although individual ages ranged from twenty-five to over sixty. None of the men were natives of Ifẹ̀. They had all come there to work as mechanics, and a third of them had served apprenticeships in Ifẹ̀ as well. In this regard the mechanics resemble the farmers in Abàkinní and Abúlékejì, who had also left their hometowns to seek out favorable opportunities for self-employment, rather than the teachers, many of whom had managed to get job assignments in or near their hometowns. Each of my informants specialized in some particular aspect of motor vehicle maintenance and repair: some worked only on motorcycle or truck engines rather than on automobiles; others specialized in panel beating, welding, or electrical work. In terms of assets and volume of business, they ranged from several motorcycle mechanics who owned less than ₦100 worth of tools, employed only one or two nonpaying apprentices, and earned perhaps ₦100 a month, to one mechanic and one panel beater, each of whom employed about thirty people (apprentices and paid workers), owned tools and buildings worth ₦5,000 or more, and earned about ₦2,000 a month net of business expenses (table 6–2).

Like most mechanics in western Nigeria (Àlùkò, 1972; Köll, 1969), all but one of my informants began their careers as apprentices. (The one exception had attended secondary school for three years and then entered the Trade Center at Òṣogbo where he completed the three-year course.) All but the eldest had attended primary school; sixteen had completed it and half of those had had some secondary schooling as well. Like the young factory workers whom Adrian Peace (1979) interviewed in Lagos, a number of my informants decided to become apprentices only because they were financially unable to continue in school. Akin (who happened to come from Ìreé) had, for example, been born in Ghana where his parents were traders. When he was five years old his mother decided to return to Nigeria and took him along because he was so young. He attended primary school in Ìreé for four years; then, as his father was still in Ghana, he went to live with an uncle. He moved again after two years to live with a cousin and completed primary school in Lagos at the age of fourteen. The cousin then went abroad, leaving Akin with her mother (his aunt). His own mother was ill at the time and unable to contribute to his school fees, and the aunt had three children of her own in secondary school and was unable or unwilling to help her nephew. So, although he passed the secondary school entrance exams, he was unable to attend; instead he worked as a houseboy and used his wages (of £5 a month) to attend modern school classes in the evening. After two years on this schedule he became discouraged and decided to become a mechanic. His story, while not necessarily representative of the entire group, is similar to the stories of several others.

Once it had been decided (often by a boy's parents or other kinsmen) that he should learn to be a mechanic, a master was found for him by his relatives. The master agreed to teach the boy his craft in exchange for a fee and, more important, the promise that the boy would remain with him for three to five years, working in effect as an unpaid laborer. The fees varied according to the status of the master, his relationship with the boy's sponsor (usually an elder agnatic kinsman), and whether or not the master undertook to feed the boy during the apprenticeship period. In general, the fees were not very large compared with, say, school fees: ₦25 to ₦50 for three to four years was typical for most of my informants' own training in the 1950s and 1960s, and even the most successful masters charged their own apprentices no more than ₦50 a year in 1979. Much more important from the master's point of view was the apprentice's labor. All but four of my informants had apprentices at the time of my interviews; the majority employed no other type of labor. Although apprentices were not very skilled or efficient, the fact that they did not have to be paid was crucial in a trade where receipts are likely to be irregular and working capital is therefore implicitly expensive. My informants often knew little about the terms of their own apprenticeships, which had invariably been arranged between the master and the apprentice's senior relatives, but the terms on which they themselves later engaged apprentices illustrate the importance of apprentice labor for reducing a master's financial risks. Several mechanics said, for example, that they required their apprentices' relatives to assume responsibility for any damage the apprentice might do to the master's tools or to customers' vehicles, and some said that they charged higher fees to apprentices who wanted to remain with them for only two years, instead of the customary three to five, because of the shorter period of service.

Apprentices are bound labor for the term of their training. They may be asked to run errands and perform household tasks (especially those who live with their masters); they are at their masters' beck and call at all times; they may be disciplined by flogging, though not all masters choose to inflict corporal punishment. Their status is expressed in rhetoric and ritual as well as in daily routine. When an apprentice completes his term of service he "becomes free." (Usually the English word is used, even in Yorùbá conversation: "ó tó *free*.") To mark the occasion, the freed apprentice and his relatives are expected to give a party for the families and friends of both master and apprentice. Often the amount spent on the freedom ceremony is two to four times the amount of the apprenticeship fee, marking the significant change in the young man's status implied by his freedom.

Once freed, a young mechanic must decide where and how to establish himself in his chosen trade. Location is an important issue. As noted above, all the mechanics I interviewed in Ifẹ̀ came from other hometowns; they had selected Ifẹ̀ as a promising place to pursue their trade. Ifẹ̀ had been an administrative (divisional) headquarters during the colonial period and, from the 1920s, was a fairly active center of cocoa marketing as well. The volume of cocoa produced in Ifẹ̀ Division rose dramatically in the late 1950s as the result of extensive new plantings after World War II by migrant farmers such as those in Abàkinní and Abúlékejì. The growth of the cocoa trade through Ifẹ̀ increased the flow of truck traffic—and hence the demand for the services of mechanics—but automobiles were not very numerous until the University of Ifẹ̀ opened in the late 1960s. The eldest of my informants, an illiterate son of Ìbàdàn who came to Ifẹ̀ soon after the end of World War II, bore witness to the late development of the motor vehicle business there. He had begun his career in Ìbàdàn repairing vehicles for the Nigerian police, served in the army during the war, and then migrated to Ifẹ̀. He decided against planting cocoa there "because the work was too hard"; instead, he joined the Public Works Department. In 1948 he quit, "because there was no chance for an uneducated man to advance" in that department, and became self-employed. "In those days there were only three mechanics in Ifẹ̀ and so few cars that one could sleep in the road until dawn in safety. We spent most of our time drinking five kọbọ palm wine."

Political largesse during the turbulent days of party politics enlarged the vehicle population of Ifẹ̀ to some extent, but it was the university that brought the largest influx of cars, motorcycles, "danfos," taxis, and buses to the town. Although "three" may be a metaphoric rather than a literal indication of the number of mechanics in Ifẹ̀ in the late 1940s, there is no doubt that the trade grew enormously in the late sixties and seventies. A census of small-scale industries in 1971 reported thirty-six firms engaged in motor vehicle repair in Ifẹ̀, with a total employment of 212, including proprietors, journeymen, and apprentices (Àlùkò et al., 1972). In 1979 the Ifẹ̀ Mechanics' Association, which does not admit apprentices, had more than 1,200 registered members.

About half of my informants had served apprenticeships in Ifẹ̀, and their reasons for doing so reflect the history of the market for mechanics' services there. Those who had come to apprentice in Ifẹ̀ before the late sixties had usually done so because they could live or train with relatives. Young men who served their apprenticeships in Ifẹ̀ during the seventies had been brought there by their relatives to take advantage of a growing market. "I came to Ifẹ̀ to learn mechanics' work because Ifẹ̀ is more civilized than Ìwó," one young man explained, and others' accounts were similar.[5] Several of the most successful of my informants had served apprenticeships in Ìbàdàn during the early sixties, then "followed the university to Ifẹ̀" to establish their own firms. Alfred, a highly successful panel beater, spent a few months with an expatriate firm in Lagos after completing his apprenticeship in Ìjẹ̀bu Waterside; he then joined a friend in Ìbàdàn, where he learned in a dream that he would "find prosperity in Ifẹ̀." He opened his first shop in Ifẹ̀ in October 1967, and, by 1979 he was employing thirty apprentices and estimated his net monthly income at somewhere between ₦1,800 and ₦2,500.

To make a living, even as an early entrant into an expanding market, a mechanic needs, in addition to adequate training, a place to work, tools, and customers. Like cocoa farmers, mechanics must have some means of support while they are getting established. Men who have left their hometowns to make a living elsewhere may not be able to live and eat with relatives until their firms are established. In short, a mechanic needs some initial capital before he can become self-employed. Since apprentices are not paid, they have little opportunity to acquire tools, build a shed or a shop, or save up working capital until after they are freed. Sometimes relatives are able and willing to supply part of a mechanic's initial capital, but more often a young man must finance his own tools and shed out of savings. To save enough to get established, most of my informants sought some form of paid employment after completing their apprenticeships. The majority worked as journeymen (often for their former masters and usually for a share of the master's proceeds), but a few took jobs with expatriate firms or government agencies. One mechanic had spent six months as an agricultural laborer, earning enough to purchase a minimum stock of tools.

On the whole, the type of enterprise in which a mechanic was employed before establishing his own business bore no apparent relationship to the subsequent growth or profitability of his own firm. Of the six most successful men in my sample, only two had worked in the "formal" sector before setting up on their own. The others had served as journeymen for self-employed mechanics. Likewise, the man who bought his initial stock of tools with money earned as a farm laborer had done quite well as a mechanic and purveyor of windshields until the autumn of 1978. Then a loaded truck belonging to the recently opened Trophy Brewery of Ilésà ran off the road and toppled onto his shop, smashing over N8,000 worth of tools, structures, and spare parts, including his entire stock of windshields.

Although my sample is much too small to be representative of the mechanics' trade as a whole in Ifè, let alone all western Nigeria, the occupational histories of my informants shed some light on the question of how access to initial capital influences subsequent performance of the firm. In his study of migrant factory workers in Ìkẹjà, Peace (1979) shows that while most of his informants aspired to eventual self-employment, they found it extremely difficult to save enough money to establish viable firms. He attributes the difficulty to a combination of factors: low wages, intense competition from established trade and service enterprises in the urban market of Agége, and the fact that migrants' friends, kinsmen, and hometowns tend to place increasing demands on their resources the longer they remain in wage employment. Journeymen in Ifè were probably not much better paid than factory workers near Lagos,[6] yet most of my informants had worked as journeymen for less than two years and had then gone on to build ultimately viable and, in some instances, quite successful businesses. Moreover, they often began with amounts of initial capital as low as N40 or N50, substantially less than the sums of N200 to N400 which Peace's informants considered necessary to establish similar kinds of enterprises in Agége about 1970.[7]

We might expect initial capital requirements to be lower in Ifè than in, say, Lagos or Ìbàdàn, because the cost of living is lower there, though the difference is not likely to be substantial. In my opinion, aspiring mechanics in Ifè derived a further advantage from their previous employment as apprentices and journeymen rather than as factory employees. To establish a viable enterprise, a mechanic (or any other artisan) needs customers as well as equipment. In the highly competitive environment of the urban informal sector, the average mechanic is not likely to attract enough customers to make a living simply by hanging out a signboard. He also needs to build up a clientele of loyal customers who can be counted on to do business with him, time and again, rather than with his competitors. As one of my informants put it, a "regular customer is someone who sends for me when his car breaks down in Ìbàdàn," rather than getting it repaired by one of the hundreds of mechanics in Ìbàdàn.

Working as a journeyman may not pay very well, but, as a number of my informants pointed out, it affords the young mechanic an opportunity to begin to accumulate customers who will one day follow him when he sets up on his own. With such a clientele, a young man can establish his own business with less initial capital than would be required if he had to maintain himself for several months while trying to develop business. Factory workers, who have little opportunity to form contacts with potential customers, require a larger stock of initial working capital to tide them over the establishment period. Initial employment in the informal sector may therefore serve as a partial substitute for savings in the establishment of one's own firm.

This observation points, in turn, to some similarities between the establishment of small nonagricultural enterprises in Ile-Ifẹ and neighboring towns and the development of cocoa farming. Like most cocoa farmers and many Yorùbá traders, mechanics often left home at an early age for areas where market conditions were more conducive to successful pursuit of their trade (see Eades, 1980; Peel, 1980; Berry, 1975a; Sudarkasa, 1979). Even away from the hometown, however, home-based relationships continue to play a crucial role in the process of becoming self-employed. Kinsmen and hometown neighbors provided the contacts that enabled young men without means to exchange their labor for access to uncultivated land or for acquisition of commercial or mechanical skills. Similarly, relatives and friends from home often provided food, shelter, patronage, or financial assistance during a young man's initial period of training and capital formation. Both in and out of the agricultural sector, young men provided labor—on an elder's farm or in the master's firm—in exchange for the means to establish themselves as independent producer-entrepreneurs. Farmers and traders were more likely to work at first for a senior kinsman than were apprentice mechanics, but the difference was one of degree rather than of kind: some cocoa farmers worked for nonkin while getting established and some mechanics served apprenticeships with relatives. In addition, such relationships played an integral part in the process of initial capital formation, for services and contacts provided by relatives or fellow townsmen often reduced the amount of working capital a young man needed to raise through wage employment. Insofar as the process of getting established influences a producer's subsequent use of income, we might expect mechanics, like cocoa farmers, to maintain economic and social ties with their home compounds and communities even though they live and work somewhere else.

Getting ahead.—Over a lifetime, however, a person's use of resources is influenced by more than just those relationships he relied upon in launching his career. Other ties, with individuals or institutions, may come to be important in the operation and expansion of the original enterprise, and of course opportunities for diversifying or even changing one's economic activities and assets are likely to alter over time. The fact that Yorùbá farmers, traders, and artisans often used similar methods of getting established does not necessarily imply that they also employed similar strategies for getting ahead.

Although the market for their services has grown rapidly in recent years, the individual mechanic faces a number of difficulties in developing a viable enterprise. Because barriers to entry are relatively low, the market is highly competitive. Customers are hard to find and to keep; demand, even from regular customers, is unpredictable in the short run; and it is difficult to enforce unwritten contracts with customers, employees, and suppliers of spare parts. Accordingly, mechanics must rely heavily on personal relationships to increase revenue and reduce some of the risks, or the costs of risk bearing, associated with doing business in a competitive and informal market. Cultivation of personal loyalties—with customers, suppliers, employer, partners, and colleagues—is one of the principal strategies mechanics employ to expand their own firms and to try to regulate the market for their services.

One of the most important conditions of business success is, as we have seen, the accumulation of loyal customers. Building a clientele depends not only on a mechanic's reputation for skill, honesty, fairness, and dispatch, but also on whether or not people like to do business with him. The success of an enterprise can thus be augmented through the adroit use of culturally sanctioned modes of interpersonal behavior. As one customer, commenting on the popularity of the mechanic mentioned above, put it, "He doesn't know everything there is to know about Volkswagens, but he is a very respectful young man." This particular mechanic spent a good deal of time visiting regular and prospective customers, and he avoided any course of action which might lead to ill feelings. When I asked him if he had ever had recourse to a debt collection agency to recover money owed him by a customer, he replied in the negative: "I do not want to fight anyone about money. After all, who knows when we may meet again or whether I might someday need his help?" Others, though not so reluctant to press their interests, also spent a good deal of time and money in cultivating customer loyalties.

Regular customers often find it to their own as well as their mechanic's advantage to remain loyal. A vehicle owner in a moderate-size town such as Ifẹ̀ (estimated population was 130,000 in 1963) has literally hundreds of mechanics, welders, battery chargers, vulcanizers, panel beaters, electricians, and other specialized servicemen to choose from. Far from being a paradise of consumer sovereignty, however, such a market presents the vehicle owner with a formidable problem of information, for there is no institutional mechanism for guaranteeing or standardizing quality of service. Without prior information the customer does not know until afterward whether any particular mechanic can be counted on to do a good job. To obtain such information in advance, most vehicle owners rely on the advice of fellow consumers. Accordingly, the more loyal customers a mechanic has, the more people are likely to recommend him to their friends and the larger his volume of business is likely to be. Developing a sizable clientele is especially important because individual customers' needs for repair services are inevitably irregular. In order to foster the loyalty on which their revenues depend, therefore, mechanics tend to offer more or better services to their regular customers. As one informant put it, "If someone is a regular customer, I have to repair his vehicle, even if he owes me money."

Mechanics also find it advantageous to cultivate special relationships with suppliers of spare parts. Such suppliers rarely extend credit— most mechanics avoid the expense of stocking parts by buying them only as needed with money supplied by the customer—but since most parts are imported, supplies are not always regular and prices are subject to sudden change. The mechanic who knows his suppliers may be able to get parts more quickly, and at a better discount on black-market prices, than one who does not. He is therefore able to offer better service to his customers.

In addition to cultivating good personal relationships with individual customers and suppliers, mechanics sometimes cooperate with one another to reduce risks or increase returns. As I point out earlier, most mechanics specialize in one aspect of motor vehicle maintenance and repair—engines, electrical systems, body work, tires—so that a customer with more than one type of work to be done may have to go to several different shops. One strategy a number of my informants used to attract customers was to form partnerships with men whose specialties were different from their own. Among my informants, seven were maintaining partnerships at the time of my interviews and two others had had partners in the past.

Most of the partnerships about which I obtained information consisted of a mechanic and a panel beater, though one mechanic had invited an electrician to join him in his shop. One young panel beater rented space in a large shop built by one of the most successful mechanics in my sample (who had several other partners as well) and derived a good part of his business from customers of his senior partners. He also helped to pay the taxes that were levied on the shop as a single firm. In other instances the junior partner paid no rent but simply shared the workshop with the owner, who felt that he derived sufficient benefit from being able to provide his customers with more than one type of service on the premises. In all partnerships each partner owned his own tools; in most, each employed his own apprentices and journeymen. Jobs were contracted for independently, and the partners' financial transactions were kept separate, although one partner might accept money on the other's behalf if their relationship was an especially good one. (An apprentice rarely accepts payment on the master's behalf; to do so would render him liable to accusations of theft.) I found only one example of partners who pooled receipts, and that partnership had broken up acrimoniously (see Köll, 1969).

Customer loyalty is not, of course, unwavering. In a relatively open market, price competition is inevitable; in addition there is the problem of managing credit relations. Most mechanics do not stock spare parts but buy them as needed with money furnished by the customer, thus minimizing their own need for working capital. However, willingness to supply parts and services on credit can help to attract customers. The mechanic faces a continual choice between short-term and long-term gains: Should he risk immediate loss by cutting prices or accepting delayed payment in order to expand volume now and in the future? Like capitalists in other economies, mechanics in Ifẹ have relied on combination, as well as individual initiative, in an effort to reduce risks and increase returns. In addition to partnerships of two or more mechanics, the Ifẹ Mechanics' Association (IMA) seeks to regulate the market and represent all mechanics' interests in local affairs.

According to its present officers, the IMA was organized in the mid-fifties to regulate the trade and maintain the quality of motor vehicle services in the town. In principle, the association will apply sanctions against mechanics whose workmanship or honesty is below standard or who overcharge for their services. Price lists for various repair jobs are distributed by the Association to its members, and customers may, if they wish, bring complaints to the association, whose officers and executive members undertake to investigate and carry out sanctions if needed. One sanction is to withdraw the association's protection from the delinquent mechanic. In an actual case in which a mechanic had offended the association's leaders (not, in this instance, through abrogation of professional standards, but through failure to demonstrate sufficient loyalty to the organization), the leaders simply told the local police that "if this man gets into trouble, we will not help him."

In practice, it is nearly impossible for the IMA to fix prices. Also, I never heard of an actual case in which it dealt with customers' complaints about the quality of workmanship. The association does, however, play an important role in helping individual mechanics cope with some of their business risks. As the example just cited suggests, the association acts as a patron for members who may get into difficulties with local authorities; this service is especially valuable to mechanics who are not members of Ifẹ̀ descent groups (see Peace, 1979). In addition, the IMA helps members recover bad debts and stolen goods by blacklisting delinquent customers and helping to trace thieves.

To perform such services effectively, the association must be able to count on the loyal cooperation of its members in giving information about stolen property or refusing to serve customers who owe money to fellow mechanics. In fact, much of the routine activity of the IMA and its officers is directed toward fostering or reaffirming members' loyalty to the organization. This was the dominant theme, for example, in the association's policies and procedures concerning initiation of new members and attendance at fortnightly meetings. In addition, most of the time at these meetings was taken up by discussion and settlement of cases in which particular members' loyalty to the association was in doubt. The following examples, from my own observations, illustrate the importance of loyalty to the association and the mechanisms used to ascertain and reinforce it.

Any apprentice who trains in Ifẹ̀ automatically becomes a member of the association on attaining his freedom. Outsiders who come to Ifẹ̀ to practice their trade are strongly encouraged to join the IMA, although they may be asked to pay an initiation fee because, as the secretary put it, "we don't know their training." Admission to membership nonetheless involves a certain amount of ritual, in which the newly freed apprentice is introduced to the association by a sponsor who is already a member. The sponsor vouches for the applicant's training and good character and, if the applicant has trained in another town, may plead with the executive to waive or reduce the initiation fee. (Young men who apprentice in Ifẹ̀ are likely to be sponsored by their former masters, for whom they may continue to work as journeymen until they are ready to establish their own businesses.) In the initiation ceremonies I observed, each applicant prostrated himself before the officers of the association while his sponsor negotiated on his behalf; he then swore, on either the Bible or the Koran, to obey the association's rules and accept the authority of its leaders. He then received his identity card and a copy of the printed price list. The ritual of sponsorship serves primarily to establish the young mechanic as a client of the association's elders (through his dependence on his sponsor), a relationship in which a patron's protection is contingent upon the client's loyalty and deference. The actual ceremonies were accompanied by a good deal of joking about the ritual, with senior members of the association shouting for the applicant to prostrate himself further and for the sponsor to plead more eloquently, and so on. The elders' attitude toward the new recruits was humorously but firmly paternalistic.

Once accepted as a member, a mechanic is expected to demonstrate his loyalty to the association by observing its fortnightly meetings, which are held on alternate Friday mornings from nine o'clock to noon. Observance of the meeting is not the same as attendance. Although in June 1979 the IMA alone had 1,256 registered members (panel beaters, electricians, welders, etc., each have their own "meetings"), there were never more than about 200 persons present at any of the meetings I attended, and often the number was smaller. Except for the officers and an executive composed of eight or ten senior members of the organization, members did not usually attend meetings unless they had business to bring before the association. Members who attended a meeting were asked to pay dues, and those who had missed one or more meetings in the past were fined, but the amounts demanded were trivial—"ten ten kọbọ"—and clearly played no part in a mechanic's decision as to whether or not to attend. Members were, however, expected to demonstrate their solidarity with their colleagues and respect for the association by abstaining from work while a meeting was in session. As the rule did not apply to apprentices, most mechanics' shops remained open during meeting hours, but with the master away from the shop little work actually got done. In principle, at least, mechanics thus sacrifice a morning's potential earnings every fortnight as a gesture of solidarity with the IMA. In practice, of course, there is nothing to prevent anyone from working overtime at other hours in order to make up the income forgone on alternate Friday mornings, so that the sacrifice is more symbolic than real. The gesture is taken seriously by the association, however. If a mechanic is found working during meeting hours the IMA impounds his tools, and he may be forced to pay a substantial fine (on the order of ₦10) as well as tender a public apology to the association's leaders in order to get his tools back.

The symbolic nature of members' normal participation in meetings of the IMA corresponds to the nature of the benefits that follow upon active membership. In effect, the IMA acts as a kind of insurance agency, whose transactions are carried out in kind rather than in cash. Members contribute to the assets of the organization through periodic demonstrations of loyalty (abstention from work during meetings) in exchange for the right to claim assistance in recovering bad debts or stolen goods. This assistance, in turn, consists not of a cash payment, but of the association's use of its power to bring collective pressure to bear on debtors or on local authorities.

As these examples suggest, the personal relationships and loyalties through which mechanics seek to increase their returns and reduce the risks of doing business are not the same as those they used in getting established. Mechanics do not, as a rule, do business with their relatives: neither the Ifẹ̀ Mechanics' Association nor individual partnerships are organized on kinship or community lines. Thus the growth of the informal sector in western Nigeria would seem to have created new forms of social relationships and institutions which do not necessarily coincide with or draw upon preexisting ones. To the extent that these new relations have facilitated capital accumulation, by allowing individual mechanics to expand their revenues and regulate certain features of the market in which they do business, we would expect them to influence mechanics' uses of income and patterns of collective action.

There are, however, limits to the degree to which mechanics have succeeded in controlling either the conditions of their market or the performance of their firms. The IMA may be able to help its members recover bad debts or stolen goods, but it does not control either prices or the quality of workmanship in a market as large as that of Ifẹ̀. Moreover, most of the mechanics I observed—like many of the small firms described in the literature—had not succeeded in developing very effective methods of managing their workers or their finances, other than that of constant personal supervision.

As noted earlier, none of my informants employed hired labor in the sense of workers paid on a time or piecework basis. The majority of their employees were apprentices; the rest were journeymen who received a share of the firm's proceeds. Employment of both apprentices and journeymen is financially advantageous to the artisan because apprentices are not paid at all and journeymen usually receive a share of the firm's profits. Neither creates a fixed claim against the fluctuating and unpredictable cash receipts of the firm. By relieving the mechanic of the expense of maintaining a cash reserve,[8] such labor contracts effectively increase the internal rate of return on the firm's assets, but they also provide relatively weak incentives to employees, especially apprentices, to maximize their productivity.

Other examples of managerial inefficiency abound. Most mechanics did not trust their apprentices or their journeymen to handle money; hence they received payment for services rendered only when they were actually in their shops. Few kept any form of written records—at most a journal of daily receipts—or felt that records were useful for any purpose other than that of obtaining credit from institutional sources. One man said that he had kept records for a couple of years but quit when his application for a bank loan was turned down in spite of his bookkeeping efforts. Another informant's description of his (mental) accounting system is especially revealing. When I asked what he earned from his business, net of expenses, he replied that out of average gross weekly receipts of about ₦50 he spent ₦35 on maintaining his family, which left ₦15 "for myself. I use this money for rent, tools and entertainment."[9] For this man, as for many others, capital accumulatin was clearly a central personal goal, but cost accounting has not perceived as a means to further that end.

Similarly, labor productivity depended heavily on the master's physical presence in the shop. Methods of production in most of the firms I observed were highly labor-intensive. One mechanic who specialized in Volkswagens had one hand-operated hydraulic jack in his shop, which was used principally for larger models. If a beetle needed to be raised while the jack was in use, four apprentices were mobilized to lift up one end while a fifth pushed a discarded engine block under the axle. The time that it took to organize such an operation was noticeably longer when the master was not in the shop, for one or more of the five apprentices were likely to be building a fire, washing clothes, transacting business with a passing food vendor, joking or wrestling with a fellow apprentice, or simply waiting for someone in a suitably senior position to organize the whole undertaking. (Most apprentices in my sample of shops were teenagers, and some were as young as eleven or twelve.) If a vehicle is brought to a shop when the master is not there, it must usually await his return before work can be started at all, even if the apprentices are not then occupied on other work. Time spent idle in this way often reveals, not the laziness or recalcitrance of the apprentices, but the master's inability to delegate authority. To avoid damage to customers' vehicles apprentices are told never to work on them without specific instructions; accordingly they wait until someone is there to tell them what to do. In firms that employ journeymen, apprentices may waste less time, but financial control is likely to be less effective, if not a cause of outright dispute between journeyman and master.

The weaknesses of artisans' managerial performance are not, I think, simply a matter of inexperience (Harris, 1971) or of culture (Kilby, 1969), though both contribute to the ineffectiveness of management. The failing is also a direct consequence of the strategies used by small-scale entrepreneurs to increase their clientele and to reduce risk-bearing costs. Building loyalties with customers, suppliers, and fellow mechanics frequently requires the mechanic to spend time away from his shop, either to make ceremonial visits or, more often, to negotiate and carry out transactions in person. The necessity for a mechanic to be away so frequently reveals the inadequacy of communications facilities in Nigeria as well as the high value placed on personal contact and interchange in Yorùbá culture (see Aronson, 1978; Eades, 1980). Similarly, diversification of an enterprise into complementary undertakings, such as dealing in spare parts or transport, may help to reduce costs or increase returns to the entrepreneur's technical skills,[10] but it may also reduce the amount of time he spends supervising labor in the initial enterprise.

Several students of indigenous forms of enterprise have suggested that relations of production and exchange in Africa are frequently based, literally or in principle, on relations of descent. Studies of commercial enterprises in West Africa, for example, have emphasized the importance of kinship or common origins in facilitating communication and the use of credit in long-distance trade (Baier, 1980; Cohen, 1969; Curtin, 1975; Eades, 1980; Leighton, 1979; Lovejoy, 1980). This view has been echoed in the literature on small manufacturing and service enterprises. In particular, it is frequently argued that the extended family serves as both a source of capital and an incentive to accumulation, rather than as an obstacle to profitable production (Nafziger, 1977; Callaway, 1973). In one study of a large sample of craftsmen in Ìbàdàn, Michael Köll (1969) spelled out the organizational similarities between family and firm. He found (p. 57), for example, that small groups of craftsmen often

associate ad hoc or permanently to share certain things or to do certain things together, without abandoning their economic independence. . . . Since recruitment into a craft is no longer through kinship, such partnerships are apparently of a contractual nature; but in fact they have more in common with kinship relations than with typical contractual relations since prospective partners take years to judge each other's moral behavior and technical skills; once established, the partnerships rest on mutual trust and understanding rather than on formalities.

The evidence presented here suggests a somewhat more complex historical relationship between kinship and business organization. Although nearly all my informants had been assisted by their relatives in getting their training, and several had also received help in purchasing tools or constructing a shed, none of them had chosen relatives as partners or paid employees, and most of them avoided taking relatives as apprentices. Several informants did say that they had been under some pressure to accept junior kinsmen as apprentices in return for their elders' assistance in arranging their own training. Most felt, however, that once they had trained two or three junior brothers or cousins they had discharged their obligations to the family. The reluctance of mechanics to use kinship ties in managing their firms reveals the contradictory nature of kinship and relations of seniority. As

Aronson (1978) points out, "any senior has a right to unquestioned service, deference, and submissiveness from any junior" (p. 94)—but not necessarily to efficiency. A senior may discipline a junior relative for disobedience or even laziness, but not for low productivity. Indeed, enterprise or innovativeness may be interpreted as a sign of insubordination, and neither is encouraged among junior people. Such norms are not, of course, confined to descent groups; they govern relations between superiors and subordinates throughout Yorùbá society and thus, to some extent, limit the authority of a master over his apprentices, whether or not they are related to him. His obligations to junior kinsmen are, however, more compelling than those to subordinates who are not members of his descent group. In taking relatives as apprentices, he therefore gains little in the way of effective control over their productivity, and he may have to spend more in providing for them than he does for nonkin. Similarly, there is little to be gained by taking kinsmen as partners; if a cousin absconds with money or tools from the firm, the family is likely to put pressure on the proprietor not to prosecute him, which they would not do if the culprit was not a relative.

In short, although my observations seem to bear out the view that Yorùbá artisans are not always effective managers, they do not support either Kilby's (1969) suggestion that their early socialization creates emotional inhibitions against mastering technical and organizational skills, or Callaway's (1973) argument that family takes precedence over firm in Yorùbá artisans' decisions about how to use resources. Such decisions were shaped by the economic, social, and cultural conditions under which they were made, rather than by the innate characteristics of the men who made them. Moreover, the resulting patterns of resource allocation often affected the conditions of production and accumulation in contradictory ways. In Ifè, at least, the strategies mechanics have devised to solve their problems of marketing and risk aversion often aggravate those of labor control, to which kinship and culture provide no ready-made solutions.

Uses of Income

From the preceding discussion it is clear that inefficient management is not a symptom of Yorùbá artisans' indifference to profit. The mechanics described here are not target accumulators, whose capitalist propensities are blunted by cultural norms or social obligations. On the contrary, for most of my informants, business expansion was a central personal goal, a point illustrated by the mechanic who described his income net of family expenses as income "for myself," to be reinvested in his firm. Their prospects for accumulation are limited, however, by the structure of the market and by their own strategies for improving the terms on which they participate in it. The questions, then, are how far they manage to transcend those limits through economic, social, or political transactions outside the market in which they earn their living, and how their success in this regard compares with that of farmers and teachers.

Although much of the aggregate demand for motor repair services originates from government expenditures, mechanics' economic dependence on the state is mediated through the market; unlike schoolteachers or even cocoa farmers before the oil era, therefore, they cannot bargain directly with the state over the terms of their participation in Nigerian economic expansion. Also, in contrast with the situation of teachers, their individual prospects for prosperity and social mobility are not directly tied to their educational qualifications. Their limited schooling tends to restrict their chances of upward mobility, but their incomes are sometimes higher than those of many schoolteachers, whose salaries are fixed according to level of schooling. Among my informants, the poorest farmers and mechanics earned less than the lowest-paid teachers, but successful mechanics reported earnings as high as ₦2,000 per month. If this figure is average, these men earned six times as much in a year as the highest-paid teachers. Although I have no reliable estimates of farmers' annual incomes, the only man from Abúlékejì whose reported assets were comparable to those of the most successful mechanics was the man who had left the village to trade in Òṣogbo and had made a small fortune dealing in cement. In other words, though mechanics as a group exert little or no political power vis-à-vis the state, in economic terms they probably benefit more from ruling-class expenditures than either farmers or schoolteachers.

Mechanics' uses of incomes reflect—and influence—their relations with both agnatic and affinal kin. As they usually prefer not to employ relatives, marriage does not augment their productive resources directly, although wives' earnings may help to cover household expenses, but it does entail extra financial responsibilities. As we have seen, most mechanics postponed marriage until they were established as independent artisans earning enough to maintain a wife (or wives) and children. Only two of my informants married before they were financially independent; at the other extreme, one man waited ten years after finishing his apprenticeship, thereby accumulating enough capital and customers to open a large shop in a choice location and to marry at the same time. Unlike the factory workers whom Peace (1979) interviewed in Lagos, mechanics do not seem to have been pressured by their families to marry before they were self-employed. Clearly, they were not capable of supporting dependents until they were established, whereas factory workers were perceived by their kinsmen as receiving a steady income and therefore capable of supporting wives and children, regardless of their aspirations toward self-employment. In this respect, the position of schoolteachers vis-à-vis their relatives is similar to that of factory workers.

Once established, my informants tended to accumulate dependents rapidly. All were married and a third of them had more than one wife, compared with 45 percent of the farmers and 5 percent of the male teachers I interviewed. Eighteen men had a total of 27 wives and 85 children, or 3.2 living children per wife.[11] Like both farmers and teachers, mechanics also contributed to the maintenance and education of other people. If we omit the two oldest men, whose answers on this score were vague, the mechanics maintained an average of 9.5 people each, including parents, other agnates, and apprentices, as well as their wives and children. This economic dependency ratio is higher than those for either the married male teachers (8.3) or the farmers and village traders (7.2) whom I interviewed. Mechanics were also more likely than either farmers or teachers to have given trading capital to their wives.

On the other hand, mechanics' contributions to the educational expenses of their children or junior siblings were somewhat lower than those of both teachers and farmers. The mechanics I interviewed had helped to educate 2.7 persons, on the average, at the secondary level or above, compared with averages of 3.0 for farmers and 3.4 for teachers. To some extent this difference is a matter of age and family structure. Mechanics had married somewhat later than men in the other occupations, and it remains to be seen how high their expenditures on education will rise as their own children reach secondary school age. However, when we consider the educational outlays of younger schoolteachers, many of whom were single, it appears that there may well be a significant relationship between occupation and individuals' investment in education. As far as wives are concerned, mechanics are clearly in a position similar to that of schoolteachers. They cannot employ their wives directly and hence stand to gain more by assisting them to become gainfully self-employed than do farmers or even traders. As a rule, however, they did not marry women whose educational qualifications were sufficient for clerical or teaching jobs. Virtually all their wives were traders, whereas only 52 percent of teachers' wives were in that occupation. Accordingly, mechanics were even more likely than teachers to contribute to their wives' trading capital.

One notable difference between the expenditures of mechanics and those of my other informants was the extent to which the former invested in the expansion of their firms or diversification of their productive activities into complementary forms of enterprise. Both teachers and farmers did, of course, invest in their respective sectors of the economy to some extent. A number of my rural informants had used the proceeds of their initial cocoa farms to acquire additional farms or to enter rural trade. That many of them were not doing so in 1979 was primarily a reflection of declining incomes in the cocoa-growing sector. Also, though most married schoolteachers were no longer allocating income to their own further education, they were spending considerable sums on school fees for their children or junior siblings. The fact remains, however, that at the time of my study, mechanics were most likely to be investing in their own income-earning capacity.

Most mechanics began by building up their motor repair businesses and then diversified into related trades. All my informants had financed the construction of their workshops and the purchase of tools almost entirely out of their own savings. Over half of them had built more than one workshop since becoming self-employed; as their businesses prospered, they had moved to more favorable sites, usually from a location inside the town to one near the outskirts on the main road. Such sites are more convenient both to customers from the university, which is outside the town, and to vehicles engaged in inter-city passenger and freight transport. One especially successful man had also opened branch workshops in Ìbàdàn, Iléṣà, and Òṣogbo. In addition, two-thirds of my informants had invested in at least one other enterprise. Most second enterprises were functionally related to the first, involving trade in motor vehicles or vehicle parts. Nine of the mechanics I interviewed were dealing in spare parts; six bought, reconditioned, and resold used vehicles; and four had tried purchasing vehicles to be used for transport. Thus, while diversification certainly placed additional burdens on an individual mechanic's managerial capabilities, it also enabled him to capitalize on technical expertise and contacts developed through his repair business.

Transport was by far the riskiest of the secondary enterprises under-taken by my informants. Three of them had purchased taxis and hired drivers to operate them. It was physically very difficult to super-vise drivers effectively; when asked how they prevented drivers from cheating them out of a major proportion of the taxi fares, my infor-mants admitted that it was virtually impossible. In fact, the three men who had tried investing in taxi ownership had given it up as a losing business. The one man who had made a success out of transport was a specialist in truck repair who had gone into the timber-hauling business. At the time of my interview he owned only one truck, though he had had three or four in the past. He had purchased it secondhand for N2,500, reconditioned the motor, and used it to haul logs from timber-cutting camps in the forests south and east of Ifẹ̀ into town, where he sold them to sawmills. He estimated his net earnings at between N75 and N100 per load; his truck handled anywhere from eight to twenty-four loads a month, depending on weather and market conditions. One truck alone earned him from N600 to N2,400 a month, considerably more than he was making from his motor repair business in 1979.

A few of the mechanics I interviewed had used some of their earnings to invest in real estate. The truck owner had built a substantial house in Ifẹ̀, where he lived with his sizable family (two wives; fourteen children, ten of whom were living at home in 1979; a junior sister and her six children; and one of his deceased father's wives). Five other men had built (or were building) houses in their hometowns for the use of relatives, friends, and their own eventual retirement. In addition, two of these men and two others had acquired building sites in Ifẹ̀, and two of them had already built houses on their lots. An older man had invested N23,000 in a house where he accommodated his family and also rented out rooms to tenants; another had built a block of four flats (at an estimated cost of N78,000 to N80,000) to rent out. At the time of my interview he and his family were living in the servants' quarters behind the flats and he was seeking tenants for the flats.

The other two planned to build on their plots but had not yet started to do so. Investing in real estate was not without risks. One man had arranged to purchase two plots of land in Ifẹ̀ in 1972 and 1973 for N200 and N350, respectively. In order to complete his acquisition of the first plot he had had to spend N700 more than the price originally agreed upon in a dash (gift) to the owner and on clearing the site to establish his claim. The Ifẹ̀ Local Government Authority subsequently expropriated him, in return for the promise of an alternative plot as compensation; so far, no plot had been forthcoming. He still held title to the second plot in 1979, although it too had cost him N650 more than the original price in bribes, clearing costs, and the like. Furthermore, he would have to start building soon in order to demonstrate effective use of the site to forestall government expropriation under the Land Use Decree of 1978.

In seeking to take advantage of the rapidly growing demand for housing and motor vehicles, mechanics' investments in expanding and diversifying their businesses and in real estate reflect and reinforce

the prevailing trend toward tertiary rather than industrial expansion
in the Nigerian economy, just as cocoa farmers' investments in more
farms or in rural trade reinforced rather than transformed the structure of the rural economy. My argument in chapter 5, however,
suggests that the payoff in terms of potential socioeconomic mobility
may be higher for investment in education in contemporary Nigeria
than it is for investment in small-scale service enterprise, even if the
latter is more profitable in the short run. To the extent that mechanics
invest relatively more in small enterprise than in education, therefore,
they may be limiting their children's prospects for upward mobility.

Whether or not mechanics' uses of income may be interpreted in
this way is not yet clear. Most of my informants are relatively young,
married somewhat later than men in the other occupations I studied,
and do not yet have many children old enough to attend secondary
school. Thus it is entirely possible that their investment in business
now will increase the income available to them later on, enabling them
to provide secondary or higher education for their children, and that
their children will then have as good a prospect of upward mobility
as the children of teachers, clerks, and other *akòwé* of modest incomes.
If, on the other hand, they continue to act on the belief expressed by
the eldest of my informants—that his children who had gone into
trade "are more prosperous now than educated people"—they may
contribute to the emerging division of Yorùbá society into educational
haves and have-nots. The implications for the future class structure
or the form of political conflict in western Nigeria depend not only
on how artisans' patterns of resource use change over the lifetimes
of individual entrepreneurs and in the course of Nigerian economic
and social change in general, but also on their political responses to
their socioeconomic circumstances.

Forms of Collective Action

It has become commonplace in the literature on contemporary Nigeria
to point out that economic inequality has increased since independence
and that opportunities for upward socioeconomic mobility are gradu-
ally being restricted to certain groups or classes. Radical scholars in
particular, after studying instances of class-based protest against
foreign capital or the state, have predicted that these circumstances
will give rise to militant class action among the masses (Williams, 1976;
Beer, 1976; Cohen and Sandbrook, 1975; Peace, 1979). From studies
of industrial strikes in major cities or of farmers' uprisings such as
the Àgbékòyà movement of the late 1960s, some authors have concluded that the growth of neocolonial state capitalism in Nigeria is

creating a climate for a revolutionary alliance among workers, peasants, and the urban self-employed, and that sooner or later such an alliance will pose a serious threat to the existing order.

Very few signs of such a movement were apparent in the activities of the people I studied for this book. Discontent with the extravagant and, to many, undeserved levels of wealth and consumption of the ruling class was widespread (see Barber, 1982), but popular expressions of the discontent had not coalesced into an organized struggle against the existing economic and political order. Certainly farmers and nonagricultural workers have engaged in occupational-based forms of collective action—strikes, work slowdowns, demonstrations, and violent protest—and have often achieved higher incomes or a measure of local autonomy in consequence. Yet the fact that different occupational groups have sometimes combined to exert pressure on those who employ or tax them does not imply that together they constitute an ongoing revolutionary movement. The multiplicity of strategies with which people typically pursue economic and political interests produces a certain fragmentation of collective effort, even within the confines of a single industry.

For example, farmers have combined on several occasions to improve their terms of trade or protest excessive exactions by the state. In recent years, however, farmers' organizations have become increasingly fragmented,[12] on the local as well as the regional level, while the structure of power within rural communities has been influenced by the process of class formation and the changing basis of political power in the larger society. In particular, the growing importance of education as a condition for access to and influence with the state has increased the power of educated people within their own descent groups and in their hometowns at the expense of their uneducated elders. Farmers are well aware of the disadvantages springing from their lack of education, but they seek to counter them by sending children to school rather than by challenging the power and privileges of educated people.

Similarly, artisans use occupational and community relationships to cope with the risks of doing business and the problems of getting ahead. Such uses are not confined to commercial issues, such as debt collection or credit mobilization; the Ifè Mechanics' Association, for example, acts to resolve disputes among its members and tries to regulate their participation in local political affairs. Mechanics also support community-based efforts to lobby the state for resources and opportunities and, as I show in more detail below, communal interests and strategies sometimes enter into the handling of occupationally related issues as well. In both modes of action, mechanics' influence is limited by the structure of their trade and the level of their assets, including formal education. Nonetheless, their efforts reinforce attitudes and relationships that keep sectional divisions alive.

In handling disputes or signs of potential disaffection among IMA members, the leaders of the association draw heavily upon prerogatives associated with their seniority among their fellow mechanics. At one of the meetings I attended, a man who had provoked a quarrel with another member was called upon by the chairman to apologize. When he refused, his former master, who was also present at the meeting, stood up and admonished him to apologize in order to demonstrate his respect for the chairman "who is senior to us all." When the offender still refused he was ejected from the meeting; the chairman shouted disapproval of his conduct and several members, who had also apprenticed under his former master, actually pushed him out the door.[13] After an hour or so he changed his mind and decided to apologize after all. Because he had been formally ejected from the meeting someone had to intercede for him and obtain permission for him to reenter the building and tender his apology. The man selected for this purpose was a friend of the penitent's former master and a former apprentice to the chairman. He duly spoke up, obtaining permission for the penitent to apologize, whereupon the latter made his apology to the mechanic he had offended and to the association as a whole.

I have described this incident in detail because it illustrates dramatically the way in which customary Yorùbá principles of social interaction are often applied to relationships stemming from economic and political situations. In this instance the principle of seniority was invoked to settle a quarrel between peers, as often happens in disputes settled within descent groups or through the traditional political apparatus. The people involved, however, were related to one another solely through their occupation; seniority was determined by master-apprentice relationships and by individuals' status within the Ifè Mechanics' Association rather than in the Ifè community. Indeed, since many members of the IMA do not belong to Ifè descent groups, their standing within kinship or community networks is largely irrelevant to their role in the association. Actual kinship and community relations played no part in either the quarrel or its resolution, but the principles and procedures used to resolve the dispute derive from those employed within kin groups and communities before Yorùbás ever set eyes on a motor vehicle.

Disputes between individual mechanics can be settled fairly quickly through the intervention of the association's elders. A more serious and lengthy case involved a possible defection from the IMA of a group of mechanics based in a section of Ifẹ̀ known as Modákẹ̀kẹ́. In physical terms, Ifẹ̀ and Modákẹ̀kẹ́ are parts of the same town. Politically, however, Ifẹ̀s consider Modákẹ̀kẹ́ to be just a quarter of their city, whereas Modákẹ̀kẹ́s prefer to speak of "our town," emphasizing their independence from and equality with Ile-Ifẹ̀ proper. Modákẹ̀kẹ́ was founded by immigrants who left Ọ̀yọ́ during the upheavals of the early nineteenth century and sought protection at Ile-Ifẹ̀, both from enemies at home and from the roving armies that often preyed on refugees or on established towns during this period (Mábòdgùnjẹ́ and Omer Cooper, 1971; Johnson, 1921; Law, 1977). Subsequent disputes between the strangers and their hosts led on more than one occasion to the Modákẹ̀kẹ́s' dispersal from Ifẹ̀. Even after the colonial administration effected a permanent reunion of the two communities on the present site, their separate traditions of origin continued to provide a focal point for political conflict within the town (Berry, 1975a; Oyediran, 1974; see also Barber, 1979). The news that a group of Modákẹ̀kẹ́s were trying to break away from the Ifẹ̀ Mechanics' Association to form their own organization therefore alarmed the IMA's leaders, who are familiar with the divisive potential of linking other issues with traditional community differences.

Accordingly, the secretary of the IMA organized a delegation to visit the Modákẹ̀kẹ́ mechanics and find out what was going on. It transpired that the Bálẹ̀ (head chief) of Modákẹ̀kẹ́ was building himself a new palace and seeking contributions to that effort from every available source within the town. Descent groups residing in Modákẹ̀kẹ́ had been asked to contribute, and the Bálẹ̀'s representatives had also approached members of each trade and craft practiced in the town. Accordingly, a group of about fourteen mechanics gathered to decide what to contribute and how to collect it, "since others, like carpenters, blacksmiths, bricklayers, and so on, were all doing the same." Queried by the representatives of the IMA, the fourteen Modákẹ̀kẹ́ mechanics denied any intention of forming a separate association or engaging in any other expression of disloyalty to the parent organization, and they readily agreed to say so publicly at the next meeting of the IMA. Although it ultimately proved to be rumor, the threat of secession was sufficiently alarming to keep people aroused for some time thereafter; public statements of loyalty by the Modákẹ̀kẹ́ fourteen were a regular event at the association's fortnightly meetings for weeks after the initial inquiry.

In one sense, the mechanics who came to be looked on as potential defectors from the IMA hardly represented a Modákẹ̀kẹ́ faction within the organization. Like many mechanics in the association (and all my informants), most of them were not originally from Modákẹ̀kẹ́; they

simply worked there. They felt that they should contribute to the
Bálè's palace in order to maintain good relations between their fellow
artisans and the traditional authorities that had jurisdiction over their
place of work. On the other hand, as we shall see in more detail in
chapter 7, building a palace is a political gesture in Yorùbá society; it
reaffirms the status of a traditional ruler and his people as an independent jurisdiction, thereby strengthening their claims on the resources of the state. The fact that individuals among the Modákèkè
fourteen were not necessarily Modákèkès by birth does not, therefore,
preclude the possibility that they might be recruited to the cause of
Modákèkè independence or that their commitment to such a cause
might someday come into conflict with their loyalty to their occupational colleagues. In insisting on repeated assurances of the Modákèkè
mechanics' loyalty to the IMA, the officers of the association demonstrated their keen awareness of local political realities rather than
simply their preoccupation with traditional rituals of solidarity and
subordination.

Other disagreements—including an elaborate series of negotiations
between two rural branches of the IMA which disagreed over the
venue of their joint fortnightly meeting—were also handled in ways
that tended to restore harmony among the disputants and to preserve
the solidarity of the association as a whole. In the IMA, as in their
individual firms, mechanics spend a good deal of time cultivating
and maintaining good relations with their customers, colleagues, and
patrons, often according to specifically Yorùbá norms of social interaction. In part, such activities are substitutes for more formal and imper-
sonal methods of transmitting information, organizing credit relations,
or regulating market conditions, which are characteristic of advanced
capitalist societies (see Cohen, 1969; Eades, 1980). They may also help
to solve problems of conflict resolution or political mobilization not
directly related to mechanics' income-earning activities. In the cases
I observed, the focus of such political activity was local or purely
internal; I found little evidence that mechanics in Ifè were seeking a
wider coalition with other occupational groups or other communities.
The IMA, for example, sends delegates to the annual meeting of the
national Mechanics' Association, but beyond that it does not seem to
be actively concerned with or influenced by the national organization.

Mechanics also maintain connections with their home communities.
Approximately two-thirds of the mechanics I interviewed regularly
attended family meetings; one-third participated in at least one other
society, of a religious, social, or financial nature, in addition to holding
membership in the IMA. Aside from the IMA, however, there was
no evidence that any of these men were looked upon as leaders within

their descent groups, hometowns, or other organizations. Although the sample is too small for this fact to carry weight by itself, it is consistent with my observations of the sources of leadership in community-based institutions in Ìreé and Ẹripa. Prosperity of modest proportions, though always welcomed by a person's kinsmen and neighbors, is rarely sufficient in contemporary Yorùbá society to qualify the person for positions of community leadership. Seniority, education, and political connections are of much more significance, and the first of these is rapidly becoming dependent on the latter two (see chap. 7).

In short, the mechanics I interviewed take part in occupationally and communally based efforts to improve their economic position, but they show little evidence of involvement in any wider process of political mobilization against the existing order. Their inactivity does not stem from any widespread popular belief in the justice of that order; instead, it reflects the strategies mechanics have used to work and live within the system. The conditions for doing business in western Nigeria favor strategies of investment and productive organization which restrict increased productivity. Hence the very process of building up a firm fosters constraints on business expansion and helps to perpetuate social relations that often divide people in similar economic circumstances. As aspiring accumulators, mechanics in Ifè find themselves face to face with the contradictions of a situation in which, because accumulation and differentiation are so closely linked to access to the state, the resulting process of class formation engenders sectional conflict, which tends to forestall the consolidation of class interests into an effective political program for economic and social change.

7

Building the Oba's Palace: Community Development and Class Formation in a Rural Town

As explained in earlier chapters, farmers, teachers, and artisans all maintain fairly regular contact with their hometowns and compounds. They do so not in the expectation of deriving immediate, tangible benefits, but rather to maintain a set of relationships which may some-time prove useful in coping with misfortune or taking advantage of opportunity. For many, the attachment to kin and community of origin is not only emotional and rhetorical; it also involves the transfer of real resources to build a house, contribute to family ceremonies, assist a needy relative, donate to community projects, take a title, or simply court a following. Let us now turn our attention back to Ìreé and Ẹripa to see what has come of emigrants' carefully fostered connections with their hometowns in terms of individual advance, the development of community resources, and political leverage. In this chapter I describe the ways in which various groups of emigrants have participated in hometown affairs and investigate the uses of community surplus. I also consider the implications of emigrant participation for the role of community identity and institutions in regional processes of economic and political change. In particular, I attempt to show to what extent descent-based strategies of resource allocation have resulted in communal progress and how differentiation is being enhanced by some of the relations and values often believed to prevent it.

Religion and Social Conflict, 1900–1945

During the colonial period Ìreé and Ẹripa were relatively remote from the main arteries of urban and commercial development. Men and women of the two small towns who wanted to participate in the expanding commercial and agricultural economy had to leave home to do so, and the towns depended almost entirely on emigrants' remittances for increased levels of consumption or investable surplus. As no colonial administrators were stationed in Ìreé, appeals for public amenities or for state adjudication of local disputes had to be referred to the authorities in Ìkìrun, Òṣogbo, or Ìbàdàn. The only other institutional source of external resources and opportunities to which the people of Ìreé and Ẹ̀ripa had access was the American Baptist Mission in Ogbómọ̀ṣọ̀.

Missionaries based in Ogbómọ̀ṣọ̀ often traveled out into the rural areas to seek converts and spread the Gospel. C. E. Smith preached in Ìrèṣì, Ìgbájọ, and Ìreé in 1898 (Ogbómọ̀ṣọ̀, 3), and George Green, the first medical missionary in Ogbómọ̀ṣọ̀, obtained permission from the oba of Ìreé to organize a church there in 1907 (Ogbómọ̀ṣọ̀, 2; Omíladé, 1967). The first converts were men who had adopted Christianity while working on the railway near Lagos (see Berry, 1975a), but they were soon joined by a handful of Ìreé residents. In 1910 three converts from Ìreé attended the mission school in Ogbómọ̀ṣọ̀. Two years later Dr. Green baptized forty people in Ìreé, in a "veritable turning to Christianity" (Ogbómọ̀ṣọ̀, 2), and helped measure land for the foundations of a church building.

From the first, the presence of converts in the town was a potential source of conflict. Like the missionaries themselves, the people of Ìreé tended to perceive social interests and processes in religious terms. To the missionaries, their own social impact was measured in numbers of conversions and the size of converts' contributions to the church, as they described and explained local politics in terms of people's attitudes toward Christianity.[1] Mission archives are filled with reports of local conflicts described as "persecution" of the mission's converts by various "heathen" elements in the community. For the Yorùbás, converts' actions may have seemed to threaten the established order in more than one way.[2] Yorùbás rely on their gods for good fortune; prayer and ritual are directed toward appeals for health, fertility, and prosperity. As there is no presumption that the power to bestow these benefits is limited to particular deities, so there is no prejudice against individuals who decide to worship the Christian god in addition to their òrìṣà. Òrìṣàs (like people), however, derive stature and influence from the worship of their devotees (Barber, 1981). To the extent that Christians abandoned or neglected their òrìṣà, then, their conversion may have seemed to threaten others who worshiped and depended upon those deities.

In addition, the status and authority of titled men and women were ritually sanctioned; conversion could thus be seen as a potential source of disobedience or disaffection from constituted authorities. Converts' loyalty to local chiefs seems to have been at issue in several outbreaks of violent conflict between Christians and non-Christians in the period 1910–1916. In each incident the non-Christians were led by *babaláwos* or by members of chiefly houses. In 1916, for example, violence erupted when a close associate of the Areé's family converted to Christianity and renounced his membership in a society of the "king's descendants" (Ẹgbẹ́ Ọmọ Ọba) (Omílàdé, 1967; Ogbómọ̀ṣọ̀, 1 and 2). The oba arrested Christians, and in the ensuing melee a wife of the controversial convert was fatally beaten.

In each of these outbursts the British authorities eventually intervened on the side of the Christians, although in the 1916 incident they did so only after the Christian combatants had been detained in Ìkìrun and had appealed to Ìbàdàn. On that occasion the oba of Ìreé was detained, in turn, as punishment for the treatment meted out to the Christians. After that the Christians were let alone. By the time overt religious conflict broke out again in Ìreé, some of the Christians had become chiefs and the lines of controversy had shifted. Nonetheless, the close association between religious differences and political conflict was to remain a characteristic feature of Ìreé affairs throughout our period.

If early conflicts between Christians and non-Christians grew out of the former's challenge to the authority of titled men and priests in Ìreé, subsequent religious strife reflected a growing correspondence between religious affiliation and differential access to economic and educational opportunities outside the town. The Baptists built churches in Ìreé, and in 1923 they established the first primary school there (Omíládé, 1967); by 1929 it had enrolled 104 pupils (Ogbómọ̀ṣọ̀, 2). The mission also encouraged converts to attend Baptist institutions outside Ìreé for further training—usually as pastors, schoolteachers, or medical aides—and sometimes helped to sponsor them. In 1945 the mission opened a maternity clinic in Ìreé, which attracted patients from a considerable distance and, for some years, trained midwives as well. In short, the American Baptist Mission and its converts served as a useful channel for access to educational and economic opportunities and resources.

The importance of the mission in this respect was enhanced by the relative insignificance of Ìreé and Ẹripa in the colonial hierarchy of local jurisdictions. Since the colonial regime provided virtually nothing in the way of amenities or infrastructure for towns as small and remote as these, the mission loomed large in the eyes of the townspeople as a source of such benefits. It was only much later, and with the advantage of hindsight, that some educated *ọmọ* Ìreé perceived the limitations of the kinds of training and opportunity provided by the Baptist Mission. Explaining the "backwardness" of Ìreé in the late 1970s, an informant who is a lawyer declared that because most educated sons of Ìrcé had become pastors or teachers, they had spent much of their lives in rural areas where the "light of civilization" shone but dimly, while those who did go on to seek professional training suffered from the lack of fellow townsmen to help them along in private employment or the civil service (see Peel, 1978). During the period of official austerity mandated by the depression of the 1930s and World War II, however, opportunities in the professions and the civil service were limited, so that the disadvantages of teaching and the ministry were not readily apparent. Before 1945 there is little evidence of conflict within the towns arising from Baptist domination of access to external opportunities. Documentation for this period is sparse and may simply omit significant incidents, but it also seems likely that the Baptists were not seriously resented at a time when so few opportunities were available to residents.

Cocoa, Decolonization, and Community Development, 1946–1965

Religious differences, like traditions of origin, are potential sources of social division and conflict in Yorùbá society, but they often lie dormant unless they happen to coincide with differential access to wealth and power (see Melson and Wolpe, 1971). In Ìreé, because of the town's comparative insignificance in the colonial hierarchy of Yorùbá communities and the Baptist Mission's corresponding importance as a source of external resources, differential access to opportunity crystallized around differences in religious affiliation, leading to a history of religious antagonism and strife unusual in Yorùbá society. The process unfolded during the era of decolonization.

As we have seen, conditions in the regional economy improved dramatically after 1945. Cocoa prices rose steeply, and many men and women from Ẹripa and Ìreé joined the exodus to the forest belt to plant the newly profitable crop. By the early 1950s some of their farms were beginning to yield a harvest, and over the next decade remittances from them generated a substantial flow of resources into Ìreé. Much of the money was spent on consumption, education, or construction of family houses, but cocoa farmers also made significant contributions to community projects. At the same time decolonization created new political opportunities at the local as well as the regional and national levels of government. In particular, the establishment of regional and national parliamentary institutions and the transfer of power to Nigerian politicians and civil servants not only afforded new employment opportunities to many but also intensified popular competition over defining and controlling channels of access to the new state apparatus. In other words, decolonization imparted new life to the issue of jurisdictional boundaries and hierarchies, as communities sought to take advantage of the reorganization to advance their claims to state resources and to expand their spheres of influence. The spirit of the times is reflected in a letter written in January 1953 by the district officer to the chiefs of the old Ifẹ́lódùn District Council. In anticipation of local government reform, many of the towns represented on the council began agitating to have the district divided into two parts. Specifically, the majority of towns, Ìreé and Ẹripa included, wished no longer to be subordinate to Ìkìrun. In the midst of the ferment, several chiefs requested permission of the district officer to "discipline" the Areé of Ìreé, who had opposed division against the wishes of many of his own constituents. The specific complaint against the Areé was that he had failed to attend council meetings on a regular basis. The district officer, though acknowledging that the chiefs had a legitimate complaint, advised that "in view of the possibility of reorganization in Ifẹ́lódùn, you may consider it wiser to do nothing" (Nigerian National Archives, Ọshun Div. 1/1/1331). Reorganization took place in due course, and the headquarters of the new Ifẹ́lódùn Council were established in Ìreé.

In the atmosphere of expanding economic and political opportunities that characterized the late 1940s and early 1950s, interest in community development intensified in Ẹripa and Ìreé. Cocoa farmers remitted part of their rising incomes to their hometowns, for family use as well as for town improvement projects. Men who had been to school and had left the towns in the thirties and early forties to seek employment appropriate to their educational qualifications also began once again to turn their attention homeward. Some sought employment as clerks or teachers or opened shops in anticipation of the increased flow of remittances from emigrant farmers and traders; some ran for local office when elections were held or chieftaincy titles fell vacant, and many campaigned actively in these contests. The returned emigrants also made efforts to lobby external institutions for amenities and political advantage for the towns. Much of this activity was channeled through the Ìreé Progressive Union (IPU), an organization of townspeople whose aims were to promote "progress in business aspects of the civilians" of Ìreé, to construct roads and buildings in the town, to promote education, and to "represent the taxpayers" of Ìreé (Nigerian National Archives, Ọshun Div. 1/1/804).

The IPU was established in 1936 by a small group of pastors and teachers.[3] Such organizations were common in Yorùbá towns in the colonial period. In larger, more commercial towns they were often founded earlier and dominated by traders, some of whom were also educated Christians; examples are the Ìbàdàn Progressive Union and the Ẹgbẹ́ Àtúnluse in Ilésà (Hopkins, 1966b; Post and Jenkins, 1973; Peel, in press). The Ìreé Progressive Union accomplished little before the war, but in the late 1940s it embarked on a series of projects, including the employment of a night watchman for the town and the construction of a small post office and a town hall. Branches of the IPU were established among emigrant ọmọ Ìreé, not only in major cities, but also in rural areas where ọmọ Ìreé had congregated, such as Àlàrí near the Dahomean border, parts of Ghana, and the cocoa-farming districts of Ifẹ̀ and Ilésà. Thus, while the Lagos and Ìbàdàn branches were dominated by educated members, farmers and traders were in the majority.

During the 1950s and early 1960s the activities of the IPU in Ìreé were financed primarily by contributions from emigrant farmers and traders, but the organization was led by the same small group of educated men who had swept the local government elections of 1953. Most of them had been trained by the Baptist Mission and pursued occupations such as teaching, clerical work, pharmaceutical work, and the ministry.[4] As educated men with professional or commercial careers, they were similar to the political elite of the Western Region as a whole (Abernethy, 1969; Imoagene, 1976). In Ìreé, however, as the members of this elite were also invariably Baptists, many of them mission protégés, the intensification of competition over new political opportunities engendered considerable antagonism between Christians and Muslims, which was not true elsewhere in the region. As early as 1952, when one of the most senior chieftaincy titles in the town fell vacant, a rancorous dispute developed over the choice of a successor; the rival candidates were a Muslim and a Baptist, and religious affiliation tended to override ties of kinship in determining who supported each candidate.

The Baptist elite of this period had a particularly able and energetic leader in the person of the Reverend E. A. Omíládé, pastor of the First Baptist Church in Ìreé, who was born in Ìreé in 1908 and educated at the Baptist Theological Seminary in Ogbómòṣò̀ (Ogbómòṣò̀, 1). After serving in several other towns Omíládé was called to Ìreé in 1936, where he lost no time in taking an activist stance on a number of issues. He was, for example, instrumental in founding the IPU, and he sought unsuccessfully to persuade the district officer to establish a government dispensary in Ìreé. In 1944 the Baptist Mission did agree to open a maternity clinic in the town, under the direction of an American missionary whom Omílàdé had known while he was a student at the Baptist seminary in Ogbómọ̀ṣọ̀. Omíládé also claims to have played an important role in the government's decision, in 1954, to make Ìreé the headquarters of the newly constituted Ìfẹ́lódùn District Council (Omíládé, 1967). In short, he took a prominent part in several efforts to increase Ìreé's access to external resources, by lobbying the government and the Baptist Mission for amenities and by maneuvering to advance Ìreé's position in the hierarchy of administrative jurisdictions under the new regional government.

Omíládé's interest in bringing new services and opportunities to Ìreé was shared by most of his fellow townsmen. His efforts aroused controversy only when they were perceived as benefiting some groups within the community more than others, either politically or economically. Projects that provided jobs for educated individuals or seemed to enhance the status and influence of Omíládé's associates within the community were looked on with suspicion and resentment by those who were not so benefited. The growing tension between Muslims and Christians in Ìreé, which was fed during the 1950s by such perceived inequities, came to a head over the issue of building a secondary school in the town.

As early as 1948 Omíládé was exploring the possibility of getting the Baptist Mission to sponsor a high school in Ìreé. To justify the project it was necessary to canvass a wider area than Ìreé and Ẹ̀ripa alone, both for local contributions toward the cost of construction and for potential students. Accordingly, Omíládé approached the Bethel Association, a group of Baptist churches in the Ọ̀ṣun area. Bethel was receptive, but some of the members—notably those from Ìrágbìjí—balked at locating the school in Ìreé rather than in their own town. As Omíládé was not prepared to compromise, the idea eventually had to be shelved. In 1954, however, after Baptist candidates had swept the local government elections and a Christian had been installed as oba in Ìreé, the question of the high school came up again. Once more the Baptists took the lead, this time with the support of the local African Church, both in seeking official sanction for the scheme and in soliciting contributions from the townspeople. As the government required the town to put up £4,000 before construction could begin, appeals were made to every compound and association in Ìreé as well as to the emigrant branches of the IPU.

The first contribution came from a group of carpenters, all belonging to the First Baptist Church, who pledged their labor free of charge in order to "glorify Christ" (Omíládé, 1967). Not to be outdone, the other Christian churches quickly followed suit. The Muslims, however, declined on the plea that they had plans to participate in building a Muslim high school in another town. (There was, by this time, a Muslim primary school in Ìreé.) In addition, some of the prominent Muslims in the town pointed out to Omílàdé and his colleagues that, when Ìreé's first primary school was built in the 1920s, the entire community had helped construct it but the school had been named the Baptist Day School. Similarly, the maternity clinic was also established through community effort, but in the end it was named the Baptist Welfare Center. The Muslims of Ìreé were not interested in contributing to another community project that, when completed, would be claimed as a Baptist institution.

The Muslims' refusal touched off a round of intense lobbying. Influential Christians, including the oba (a Catholic), put pressure on leading Muslims to contribute, assuring them that the high school would be for the whole community. According to some informants, the plans for a Muslim secondary school at Ìrágbìjí also fell through at about this time. In any event, the Muslims finally relented and raised several hundred pounds toward the cost of the school. The truce was only temporary, however. The school opened in 1959 with thirty-four pupils, a principal and teachers recruited and partly paid by the Baptist Mission, and the official name of Ìreé Baptist High School. Money was also raised to send a few young men from Ìreé to universities abroad in order to train local sons for the high school staff. Needless to say, those sent were all Baptists.

The Muslims felt betrayed. Once again, it seemed, the Baptists had managed to gain control of a key community project and were using it to advance the personal and collective interests of their own followers and protégés. The Muslims, lacking the resources to build another school, could do little at the time. Even after 1962, when the regional government assumed responsibility for paying the teachers' salaries, the Muslims were unable to get the word "Baptist" deleted from the name of the school. The legacy of resentment and bitterness between Muslims and Christians in Ìreé flared up repeatedly in subsequent political crises, often influencing who sided with whom in conflicts over political matters and the allocation of resources to community projects.

Religion was not the only basis of differential advantage, however, either with respect to external resources or in terms of the internal power structure of the town. Class differences independent of mission affiliation emerged during the 1960s and 1970s as an increasingly significant feature of local politics. The political turmoil of the mid-

sixties, which engulfed the entire Western Region and reflected complex forces, was an early indication of the growing importance of class
interests in Ìreé. Conflict broke out initially over the familiar issue of
administrative jurisdictions, but the dispute soon became enmeshed
in party politics and in the growing regional and national crisis that
led to violent civil strife in late 1965 and to the collapse of the First
Republic in 1966.

The local crisis was parochial enough in its inception. In 1963 a
majority of towns with representatives on the Ìfẹ́lódùn District Council
decided to move the council's headquarters from Ìreé to Ìrágbìjí.[5]
The people of Ìreé felt the loss of status acutely, fearing that it might
prove costly in terms of future access to state resources. In an effort
to salvage the situation Omíládé went to see S. L. Akíntọ́lá, a former
classmate and a fellow Baptist who also happened to be premier of
the Western Region (Omíládé, 1967). Akíntọ́lá declined to intervene,
but Omíládé persisted, with the active support of the officers of the
Ìreé Progressive Union, to press his cause with the regional government. When it became clear that nothing would be done to return
the district offices to Ìreé, the Baptists changed their tactics and begged
that Ìreé and Ẹripa be constituted as a separate local government
jurisdiction.

The Muslims of Ìreé, fearing that the establishment of a separate
local council would further strengthen the hegemony of the Baptist
elite within the town, formed an opposition group. Several prominent
Muslims publicly advocated reconciliation with the rest of the towns
in Ìfẹ́lódùn District, suggesting that it might be effected through personal contacts they had in Ìbàdàn, at no disadvantage to Ìreé. Nothing
came of their efforts, however. Meanwhile the Baptist faction succeeded in getting the divisional officer to schedule public hearings on
the issue of a separate local council for Ẹripa and Ìreé. Soon after the
hearing, held in February 1965, the premier authorized creation of
a new administrative unit to be called the Ìreé-Ẹripa Provisional
Authority.

After the premier's decision was announced, Omíládé publicly
urged the townspeople to cooperate with the regional government in
order to show their gratitude. By the summer of 1965 tension between
Akíntọ́lá's Nigerian National Democratic Party (NNDP) and the Action
Group was acute, and the government was not above granting local
administrative favors as a strategy for mobilizing popular support.
Action Group sympathizers in Ìreé certainly interpreted Omíládé's
position as an effort to pressure the people of Ìreé into voting for the
NNDP in the upcoming elections. They criticized Omíládé for his

support of the government and accused him—with what justice it is impossible to say—of participating in the corrupt tactics of his patrons. As the elections approached the campaign became increasingly turbulent throughout the Western Region, and Ìreé witnessed its share of strong-arm tactics. Party stalwarts solicited contributions from patients seeking to visit the Welfare Center, and tensions ran high. When the premier showed up unexpectedly at a rally scheduled for an Action Group candidate, one infuriated Action Grouper is said to have traded blows with Akíntọlá as the latter stepped from his car, causing a minor riot in the town. After the NNDP claimed victory in what is widely acknowledged to have been a fraudulent election, Omíládé was physically attacked by Action Group sympathizers and forced to flee Ìreé.

The hostility directed toward Omíládé during the political crisis of 1965 was not simply an outburst of suppressed Muslim antagonism against Baptist aggrandizement. Indeed, many of the town's most active Action Group sympathizers were Baptist. Muslim informants whom I interviewed in 1978–79 claimed, further, that a majority of the townspeople had been inclined in 1965 to vote for the NNDP, on opportunistic grounds if for no other reason (see Mackintosh, 1966; Sàndà, 1974). Omíládé was resented for his personal power and as de facto leader of the Baptist clique that had dominated the town politically since the early 1950s. Opposition to Omíládé stemmed not only from Ìreé Muslims' resentment against Baptists' privileged access to extralocal resources, but also from a rising younger generation of men (and some women) who were better educated and more prosperous than the Baptist teachers and pastors associated with Omíládé. Like the preceding generation of Baptist-trained school leavers, the young graduates believed themselves uniquely qualified to direct the course of progress at all levels of society. As the military regime moved, after 1966, to consolidate power in the hands of a central government increasingly dominated by graduates, so the political leverage of people with appropriate educational qualifications tended to increase at the local level. At the same time graduates sought, like their fathers, to pursue every available avenue to personal advancement and to reinforce their educational advantages with whatever political support and property rights they could claim by virtue of descent. From the end of the civil war, emigrant professionals became increasingly active in Ìreé and, by the late 1970s, they had largely supplanted the Baptist Old Guard as the dominant group in the town's political structure. Among their fellow townspeople they were often referred to, with a mixture of admiration and resentment, as "the Lagos people" or simply "the elites" (pronounced a-lights).[6]

Graduates and Chiefs: The Contradictions of Community Development, 1965–1979

From the late 1960s, Ìreé came increasingly to resemble a microcosm of western Nigerian society as a whole. Access to the state took precedence over access to the mission, both as the primary aim of local strategies of advance and as a determinant of their outcomes. Religious polarization did not disappear; on the contrary, it occurred more often in consequence of emerging class conflict, rather than serving as a source of differentiation. Local resource mobilization and conflict continued, as in the 1950s and early 1960s, to revolve around the issue of chieftaincy titles, town projects, and party politics, but the results were more clearly in favor of ọmọ Ìreé who enjoyed close ties to the state or the national ruling class.

In some respects, the men who emerged as Ìreé's new political and economic elite during the 1970s were a diverse group, including one or more senior military officers, lawyers, engineers, and architects, as well as secondary school teachers, university lecturers, civil servants, and businessmen. Most, but not all, of them had received some form of postsecondary education; many lived and worked in Lagos or other major Nigerian cities, but some were based in rural areas; most were Christian—indeed Baptist—but there were Muslims among them too. Nearly all were self-made men. Like the teachers, traders, and mechanics discussed in earlier chapters, most of them were sons of farmers and traders who had reached their present positions through their own efforts rather than their parents' advantages. What distinguished them from the majority of their fellow townsmen was not their backgrounds but their success.

A few members of this elite group had been educated at their parents' expense; for example, one man had been put through the London School of Economics by his father, a prosperous trader based in Ghana. Most of them, however, had won scholarships or worked their way through school, often by signing a bond with the Baptist Mission or the government agreeing to teach for two or three years for each year of higher education they received. Several had even managed to study abroad, supporting themselves from savings and by working while they studied. One man, after graduating from a teacher training college in Ìwó and teaching for a year, was given enough money by an uncle and a senior brother to pay for his passage to England. He took a job in London as a clerk with a firm and studied in the evenings. By the time he passed his A-level exams he had so endeared himself to his employers that they promised him employment whenever he had a vacation. His vacation earnings enabled him to complete a bachelor's degree in economics at the University of London. He then signed on with the United Africa Company (UAC) as a management trainee, at a starting annual salary of £950. In nine years he worked his way up to the position of Lagos area manager (at an annual salary of ₦12,000), and in 1976 he resigned to go into business for himself. I interviewed three other professionals who had studied abroad on scholarships or with their own savings, including one teacher who had written a textbook and used the royalties to finance his way to the United States for postgraduate study.

Apart from the UAC manager and one other man, all the emigrant professionals I interviewed were (or had been) employed by the government as civil servants or teachers or in paragovernmental enterprises, such as the Nigerian Tobacco Company or the Nigerian Electric Power Authority. Their experiences reflected the views of a group of young professionals whom I met in Lagos at the home of one of my informants. Working in the ministries, though often a tedious and poorly paid occupation, they explained, was advantageous in the long run because "after you go out [into self-employment], you know where to lay your hand on things." Those of my informants who had left the civil service to go into business were indeed doing well financially. One of them, upon retirement from a Lagos State ministry, had obtained a ₦100,000 loan from the Nigerian Agricultural Bank to start a poultry farm, just outside Lagos. He used imported chicks and feed and sold eggs to marketwomen in the Lagos area. In three years he had accumulated fixed assets worth ₦235,000 on which he earned a return of 100 percent in 1978. Another man left the Nigerian Tobacco Company in 1975 to invest ₦20,000 of his own savings in a small business distributing imported greeting cards in Nigeria. When, in 1978, the government prohibited further imports of cards, he arranged to lease designs from a foreign company and to subcontract the printing in Nigeria. The change meant lower unit costs, he said, but more red tape. However, his sales increased rapidly. After four years he had boosted his capital to ₦400,000; his sales in 1978 brought in ₦740,000. The former United Africa Company agent was equally successful; starting with ₦2,000 of his own money and a good credit rating with local suppliers of building materials (who knew him from his days with UAC), he achieved an annual turnover of ₦1,000,000 in three years.

Those who remained in government employment made less money than the private entrepreneurs, but they still enjoyed a standard of living far beyond that of their fellow townspeople. Civil servants, grammar school principals, and lecturers were often provided with housing and other benefits by their employers. Several had acquired rental properties or as yet undeveloped plots of urban land, and most of them maintained several children and other junior kin in secondary schools and universities. Their wives, too, had secondary or even professional education and either held salaried jobs—most commonly as nurses—or, like their husbands, had retired to go into business for themselves.

Throughout the 1970s Ìreé's graduates became increasingly active in efforts to expand the flow of state-controlled resources to the town and to increase and consolidate their own power within it. Their actions followed familiar patterns: chieftaincy disputes, constructing houses, and, after September 1978, campaigning for national political parties. Their growing influence was reflected not so much in the forms of local accumulation and political conflict as in the resulting distribution of power and access to resources. These trends may be traced through the history of town politics and community development in the 1970s.

Choosing a chief: the professionalization of sectional conflict.—In 1972 Oba Ọlátúnjí—a Catholic who had held the title of Areé of Ìreé since 1954—died and the townspeople turned their attention from the matter of building a palace to the question of who was to occupy it. It soon became clear that the choice would not be an easy one. In the bitter struggle that ensued, construction of the palace was postponed indefinitely and the entire town became polarized, once again, on religious lines.[7]

No quarrel arose over which house (*ilé*) had the right to present candidates for the title. The codification of local succession rules drawn up in 1956 by the Western Region Ministry of Local Government and Chieftaincy Affairs recognized six "royal" houses in Ìreé, among which the office of oba should rotate (Western State Chieftaincy Declarations). State officials, local kingmakers, and most of the six houses were agreed that it was Ilé Oyètité's turn to hold the title, and his house therefore put forward three candidates.[8] From them the town kingmakers (the five most senior chiefs after the oba) unanimously selected Matthew Oyè (a pseudonym), a retired farmer with no formal education, in a meeting witnessed by the secretary of the Ìreé-Ẹripa Provisional Authority.[9] Their decision, when announced publicly, met with immediate protest. No one doubted Matthew Oyè's good character, but a number of people questioned his qualifications for the office of Areé on the grounds that he lacked the necessary educational background. The crux of the matter was expressed in a petition to the permanent secretary of the Ministry of Local Government and Chieftaincy Affairs, written by a group called "Young-Men of Ìreé." They demanded "an enlightened oba, who can read and write in

English" as well as in Yorùbá (File on Areé, Oct. 2, 1972). Their concern was based not on reverse cultural chauvinism but on political pragmatism: as one of my informants explained in 1979, "we did not want another oba who needed an interpreter to talk to the government."

Under considerable pressure the Oyètité family withdrew Matthew's name and put forward two other candidates. One, a middle-aged Muslim who had spent much of his life in Ghana, was one of the three candidates originally proposed by the house. The other, a Baptist carpenter in his thirties who had attended trade school in England, was a son of Matthew Oyè, the rejected candidate. Neither of the newly proposed candidates had attended secondary school or received any form of professional training. On his return from England, Matthew's son had established a business in Lagos, making furniture and undertaking small construction jobs. His firm was viable but not large; it employed about ten people at the most. The Muslim candidate had been a trader and had held other relatively unskilled jobs. In short, neither man could be considered a member of the professional class.

Nevertheless, my evidence indicates that the decision to substitute a "been-to" son for his illiterate father and efforts to muster support for his candidacy rather than that of the Muslim trader were spearheaded by Ireé's emigrant professionals. Though disclaiming any official partisanship, the leaders of the IPU campaigned actively for Matthew's son. In a transparently worded letter to the kingmakers, for example, the president of the IPU declared in March 1973 that, while the IPU "as an organization" supported neither candidate, "we who support . . . [Matthew's son] do so because of his educational qualifications, his support for the IPU and his childhood residence in Ireé" (File on Areé, March 27, 1972). Members of Ireé's professional elite whom I interviewed in 1979 were also outspoken about their support for the same candidate. One career civil servant in Lagos described the installation of Matthew's son as "the greatest achievement of the educated elements" in Ireé.

In March 1973 the kingmakers met and agreed to make Matthew's son the oba on the grounds that they "knew him better" than they did his opponent, because of the latter's long absence from the town (File on Areé, March 30, 1973). Their announcement only fanned the flames of controversy. During the next few months the Ministry of Local Government was inundated with petitions supporting one candidate or the other. The lists of signatories do not reveal much about the social basis for the conflict; some were written by emigrant groups who supported the Muslim, but other emigrants endorsed

Matthew's son, and both candidates received support from groups calling themselves "Ìreé Tax Payers." Campaign tactics were not limited to petition writing. Supporters of each candidate chanted songs and slogans invoking the scandalous conduct or humble status of their rival's forebears or praising their own candidate's past contributions to community projects. Questions were raised by each side about the exact genealogy of the rival candidate, in an effort to cast doubt on the legitimacy of his claim to office. Appeals were made to distant kinsmen with little previous connection with the town. One candidate prevailed on a wealthy brother-in-law, who was not from Ìreé, to use his influence with the government in that candidate's favor, while relatives of the other visited towns from which their distant ancestors were thought to have migrated in the hope of finding new allies there. Most of all, efforts were made to mobilize support for or rouse opposition to each candidate on the basis of his religious preference, a tactic that, by rekindling mutual suspicion and resentment between Christians and Muslims in Ìreé, added greatly to the intensity and bitterness of the rivalry between the candidates and their supporters.

In August 1973 the kingmakers met again. This time their votes were split evenly between the two candidates; the tie-breaking vote was cast by the most senior chief in favor of Matthew's son. Since that chief was a leading member of the First Baptist Church with a long history of pro-Baptist actions, his vote served only to aggravate the dispute. In 1974 some of the professionals who supported Matthew's son prevailed on the Ministry of Local Government to hold a public hearing on the matter. I was unable to locate any record of the proceedings, although correspondence in the files of the local secretariat indicated that, on the day of the hearing, a relative of the Muslim candidate showed up with a truckload of demonstrators (File on Areé). The outcome is well known: early in 1975 the ministry ruled in favor of Matthew's son and directed the townspeople to proceed with his installation.

To what extent the state's decision was the result of direct pressure from members of Ìreé's educated and professional elite cannot be determined precisely from available sources. Certainly the town's Muslims were not inclined to view the ministry's intervention as neutral; tension between Muslims and Christians (especially Baptists) remained high even after the new oba was installed and flared up periodically thereafter. In 1979 I was told that "the chief imam still has not visited the oba"—a "gesture" tantamount to nonrecognition under Yorùbá rules of etiquette. The educated elements, on the other hand, were elated. Soon after the new oba's installation the Ìreé Progressive Union met on a self-congratulatory note. At the suggestion

of the officers, those present voted to send letters of thanks to the
divisional officer "for the noble role he played in the chieftaincy affair
and for gracing the occasion of the installation with his august presence"; to the commissioner of Local Government and Chieftaincy
Affairs for his "discreet determination of the right candidate for the
obaship of Ireé"; and to the chief kingmaker for "successfully captain-
ing the ship of the community to a safe harbour" (IPU Minutes Book,
April 5, 1975). They also voted to resume construction of the oba's
palace and to ask the Ireé Youth Movement to provide the new chief
with a car.

Investment in housing.—In addition to the palace, emigrant ọmọ Ireé
undertook other construction projects during this period. As we have
seen, Yorùbá men often use part of their lifetime earnings to build
houses in their hometowns, both as a mark of personal achievement
and as an affirmation of their commitment to their home communities
(Eades, 1980), and my informants were no exception. More than a
third of the men I interviewed during the course of my field research
had built (or at least had started to build) houses in their hometowns,
and others avowed their intention of doing so. Houses in Ireé which
were built by emigrants were not rented out (if only because there is
little demand for rented lodgings in the town), but they stood ready
to accommodate the owner, his dependents, or his guests as needed.
The decision to build a house in Ireé was not, in other words, motivated
primarily by expectations of financial gain; instead it represented an
investment in maintaining or enhancing a man's status in his kin group
and community.

Although their incomes were vastly different, those among my informants who were most likely to have built houses at home were
cocoa farmers and emigrant professionals. The styles of housing built
by members of these two categories, however, varied even more than
their incomes. Cocoa farmers favored one- or two-story buildings with
mud-brick, cement-plastered walls, wooden window frames and shut-
ters, and corrugated iron roofs, as did traders and artisans. My informants in these occupations had spent between ₦1,000 and ₦8,000
each on their hometown houses. The most successful traders or
farmers built bigger houses, sometimes with cement floors and glass
windowpanes; otherwise their style was similar to that of houses built
by men of more modest means. Whenever possible, farmers and
traders built houses within their fathers' compounds or, if land was
not available there, immediately adjacent to other similar dwellings.
In contrast, several houses built during the 1970s by emigrant professionals and civil servants were of an entirely different type: modern
bungalows with asbestos roofs, combination tile floors, cement-block

walls, and louvered glass windows, protected by screens and alarm systems. Some were even fitted with plumbing and electric wires in anticipation of the arrival of the requisite amenities in the town.

The houses of Ìreé's professional elite are not only very different, in style and cost, from those of the majority of the town's emigrants, but their proliferation is likely to be accompanied by major changes in the structure of property rights in the town. The construction of elite housing is a recent development in Ìreé: the first house was built in the early 1970s by a high-ranking military officer; by 1979 no more than half a dozen had been built or were under construction. All were located on the western edge of the town, well apart from the owners' family compounds and, indeed, from the rest of the town's dwellings.

The breakup of large, patrilocal compounds in Ìreé antedates the latest round of elite construction. The growth of the regional economy, especially since 1950, has provided many sons of Ìreé with the where-withal to build houses of their own, and many families have run out of space for additional houses within the walls of their compounds (see Clarke, 1978; Lloyd et al., 1967). Walls have been allowed to deteriorate, and many men have had to obtain building plots from other families with land to spare. The houses built by Ìreé's emigrant professionals, however, have been erected on the outskirts of town at some remove from the owners' descent groups' compounds; to date they have all been built on the same side of town, on open land where the only other buildings are schools. The spatial arrangement of build-ings in Ìreé in 1979 suggests the beginnings of an elite suburb or, at least, a pattern of development in which the western side of town has been zoned—in fact if not in law—for professional buildings and high-cost housing.

By 1979 only a few elite houses had been constructed, and their contiguity might simply reflect a coincidental step in an unplanned process of expansion. At least some of the town's emigrant profession-als, however, saw the embryonic suburb as desirable and were actively working to expand it. Under the energetic chairmanship of a young architect from Ìreé, the Town Planning Authority for the Ìfẹ́lódùn Local Government Area had drawn up a layout for the development of Ìreé town which demarcated an extensive area west and southwest of the present townsite for future residential and industrial develop-ment. This area was to be subdivided into 500 plots which would be serviced by roads, electricity, and piped water and earmarked for elite-style housing and industrial use. In 1979 the Town Planning Authority was empowered to act only in an advisory capacity to the Local Government Council and to the chiefs and people of its con-stituent towns, so that the Ìreé layout represented a statement of the

Planning Authority's intentions rather than a blueprint for action authorized by the state. Authority officials, however, in consultation with the oba of Ìreé, had already allocated plots to 126 Ìreé emigrants, most of whom were traders, civil servants, or professionals living in Lagos or Ìbàdàn. When local families who claimed title to the land so allocated raised questions about the Town Planning Authority's actions, the latter explained that the government was taking over the land for purposes of community development and that there was nothing local landowners could do about it. In fact, there had been no confirmed state expropriation of land in Ìreé, although the state, under the provisions of the Nigerian Land Use Decree of 1978, is empowered to expropriate urban land for public use and holds final jurisdiction over all land disputes, in rural as well as urban areas. The state's control of land is qualified by the statutory obligation to award title to disputed land to whichever claimant can best develop the land commercially. The power to evaluate proposed development plans rests, however, with the state. It seems clear, therefore, that should some of the allocations of land to emigrant professionals in Ìreé be contested by local families, the professionals in the Town Planning Authority may expect the state to back their claims. In general, the Land Use Decree is potentially an effective instrument for the further consolidation of state power in western Nigeria, and the emigrant professionals of Ìreé seem determined to use it to ensure their own place in the ruling class.[10]

"For unity and progress": The Ìreé Youth Movement and the return to politics.—The role of the Ìreé Youth Movement (IYM) in the aftermath of the oba's installation illustrates even more clearly than the chieftaincy dispute itself the nature and significance of class formation in the political economy of the town. The Youth Movement was organized in 1973,[11] by a group of university students of Ìreé descent, to promote community development. To express their commitment to the town and to their forebears, the students acknowledged the IPU as a kind of classificatory parent body, but in fact they took an independent stance on most issues. They supported Matthew's son as oba while keeping aloof from the chieftaincy dispute, which they regarded, somewhat patronizingly, as illustrative of a retrogressive political culture that was detrimental to town progress. During the dispute the IYM devoted its energies to organizing elite-style fundraising events in Lagos or Ìbàdàn; after 1975, however, the group took a more active role in Ìreé. In December 1975 it donated ₦3,000 toward the cost of a car for the oba, adding another ₦1,000 the following April. In 1977 it held a series of peace meetings in Ìreé to bring together people who had taken opposing sides in the chieftaincy

dispute. To demonstrate their goodwill toward all elements in the town, members of the IYM took care to include Muslims among the group's officers and to voice support for Muslim interests in the town. For example, they pledged both moral and financial support for construction of a Muslim high school in Ìreé, as well as for providing the oba with a car and a palace. They also spearheaded a drive to have the old Baptist Welfare Center taken over by the Ọ̀yọ́ State government and converted into a hospital ("Five Years," IYM Papers).

The issue of the Baptist Welfare Center is particularly revealing of the Youth Movement's position, both sociologically and politically. In 1967, when the American missionary who had presided over the center almost from its inception retired, the mission invited a nephew of the Reverend E. A. Omílàdé to take her place. He proceeded to make the center financially independent of the mission by charging patients for consultation and for medicines. The townspeople, annoyed at the increased costs of the center's services, were inclined to regard the new policy as an effort to turn a community facility into a profitable venture for one of Omílàdé's protégés. In 1973, when the chieftaincy dispute halted construction of the palace, the local administrator for the Ìreé-Ẹripa Provisional Authority suddenly announced that the government would provide staff and supplies for a new maternity center in Ìreé if the town would build it.[12] Cement blocks, purchased with community funds for the palace, were quickly diverted to the new project; the schools were emptied for a few days to provide labor to carry the blocks to the new site; and the building was erected in seventeen days. In 1979 people assured me that "thousands" of babies had been delivered at the clinic since it opened. The competition did not, however, drive the Baptist Welfare Center out of business, and in 1977 the Youth Movement took up the cause.

In August of that year a representative of the Ìreé Youth Movement met with the Ọ̀yọ́ State commissioner for health (a former classmate) to discuss the possibility of obtaining state funds to improve the Welfare Center, primarily by hiring additional staff (File on Ìreé Baptist Welfare Center, IYM Papers). The commissioner, though sympathetic, said that the state could not give money to an institution whose staff were not accountable to a government agency; therefore the question of the ownership of the Welfare Center would first have to be resolved. The IYM then wrote to the Nigerian Baptist Convention (NBC) that the people of Ìreé wanted to turn the Welfare Center over to the government in order to upgrade its services. The NBC admitted that the center needed more staff, but it hoped to obtain state assistance without relinquishing control of the facility. The convention's annual report for 1976 pointed out that the status of all Baptist medical facilities had been called into question when the Western State was divided up in 1975, but that fortunately, "whether by accident or by invisible touch of God, . . . [the new Ọ̀yọ́ State Ministry of Health] had Baptists in all the key posts" (64th Annual Report, IYM Papers). Thus reinforced, the NBC responded to the Ìreé Youth Movement's request by appointing a committee to study the matter. The IYM, regarding this move as a delaying tactic, called a town meeting in Ìreé which voted to invite the state to assume control of the Welfare Center. Again, the Ministry of Health agreed to do so only if the Nigerian Baptist Convention had no objections—which of course they did. For a while the secretary of the Youth Movement, the proprietor of the Welfare Center, and the medical secretary of the NBC traded threats and insults, in person and in print, but to no avail (*Daily Sketch*, Sept. 12, 16, Oct. 2, 1978). At the time of my fieldwork the issue was still unresolved, partly because the IYM was awaiting the outcome of the 1979 elections.

The issue of the Welfare Center was an attractive one to the Youth Movement for several reasons. Because the proprietor of the center was widely viewed as a protégé of the Baptist clique that dominated town politics during Omíládé's time, the IYM could, by urging his subordination to the state, demonstrate their goodwill to the Muslims of Ìreé. Also, the takeover of a local denominational institution by the state accorded with the Youth Movement's beliefs not only in the retrogressive character of religious particularism but also in the progressiveness of professionalism. By working closely with a state increasingly staffed by professionals like (and including) themselves, and by bringing that state more intimately into the management of local resources, they believed they were acting in the best interests of the townspeople and advancing the cause of community development. An officer of the IYM explained to me—apropos of his own role in the state's expropriation of his family's land in Ìreé, to be used for an elite residential development—that "you have to play tricks on them."

In attempting to exploit relations of kinship and clientage in order to effect the rationalization of community development in Ìreé, the leaders of the IYM encountered obstacles arising from the prevalence of similar relationships within the state apparatus. Those who wanted the Welfare Center to remain under Baptist control also had connections in the Ọ̀yọ́ State government and were able to use them to neutralize the IYM's efforts. On May 16, 1978, the permanent secretary of the State Ministry of Health wrote the secretary of the IYM that the ministry was "prepared to integrate the Ìreé Baptist Welfare Center into the State Health Management Board system." Ten days later he shifted his ground and reiterated that, in view of the Baptist Convention's objections, nothing could be done until "the question of proprietorship was sorted out" (File on Welfare Center, IYM Papers). Evidently the permanent secretary had been lobbied by both sides, to more or less equivalent effect.

On September 21, 1978, the federal military government lifted the "ban on politics" which had been in effect since January 1966 and officially opened the campaign for the 1979 elections, which were to return the country to civilian rule. In Ìreé, the protagonists in the Welfare Center debate temporarily abandoned their lobbying efforts and turned their energies to the campaign, on the reasonable presumption that the ultimate fate of all local projects would hinge on the outcome of the elections. As one informant put it, in discussing Ìreé's as yet unsuccessful efforts to be included in the state's rural electrification program, "if a certain party wins the election, all the irregularities will be regularized."

Both the Unity Party of Nigeria (UPN) and the National Party of Nigeria (NPN) campaigned vigorously in Ìreé.[13] Efforts were made to rekindle old antagonisms as well as to woo voters with promises of tangible returns, and a number of my informants expressed anxiety lest the campaign revive open hostility between Muslims and Christians or between former supporters of the Action Group and the NNDP. Undoubtedly some old enmities were aroused, but the UPN held a trump card in Ìreé in the person of its candidate for deputy governor of Ọ̀yọ́ State, S. M. Afọlábí, who was a "son of the soil." For many voters, the overriding consideration in the election was how best to establish effective connections between the town and the new civilian government. UPN supporters played on that concern in their campaign, advising their fellow townspeople that "politics has returned and everyone must make his choice. You can choose to support your native son or you can reject him." The advantages of having an ọmọ Ìreé in the statehouse overrode many potential scruples. Several former NNDP supporters said, for example, that they would vote for the UPN candidate, "whether or not we agree with his political beliefs." Supporters of the oba also took the occasion to point out to his opponents that he would be more effective in lobbying the new regime on the town's behalf if he could boast the allegiance of a united community. The oba himself took a public stance of political neutrality, partly to avoid provoking open conflict but also to prevent his own unpopularity with some of his constituents from undermining support for the UPN.

Both the strategies of the UPN and the degree to which Afọlábí's candidacy evoked public tolerance—if not wholehearted enthusiasm—

for its platform were demonstrated at a public ceremony held at the end of March 1979 to establish a new community development fund. The launching, as the ceremony was popularly designated, was ostensibly a nonpartisan affair, organized on behalf of the entire community by the Ìreé Youth Movement. Invitations were issued to all emigrant sons and daughters of Ìreé and to anyone else considered likely to make a contribution. The state commissioner for works, who had authorized repairs to the Òṣogbo-Ìkìrun road in January,[14] was asked to preside.

On the appointed day a number of visitors and emigrant ọmọ Ìreé traveled to the town to witness the proceedings. People were assembled on the ground floor of the unfinished palace; prayers were offered by the pastor of the Baptist Church and by a representative of the chief imam. (The chief imam himself refused to attend because the oba was present.) The officers of the IYM welcomed the audience and introduced distinguished guests. Then donations were made and announced, beginning with a substantial contribution from the chief launcher, a successful businessman of Ìreé descent. After the ceremony, lunch was served to a number of visitors at the homes of an engineer and a grammar school principal and at the high school.

Both the seating arrangements at the launching ceremony and the disposition of guests at lunch were designed in accordance with the social status of the participants. At the launching, the representatives of the IYM, who acted as masters of ceremony, stood around a microphone and table facing a row of armchairs in which were seated the most distinguished persons present. These included the obas of Ìreé and Ẹripa,[15] the commissioner, the UPN candidate for deputy governor, the oba's senior brother who, with a PhD from an American university, was the most highly educated son of the town, and the chief launcher. The rectangular space between the organizers and the dignitaries was bounded on one side by a wall and on the other by the "a-lights"—professional men and women who had come home for the occasion. Directly behind the dignitaries, and somewhat less visible, sat the town chiefs, the compound heads, and an assortment of townspeople, including delegates from most of the emigrant branches of the IPU. Nonelite women, children, and others of no pretensions watched the proceedings from behind the rows of seats or through doorways and windows. Similarly, at lunch, the obas, distinguished guests, and professional ọmọ Ìreé were directed to the houses of the two emigrant professionals, while other visitors were fed at the high school.

The day's events went off peacefully and netted the town about ₦10,000 in contributions. The leaders of the IYM were pleased with the size of the turnout, which they interpreted as evidence of the progress they had made in unifying the townspeople around the cause of community development. That their success in uniting their fellow citizens was only partial (witness the chief imam's absence from the launching) occasioned them no more surprise or dismay than their recognition (reflected in the day's arrangements) of the substantial degree of socioeconomic differentiation obtaining among the towns-people. The youthful graduates of the Ìreé Youth Movement were inclined to attribute both religious factionalism and the poverty of many of their kin and neighbors to their elders' lack of education and corresponding want of "enlightenment." They regarded it as their own right and responsibility to take the lead in developing the town, since their elders were manifestly less well qualified to do so. Having launched the development fund, the leaders of the IYM simply took it for granted (much as Omílàdé and his colleagues had done in the past) that they should also decide how to use it. They planned to spend the money on the oba's palace.

⸜ Conclusion

The expansion of the colonial economy affected Ìreé and Ẹripa gradu-ally and indirectly. Before 1945 the principal effects were an increased rate of emigration to areas of opportunity for trade and wage employ-ment, and the presence of the Baptist missionaries, who trained a few ọmọ Ìreé as pastors, teachers, and dispensers. These careers brought their adherents little in the way of wealth and power. One prominent and relatively senior member of Ìreé's emigrant elite complained, in 1979, that the missionaries had held back the progress of the town by steering people into occupations with low pay and little influence. During the early 1950s, however, the potential surplus available for accumulation and economic transformation in Ìreé and Ẹripa was significantly increased as hundreds of ọmọ Ìreé migrated to the cocoa belt. By the mid-fifties farmers who had planted cocoa after 1945 were beginning to enjoy rising incomes, and they continued to do so well into the sixties, as increasing yields from maturing cocoa farms offset the effects of declining cocoa prices. Treated as strangers in the cocoa belt—with respect both to political affairs and to property rights—the migrants retained close ties with their communities of origin and contributed willingly to schemes for improvement in their hometowns.

Despite the emigrants' enthusiasm, however, the record of commu-nity development in Ìreé is notably unspectacular. Time and again, townspeople's contributions—of money, labor, building materials—

were used to duplicate existing facilities or to build political monuments, rather than for more productive undertakings. Members of the town's elite used whatever contacts or leverage they possessed with the state to influence the outcome of local political disputes, rather than to bring productive services to the town. Schemes to provide Ìreé and Ẹripa with electricity and piped water were discussed at every meeting of the IPU from 1967 on, yet by 1979 neither project had been realized. Instead, Ìreé had two maternity clinics, two post office buildings, and a high school—which together became a focus for ongoing contention over a potentially wasteful expenditure—and the oba had a car and the beginnings of a palace. Emigrant ọmọ Ìreé had added many new houses to the town, but local employment opportunities remained stagnant or may even have declined.[16] Many of the houses stood empty or were inhabited by a fluctuating population of elderly people, schoolchildren, and transient adults, whose efforts to maintain a stake in their home communities while earning a living elsewhere often absorbed their own energies and incomes in frequent travel back and forth. Like cocoa farmers' journeys among scattered plots or mechanics' perpetual travels to maintain contacts with actual or potential customers, emigrants' trips home tend to undermine the efficiency of productive activity for the sake of gaining access to productive resources.

Similar forces operate at the level of the community. As we have seen, townspeople's collective efforts to improve the material conditions of their community have engendered competition and political conflict, which in turn have absorbed the surplus collected for local improvements. The dominant position of the Nigerian state vis-à-vis the country's economic resources is clearly reflected, as well as the contradictions of a class struggle that resembles sectional conflict. The struggle to advance a community's status in the political hierarchy is both a condition of local accumulation and an obstacle to community development. In this context the educated elite is strengthened, but at the same time constrained, by its own power. Education confers preferential access to the state—sometimes in the form of official powers—which can be used to bring resources to the town and to control their use. The architect who used his position on the local government town planning commission to assume control over the allocation of local land is a case in point. Yet, under the terms of the Land Use Decree, his future ability to retain control depends mainly on those who are in power and on his connection with them, rather than on actual use of the land. By 1979 he and other aspiring graduates were devoting most of their energies to courting votes for the UPN and to building the palace, rather than to actual productive investment.

The struggle over access to the state has shaped the process of class formation as well as the form of accumulation in Ìreé. The self-defeating nature of investment in education as a strategy of upward mobility is reflected in the social history of the town as well as in the life histories of the schoolteachers described in Chapter 5. Before 1945 Ìreé's principal channel of access to external resources and opportunities was the Baptist Mission rather than the state, and local differentiation took the form of religious polarization. Scarcely had the Baptist elite consolidated its position, however, and begun to confront the divisive consequences of its zeal for community progress when it was elbowed aside by a rising generation of better-educated sons of the soil who did not hesitate to appeal both to religious cleavages and to kin-based loyalties to advance their own careers.

The rise of the graduate elite in Ìreé was fostered by decolonization, which brought the town and its people more directly into the orbit of local and national political competition. Decolonization, however, also intensified sectional forms of political mobilization and conflict. Thus, not only were the power and status of educated men constantly challenged by the educational achievements of their juniors, but they also rested on the mobilization of sectional interests which tended to undercut the elite's ability to play a progressive social role. The Ìreé Youth Movement's attempt to improve the efficiency of local health-care services by transferring control of the Welfare Center from church to state foundered on the power of religious interest groups within the state.

Similarly, the townspeople's efforts to improve the educational resources of their own children served, in part, to underscore the limits of education as an instrument of social transformation, at least in the western Nigerian context. When the high school was under construction in the late 1950s, scholarship money was raised within the town and from some of the emigrant branches of the IPU to enable local sons to attend universities and prepare to assume positions on the high school staff. As these men returned from their studies, several were hired as additional teachers, but both the Baptists and the Ministry of Education balked at discharging people already on the staff to make room for native sons. One man, disappointed in his hopes of becoming principal of the high school, tried to put pressure on the authorities by stirring up popular protest against the incumbent principal, who had been recruited by the Baptist Mission. In the process, he spread a rumor among the Muslims in Ìreé that the money they had contributed for construction of the high school had never actually been spent for that purpose; instead, it had been appropriated by members of the Baptist establishment for their own use. Although his efforts did not get him the job of principal, they did exacerbate religious antagonism in the town, intensify the subsequent conflict over the choice of a new oba, and hence reproduce existing patterns of unproductive accumulation and factional strife which undermine progressive social transformation in the town. The irony of the situation was well, if unintentionally, expressed by a member of the Ìreé Youth Movement, who described the man who wanted to be principal of the high school as "a fellow revolutionary."

Conclusion

Prosperity has proven an elusive goal in contemporary Nigeria, for the nation as well as for its citizens. Nigeria's leaders have been unanimous in professing their commitment to national economic development, yet the unprecedented oil revenues of the 1970s and early 1980s have been squandered in conspicuous consumption or in competition over control of the newfound wealth. Since the late 1970s government finances have been so overextended that whenever the world market price of oil declined the Nigerian government was unable to pay all its bills for imported commodities or the salaries of its own employees. Individual Nigerians are equally committed to material progress—"we want to do something tangible"—but the very intensity of their efforts to accumulate has increased the risks and reduced the level of their returns. Schoolteachers saw their prestige dwindle as the educational system grew; mechanics' profits were threatened by competition from their erstwhile apprentices and by their own strategies of business expansion; civil servants have suffered declining influence and perquisites as the bureaucracy has expanded; even the power of political office has frequently been adulterated by the proliferation of state and local government agencies.

Nor has economic growth proved to be a leveling force. The growing size of the national pie has not eased the intensity of struggles to divide it; neither has the accumulation of wealth by some individuals reduced the rest of the population to a uniform level of poverty or proletarianization. The strategies by which people such as those described in this book have struggled to stay abreast or advance in the general competition for wealth and influence have exacerbated inequality and promoted unproductive patterns of accumulation and resource use and management. Rising stakes have been accompanied by increased risks in all forms of economic activity and social interaction. People cannot count on the security of property rights, let alone the stability of profits, or on the loyalty of customers, co-workers, constituents, or even kin.

In this context commercialization, urban growth, and the consolidation of state power over the means of accumulation have not led to the polarization of Yorùbá society into privileged urban dwellers and a "neglected rural majority," or even into urban rich and urban and rural poor. Instead, these developments have engendered a kind of perpetual restlessness, in which no one stays anywhere for very long lest he miss an opportunity somewhere else. Low and uncertain returns to most forms of productive and commercial activity do not slow things down; rather, they reinforce the impetus to keep moving, if only to avoid falling farther behind in the economic and political lottery of accumulating good connections. People invest in access to productive resources instead of in the expansion of productive capacity.

Nigeria's political and economic syndrome of unproductive competition is, in some respects, the antithesis of the neoclassical paradigm of a market economy, in which competition erodes concentrations of wealth and power, leading to efficient resource allocation with a minimum of social conflict. In Nigeria, competition produces uncertainty, tension, and turmoil. People dissipate their energies in ceaseless mobility and their savings in pursuit of the means of competition instead of building the means of production. The articulation of capitalist and precapitalist modes of production in western Nigeria has not been a matter of traditional social formations resisting capitalist penetration and, thus, holding back capitalist development. Rather, the political conditions that surrounded and even stimulated the commercialization of agriculture and the growth of the tertiary sector also fostered strategies of accumulation and resource control which both reinforced and altered established social relations and people's understandings of them. In struggling to secure a better future for themselves and their children, Yorùbás have found money, education, patronage, and kinship equally and increasingly necessary—and less reliable than ever. The anarchy of capitalist expansion has neither fossilized nor swept away traditional institutions and practices: it has penetrated and transformed them.

In 1966 a Yorùbá farmer, in answer to my rather naive query—"Do your children help you on your farm?"—explained that "formerly sons worked for their fathers, but today we have schools and civilization, and now fathers work for their sons." His words capture much of the irony and tension of socioeconomic change in contemporary western Nigeria; they also bear on the question of why agricultural commercialization has not led to sustained economic growth and diversification, either through the efforts of farmers and their descendants or through state intervention. In the literature on Nigerian rural development, much has been made of the opposition between farmers and the state over the control of agricultural surpluses. Certainly, the government has extracted surplus from the agricultural sector in a variety of ways and has channeled most of it into nonagricultural uses, but it does not follow that the relationship between farmers and the state is exclusively antagonistic, that nonagricultural investment is necessarily unproductive, or that we can explain the pattern of economic change and political conflict in western Nigeria simply in terms of class struggles between peasant producers and state bourgeoisie (see Cooper, 1981a, 1981b).

Farmers, like most people, see the state as both an oppressor and a potential ally—a means to provide for their children's futures if not for their own current comfort. These contradictory attitudes are reflected in contradictory practices. Farmers seek to enlist the power of the state and its resources in support of kin- and community-based interests and relations, as well as to draw on the latter to enhance their access to the state. The contradictions of farmer-state relations in western Nigeria have fostered the pursuit of multiple strategies of personal and collective advance which, in turn, have contributed to unproductive accumulation, uncertainty, and social conflict. Understanding this process, through recording and interpreting the histories of men and women who are involved in it, helps us to see why peasant accumulation has not led to unimodal economic development and why state programs for rural development have accomplished so little. The issue is not state exploitation, urban bias, or peasant intransigence; it is rather the way in which farmers, bureaucrats, traders, artisans, politicians, and professionals both create and are limited by a dynamic process of unproductive accumulation, differentiation, and sectional conflict, a process that is not likely to be arrested by the unilateral action of any single class, community, or institution.

Notes

Introduction

1. The best published source of data on aggregate trends in the Nigerian economy is the Central Bank's *Economic and Financial Report*, published semiannually. For a convenient summary of data on aggregate economic performance during the 1970s, see Kirk-Greene and Rimmer, 1981.

2. Economists often use the term "structural change" to refer to shifts in the sectoral composition of aggregate output and employment. Others use it to refer to changes in relations among groups and institutions engaged in economic processes.

3. I have traced the spread of cocoa growing in western Nigeria and its impact on the organization of the rural economy there in *Cocoa, Custom and Socio-Economic Change in Rural Western Nigeria* (Oxford, 1975). Because the research for that book was carried out entirely within the cocoa-growing areas, it does not fully represent the degree to which cocoa production and cocoa farmers are integrated into the regional economy and society. The present study was undertaken, in part, to overcome that deficiency in my earlier work.

4. Most of the empirical studies demonstrating that farmers in underdeveloped economies are responsive to relative price changes show that, in the short run, farmers reallocate relatively fixed amounts of inputs among alternative crops in response to changes in relative price. There is, however, little clear-cut evidence that increases or decreases in producer price or agricultural terms of trade lead to long-term growth or decline in aggregate output (Helleiner, 1975; Askari and Cummings, 1976). Also, most of the evidence that small farms achieve higher yields per acre than large ones, which is often interpreted to mean that egalitarian agricultural growth is both possible and efficient, is also based on cross-section data. When techniques or conditions of production change, it is likely to be the larger farms who undertake and benefit from most of the increase in output (Heyer et al., 1976; Farmer, 1977; Roy, 1981).

5. Much of the rural development literature written in the neoclassical vein simultaneously criticizes governments for "distorting" resource allocation through excessive or misdirected intervention in the market and urges them to intervene in favor of more efficient resource allocation. Since the neoclassical definition of efficiency is couched in terms of perfect competition, or the absence of power, the whole idea of state intervention to bring about

greater efficiency is self-contradictory, and neoclassical economists' endless pleas for "better" price policies are a largely fruitless exercise.

6. A Yorùbá house (*ilé* or *agbo ilé*) may comprise members of one or more descent groups. In the past, the members of a house often lived within a single walled enclosure. Today, a house may consist of several noncontiguous structures, whose members come and go in pursuit of a livelihood and social connections (Schwab, 1952; Lloyd, 1954; Bender, 1970, 1972; Barber, 1979; Peel, in press).

7. The chief exception among my informants was that farmers rarely gave or even loaned money to their wives to assist the latter in establishing their own businesses. Yorùbá wives do, however, expect to receive annual presents of goods or cash from their husbands, which they may use as working capital to start a trade or a food-processing enterprise.

8. Most of the compounds in Ẹripa claim kinship with descent groups in Ìreé, and for many purposes the people of both towns consider themselves members of the same community.

1. Structural Change in the Political Economy of Western Nigeria

1. Figures for Ọ̀yọ́ State, which was formed in 1976, are compared with data for the Ìbàdàn and Ọ̀yọ́ provinces of the Western State in 1968 (Western State of Nigeria, *Current Education Statistics*; Ọ̀yọ́ State of Nigeria, *Current Education Statistics*).

2. Among them were colleges of education, federal advanced teacher training colleges, and state-sponsored two-year colleges of arts and sciences. For a useful description of the Nigerian educational system, see Margolis, 1977.

3. On the process of wage determination in Nigeria, see the debate among Peter Kilby, John Weeks, and Robin Cohen in *Journal of Developing Areas*, 1967–1968.

2. Migration and Community in Historical Perspective

1. For general discussions of Yorùbá migrations in the twentieth century, see Mábògùnjé, 1972; Eades, 1980; case studies of Yorùbá migrants in Ghana by Eades (1979) and Sudarkasa (1979); and studies of recent urban immigrants by Aronson (1978), Barnes (1976), Peace (1979), and Plotnicov (1967). On internal migration in Nigeria, see Adépọ̀jù (1976), Caldwell (1978), Olúsànyà et al. (1978), and Amin (1973).

2. The Modákẹ́kẹ́ land dispute, which occurred in Ifẹ̀ Division in the early 1950s, is a case in point. The Modákẹ́kẹ́s are descendants of Ọ̀yọ́ Yorùbás who were dislocated by the collapse of Ọ̀yọ́ in the early nineteenth century

and who fled to Ifẹ̀. Their relations with the Ifẹ̀s have never been easy. The town of Ile-Ifẹ̀ has witnessed periodic outbursts of political turmoil and sometimes violent conflict between Ifẹ̀s and Modákẹ́kẹ́s for more than a century; the most recent occurrence was in 1981. In the early fifties the rising price of cocoa and the influx of migrant farmers to the forests of Ifẹ̀ Division brought considerable income to Ifẹ̀ families in the form of tribute (ìṣákọ́lẹ̀) paid by immigrants for the right to plant cocoa on Ifẹ̀ land. Some Ifẹ̀ families took the occasion to suggest that, since the Modákẹ́kẹ́s were also immigrants or "strangers" (àléjò) to Ifẹ̀, they too should pay ìṣákọ́lẹ̀. Many Modákẹ́kẹ́s, who had been farming in Ifẹ̀ for generations without permission from any Ifẹ̀ family, objected strenuously to this idea. The dispute was eventually resolved by the Ọ̀ọni of Ifẹ̀ (at that time chairman of the Western Region House of Chiefs and an influential member of the Action Group) in favor of the Ifẹ̀s, a decision that did little to temper the Modákẹ́kẹ́s' resentment or sense of ethnic identity (Oyèdiran, 1974; Berry, 1975a).

3. Peace, 1979; Peel, in press; Olúsànyà, 1969.

4. Similarly, the argument that peasants' expenditure on their children's schooling ought to be counted as a flow of capital from rural to urban areas (Essang and Mabawonku, 1974) assumes that people who leave a farming village to seek employment elsewhere cease to interact economically with their parents, and that the entire cost of their schooling—because paid by their parents—was therefore derived from village-based agricultural income. Both assumptions are of doubtful validity for Yorùbá farming households.

5. The appropriateness is subject to qualification in both instances. Ilẹ́ṣà is not a rural area, but a town of several hundred thousand inhabitants, many of whom have farms or control land in the surrounding rural areas. At the time of his study, Peace's informants were full-time wage earners, not dispossessed workers with no alternative means of subsistence.

6. It is not clear what proportions of the towns' emigrants were included in the census count. I was shown a list of the adult male members of one house (agbo ilé) in Ẹripa, containing 153 names. Of these, only nine were actually living in Ẹripa in 1979. Abàkinní and Abúlékejì have experienced a high rate of turnover in the resident population, within households as well as in the villages as a whole (see chap. 3). In such circumstances, a community is a social and conceptual as well as a territorial entity, and the influence of community membership on resource allocation cannot be observed in a single place.

7. Women in Ìreé used to grow onions for sale outside the local chain of periodic markets, but even this local enterprise has declined in recent years.

8. Founders of some of the compounds for which I collected information in Ẹripa and Ìreé were said to have left their previous homes because of infertility or infant mortality (the àbíkú syndrome, in which the same child is believed to keep coming back to die).

9. Oríkì are oral poems that describe or dramatize the attributes of a person or house. They are sung on public and ceremonial occasions to praise or draw attention to their subject(s) (Barber, 1979, 1981; Ayọ̀rínde, 1973).

10. Some traditions say that Ẹripa was founded from Ìreé; others trace the founders of Ẹripa to Èfòn Àláyè. As we have seen, some houses in both Ẹripa and Ìreé claim Ìjèṣà origin, and the titles of the principal chiefs in both towns (Esa, Ojomo, Arogun) are associated with "forest" kingdoms, such as Iléṣà or Òndó, rather than with Ọ̀yọ́. I am indebted to J. D. Y. Peel for this information.

11. For example, ex-slaves were instrumental in spreading Islam and Christianity from Ìbàdàn and other western Yorùbá states eastward to Èkìtì after the end of the nineteenth-century wars (Akíntóyè, 1971; Gbàdàmósí, 1978).

12. This brief summary of Peel's discussion covers only points directly relevant to my analysis. His description of the changes in political interests and alignments which followed the imposition of colonial rule on Iléṣà is much richer, in argument and detail, than the outline presented here. I am grateful to Peel for allowing me to read parts of his book in manuscript. I am, of course, entirely responsible for any inaccuracies in my summary as well as for the comparative inferences I have drawn from his material.

13. In his study of economic and social change in Òkèigbó—a nineteenth-century settlement established by Ifè warriors and their followers on the western edge of what later became Òndó Division—Julian Clarke argues that the advent of colonial rule broke up the large compounds in Òkèigbó by removing the "conditions for the reproduction of the military household," namely, slave raiding and the import of firearms (Clarke, 1980, n. 18). In other towns, such as Iléṣà and Ìreé, whose history antedates the upheavals of the nineteenth century, members of large households often scattered to other towns or into the bush during the wars, and many returned to their former compounds during the early years of colonial rule. Subsequently, the old walled compounds were gradually replaced by smaller structures and households, as more men used their earnings from trade, agriculture, or wage employment to build houses. At first they did so on land belonging to their ancestral compounds, but later they moved to other parts of town as the old compounds became more congested.

14. American Baptist missionaries in Nigeria are affiliated with the Southern Baptist Convention, traditionally a federation of white Baptist churches in the southern states. They have made Ogbómòṣọ́ one of their principal centers of activity in western Nigeria, building both a hospital and a seminary there and sending evangelists out to many of the towns and villages along the edge of the savannah. Missionaries organized a church in Ìreé in 1907 (Ogbómòṣọ́, 2; Omílàdé, 1967).

15. The other principal landowner at Abúlékejì is the Ọ̀òni of Ifè, who preempted quite a number of disputed parcels of land (as a way of settling the disputes) during the 1950s (Berry, 1975a).

3. Accumulation, Family, and Class

1. For some contributions to the formalist-substantivist debate, see Sahlins (1972), Schneider (1974), and Dalton (1969). Some of the literature on

decision-making algorithms is reviewed in Berry (1977), and its relevance to economic anthropology is assessed in Ortiz (in press).

2. Cowen (1983) takes up the issue of fungibility in connection with the effects of commoditization on the incomes of peasants in central Kenya and on their standards of nutrition. Because of economic and biological lags in converting agricultural surplus into dairy cows, increased cash income does not always enable peasants to become self-sufficient in milk. A return to self-sufficiency in times of declining crop prices therefore means different things for those who do not own dairy cows, those who own them but are obliged to sell their milk to purchase staple foodstuffs, and those who can afford to consume their own milk. Thus, Cowen argues, when the lack of fungibility is taken into account, the polarizing effects of rural commercialization are less reversible than they might otherwise seem to be (see also Cowen, 1981).

3. A wife's seniority in her husband's compound depended on the time of her marriage rather than on her age (Fádípè, 1970; Bascom, 1942).

4. Actually, *isagi* (the payment made when land is shown to a prospective tenant) increased steadily as uncultivated land was increasingly planted to cocoa trees. *Ìṣákọ̀lẹ́* (annual tribute) was often designated in terms of a fixed quantity of cocoa, however, and therefore varied in value in accordance with fluctuations in the cocoa price (Berry, 1975a).

5. This was true of the majority of cocoa farmers in the southeastern parts of Ifẹ̀ and in much of Ilésà and Òndó (Berry, 1975a; Olúsànyà et al., 1978).

6. The Ọ̀ọ̀ni of Ifẹ̀ frequently claimed unused or disputed land for his own, on the grounds of chiefly prerogative or his responsibility to preserve peace among his subjects (Berry, 1975a). Tenants usually distinguished, in conversation, between the Ọ̀ọ̀ni's "family land" and land he had acquired in other ways during his tenure in office.

7. Amelonado cocoa, the type commonly planted in western Nigeria before the 1950s, begins to yield after seven years and requires twelve years or more to reach full bearing age. The hybrid varieties widely adopted by Yorùbá farmers from the late 1950s on begin to yield after only four years (Cocoa Research Institute of Nigeria, Annual Reports).

8. Even hired laborers, especially migrant farm workers, whose status in their employers' households and villages was based solely on the fact of their employment are often treated as juniors by their employers (Berry, 1975a).

9. One example is the Súlè family. Súlè was the first stranger to settle and plant cocoa in Abúlékejì in 1945 or 1946. When he arrived, he was accompanied by at least one of his sons; others were studying or preaching Islam near Lagos. When Súlè died, in the late 1950s, he divided his cocoa farm between the children of his two wives. Each group of full siblings not only inherited their respective portions of the father's farm jointly, but they have continued to work their farm jointly as well. In each case the eldest brother manages the farm, receives the money from the sale of the crops, and spends it on behalf of the entire household. Each group of full siblings lives under the same roof, together with their wives and children. The family continues

to devote a significant part of its resources to Muslim activities: three young men, now studying in Lagos or Ìbàdàn, are supported from the proceeds of the farm and some of the brothers living in Abúlékejì also preach in neighboring villages when they have time. By 1970, four of the five resident brothers had performed the hajj, and the eldest, Alhaji Súlèmánu, was the chief imam of the village. Around 1970 the family established a second cocoa farm south of Òndó. Some of the junior men now spend most of their time on the new farm while Alhaji Yésúfù, the eldest son of old Súlè's second wife, travels back and forth to supervise their work.

10. Thirty-four out of sixty-two farmers interviewed had acquired a second farm. The few men who practiced crafts—bricklaying, blacksmithing, goldsmithing, carving—had usually begun their careers as craftsmen and used earnings from those occupations to establish cocoa farms. They may, of course, have used cocoa earnings to expand or continue craft production at various times, but there was no clear way to identify such outlays from farmers' recollections.

11. See Clignet and Foster (1966), Foster (1965), and chapter 5 below.

12. See Epstein (1958). Yorùbás do not alternate between kin and class when it suits them to do so; they are compulsively involved in both.

4. The Disappearing Peasantry

1. The term "children" is used here in the classificatory sense common in Yorùbá parlance to refer to the descendants of a lineage or a community, rather than to the immediate offspring of a single individual.

2. See below, p. 000; Essang (1970, 1974); Beer (1976).

3. This is confirmed by J. D. Y. Peel's observations in Ìjèṣà villages in 1974 (see Peel, in press).

4. See Cowen (1981) and the discussion of fungibility in chapter 3, above.

5. The diversification of rural occupations did not represent, especially in the economic conditions of the 1970s, a process of progressive structural transformation of the rural economy, as I argue in a previous work (Berry, 1975a).

6. This discussion excludes the Hausa kola traders, who are all men but whose role in the village economy affects principally the Yorùbá women (see below, pp. 96–97).

7. Most of the nonresidents were sons and daughters of resident farmers, although the totals include a few wives. A number of farmers' children under fifteen were also attending school elsewhere.

5. Schoolteachers

1. A few government schools were established during the colonial period, either in major towns or in areas where there were no missionaries. Some of these schools, especially at the secondary level, continued to be financed by

the federal rather than regional or state governments after independence, and today they rank as some of the most prestigious secondary schools in the country. Admission from the pool of qualified applicants to these colleges is popularly reputed to depend on one's elite connections.

2. As Peel points out (personal communication), not only did teachers consider themselves well qualified for roles of leadership, but they may also have regarded the rewards of political office as more appropriate remuneration for their qualifications than the very modest salaries they received as teachers.

3. For an example of the political influence of members of a Christian denomination on school policy and administration, see chap. 7.

4. The point is not that a Yorùbá must come from the upper classes to get an education—which is clearly not true—but that he or she must be educated to enter the upper classes. The fact that we do not yet have much longitudinal evidence to show that education serves to maintain existing socioeconomic strata does not mean that the basis is not being laid for this to happen in the future (see Foster, 1976).

5. Of the fifteen individuals with nonteaching experience, seven had been clerks, three were civil servants, two had been actors, one a midwife, one a lab technician in a state college, and one an evangelist. Of the four men who could be said to have moved from being oníṣòwò to akòwé, one had been a trader, one a watch repairer, one had tried photography and, later, worked as a gas station attendant, and one learned weaving and worked for textile mills in Adó Èkìtì and Ìkẹjà.

6. The associateship in education at the University of Ifẹ̀ is a nondegree one-year course designed to enable teachers to increase their skills.

7. Group farming ventures mentioned by my informants included both inherited tree-crop farms, the proceeds of which were used to maintain the family house, and a couple of commercial food-crop farms. The latter represented investments by salaried or professional people in agricultural ventures in their home communities, a growing practice in the wake of rapidly rising food prices in western Nigeria. One of the farms mentioned by my informants had been organized by an accountant and produced cassava on land belonging to his extended family. A member of the family acted as manager, in charge of production (using hired labor) and sales. In 1978 the family purchased a mill and began to process their own cassava. Profits had been used for scholarships for children in the family and for repairs on the family house. Another commercial farming venture was a partnership between a female secondary school teacher and her brother. Acquiring a plot of land and receiving technical advice from the Young Farmers' Club in their hometown, they grew yam, maize, cassava, rice, and cowpeas. The first year (1976–77) the sister put up money to hire laborers and her brother supervised their work. Profits doubled between 1977 and 1978. My Ibo informant also said that his family operated a "communal" farm at home, both for subsistence and for the market.

8. Eight of my informants owned cars. With one exception, they were either secondary school teachers or primary school administrators (including three married women whose husbands earned substantial salaries). The

exception—a male primary school teacher in his fifties—evidently enjoyed significant other sources of income, but he was not willing to divulge much information about them.

9. For young factory workers in Lagos marriage is also a potential liability, often interfering with a man's efforts to save toward becoming self-employed. Peace (1979) describes how workers at Ìkẹjà tried to delay responding to family pressures on them to marry.

10. Among my male informants who could calculate their ages, the distribution of age at the time of first marriage was as follows:

Age	Teachers	Farmers
Under 25	10	20
25 or more	10	8

11. These transactions were gifts, not loans. No repayment was expected, although, to the extent that a wife's business prospered, her children stood to benefit. Whether this practice relieved the husband of some financial responsibility for the children or simply increased their standard of living and access to education, it was clearly in the husband's interest.

12. Of the rest, one woman had married a banker, one a trader, and one a chief.

13. I did not undertake a systematic investigation of conflict between husbands and wives over income, property, and the division of financial obligations; nor did I seek to determine how patterns and intensity of conflict changed with socioeconomic mobility. The fact that a few of the female teachers I interviewed had experimented with joint management of conjugal resources certainly does not preclude disagreement or even struggle. This would be a fruitful area for further research.

14. This tendency is even more pronounced among undergraduates at Nigerian universities (Beckett and O'Connell, 1978, p. 44).

15. The possibility that agnates may provide support for workers engaged in strikes or other forms of labor protest suggests that the further development of capitalist labor relations (e.g., within the state apparatus) will not necessarily undermine investment in descent-group relations in western Nigeria. I do not have evidence to show the extent of this practice, but it would be well worth further investigation. I am grateful to Fred Cooper for drawing my attention to the issue.

6. From Peasant to Artisan

1. During the year in which I did the field research for this study, my principal means of transport was an aging Volkswagen beetle which broke down regularly. My contacts with the mechanics in Ifẹ̀ thus began with a considerable amount of involuntary participant observation in my own mechanic's workshop. He, it turned out, came from Ìreé and we soon de-

veloped a circle of mutual acquaintances from his hometown. As his relations with the leaders of the Ifẹ̀ Mechanics' Association were good, he was able to introduce me to them and thus make it easy for me to obtain their permission to interview them. After visiting a few meetings of the association, I became a familiar figure to many of the mechanics in Ifẹ̀ and had no difficulty visiting their shops. The whole process took a good deal of time, however, so that the number of individual mechanics I was able to interview was not very large.

2. Studies of small-scale firms and entrepreneurs in Nigeria include Akérédolú-Àlé (1975), Àlùkò et al. (1972), Callaway (1973), Harris (1968, 1971), Harris and Rowe (1966), Kilby (1965, 1969), Köll (1969), Nafziger (1977), and Schatz (1977). For a survey of the literature on small enterprise in Africa, see Page (1979).

3. I use the term "informal sector" to refer broadly to all small-scale service and manufacturing enterprises, rather than following Steel's (1977) division of this category into an "intermediate sector" of small firms that "add to the value of output" (including manufacturing and vehicle repair) and an "informal sector" of essentially "unproductive" trade and service enterprises.

4. Akérédolú-Àlé (1975) complains that Nigerian entrepreneurs "selfishly" divert business profits to the support and education of their kinsmen, rather than using them to expand output and capital stock, activities that, he feels, would be more in the national interest.

5. John Peel (1978) has explored the connotations of economic and social progress in the Yorùbás' use of such terms as "civilization" and "enlightenment." In this particular quotation, "civilized" amounts to a synonym for "developed."

6. Shop floor workers earn low but steady wages, whereas journeymen have to share in the fluctuations of their masters' receipts. Hence, a journeyman's income in any given week or month is fairly uncertain.

7. Peace, 1979, chap. 4. Of 25 repair enterprises studied by Callaway (1973) in Ìbàdàn, 17 began with less than ₦200 of initial capital.

8. Such expenses consist either of the cost of borrowing to meet the payroll obligation when the firm's receipts are not sufficient to cover them, or of the forgone opportunity to use receipts for investment or other business expenses.

9. Entertaining friends establishes one's reputation for generosity and sociability—qualities that attract customers as well as friends and followers—and thus represents investment in the firm, just as does the purchase of tools (see pp. 138–139, above, and Aronson, 1978).

10. By stocking spare parts, a mechanic can often offer his customers cheaper and faster repair services. As the owner of a taxi or a truck he can reduce costs by servicing his own vehicle. See p. 158, below.

11. One of the eighteen claimed to have four wives and twenty-four children. If he is excluded, the average number of children per wife drops to 2.6, considerably less than the figures for either the rural wives or the teachers and teachers' wives discussed in previous chapters.

12. In addition to the collapse of the Àgbẹ́kòyà movement and the decline of village marketing cooperatives, organizations such as the Western State Farmers' Union had by 1978 lost what support they had had among the

immigrant farmers of Abúlékejì in the 1960s, although the WSFU was still
strong in some parts of Ifè.

13. In a conversation after the meeting, the secretary of the IMA emphasized that the chairman's anger with the unrepentant young man was symbolic
rather than personal; he was expressing in dramatic form the disapproval of
the entire association at the young man's apparent disregard for its authority.

7. Building the Oba's Palace

1. The diaries and letters of missionaries who preached in Ìreé and Ẹripa
give little information on local political events or processes; even today, missionaries with long experience in the towns seem to have been largely unaware
of the social forces at work there. One American missionary who had taken
Yorùbá lessons from S. L. Akíntọlá in the 1930s expressed bewilderment and
dismay at his subsequent political career. The only way she could account for
his later career was to accuse him of religious backsliding. He had, she
explained, abandoned his faith and resorted to fetishes and idol worship in
the days of his political ascendancy.

2. I am indebted to John Peel for illuminating comments on this point.

3. I collected information on the history of the IPU from discussions with
a number of its members and officers (past and present); from the Minutes
Book of the IPU, which covered meetings held between 1967 and 1978 and
which was kindly shown to me by the secretary, J. O. Ògúnrántí; from the
Ọ̀ṣun Divisional Reports and correspondence in the National Archives; and
from Omílàdé's (1967) history of the establishment of the church in Ìreé, of
the early obstacles it faced, and of developments since that time.

4. The men elected to represent Ìreé in the Ìféḷódùn District Council
included a teacher, a pastor, a retired customs officer, a dispenser, and a man
who had served as a medical aide during World War II.

5. My discussions of the establishment of the Ìreé-Ẹripa Provisional Authority is based almost entirely on interviews with resident and emigrant sons
of Ìreé. The fact of Omílàdé's contacts with Akíntọlá—though not my interpretation of their political connotations—is documented in Omílàdé (1967).

6. Peel suggests that this word should be rendered "ee-lights" and understood as an allusion to ọ̀làjú (enlightenment) rather than to Pareto's theory
of elites. Insofar as ọ̀làjú has become associated, in Yorùbá usage, with social
progress as well as education (Peel, 1978), however, it would appear that an
allusion to ọ̀làjú need not preclude the notion of upward mobility or even of
a dividing line between those who have achieved it and those who have not.

7. In addition to interviews with a number of townspeople and chiefs of
Ìreé, I consulted correspondence and memoranda concerning the chieftaincy
dispute in the files of the Ìféḷódùn Local Government Council Secretariat.

8. One other house briefly challenged Ilé Oyetite's claim but was apparently unable to muster much support (File on Areé, May 8, 1972).

9. The Ìreé-Ẹripa Provisional Authority continued to function, with personnel appointed by the military government, until the reconstitution of

elected local councils in 1976. Ìreé was then reintegrated into the Ìfẹ́lódùn Local Government Area, with headquarters in Ìkìrun.

10. These observations are borne out by Paul Francis's (1981) much more intensive study of land tenure and local politics in Ibokún, a small Ìjẹ̀sà town between Ilésà and Ìrágbìjí.

11. I am grateful to M. O. Àjàyí for permitting me to consult his files on the minutes and correspondence of the Ìreé Youth Movement, as well as for patiently answering my questions about the IYM.

12. As informants invariably referred to this incident with an air of secrecy, I was never able to discover how the government's announcement came about, although it seems improbable that it was not occasioned, in some manner, by the chieftaincy dispute.

13. Other parties campaigned in Ìreé also but, by the early months of 1979, local discussion of the elections focused primarily on the rivalry between the UPN and the NPN.

14. When I first visited Ìreé and Ẹripa, in December 1978, the main road from Òṣogbo to Ìkìrun was in dreadful condition. Two years before, the government of the newly constituted Ọ̀yọ́ State decided to commission a brand-new highway between these two towns rather than repair the existing trunk road which had deteriorated badly during the Nigerian civil war. A contract was given and a new road built, but the job was so badly done that the pavement began to deteriorate almost as soon as it had been laid down, and the commissioner of works was forced to condemn the road without its ever having been opened to regular traffic. In the meantime, the old road went unrepaired; by the end of 1978 the remaining shards of the original pavement created a rougher and more hazardous road surface than would have existed if it had never been paved in the first place. It took me three hours to travel the 25 km from Òṣogbo to Ìkìrun.

The appalling condition of the road did not, however, deter the area's émigrés from returning home for the Christmas holidays, especially in an election year. Driving from Ìreé to Ifẹ̀ at the beginning of a long New Year's weekend, I passed a steady stream of traffic heading for Ìkìrun and the smaller towns and villages beyond, which consisted mostly of the Peugeots and Mercedes of the nouveaux riches, coming from Lagos and Ìbàdàn. It was my first glimpse of emigrant professionals' participation in the affairs of their rural hometowns.

15. The Ẹlẹripa of Ẹripa was an illiterate Muslim farmer, socially out of place among the other distinguished guests of the day. His presence, however, served as a political reminder of the respect owed to chiefs and hence to the Areé of Ìreé.

16. Several informants pointed out, for example, that a number of women had, until recently, maintained a flourishing business growing onions on the banks of a local stream for "export" to urban markets. That local enterprise is now defunct (see *Daily Tribune*, March 30, 1979).

References

I. Books, Articles, and Theses

Abernethy, D. B. *The Political Dilemma of Popular Education in Southern Nigeria*. Stanford: Stanford University Press, 1969.

Adépòjù, R. "Migration and Socioeconomic Links between Urban Migrants and Their Home Communities." *Africa* 44, 4 (Oct. 1974).

Adépòjù, R., ed. *International Migration in Nigeria*. Ile-Ifè: Department of Demography and Social Statistics, University of Ifè, 1976.

Adewoye, O. *The Judicial System in Southern Nigeria*. Atlantic Highlands, N.J.: Humanities Press, 1977.

Adéyeyè, S. O. "The Western Nigeria Cooperative Movement, 1935–64." M.A. thesis, University of Ìbàdàn, 1967.

Agìrì, B. A. *Kola in Western Nigeria 1850–1950*. Ph.D. diss., University of Wisconsin, 1972.

Àjàyí, J. F. A., and R. Smith. *Yorùbá Warfare in the Nineteenth Century*. Cambridge: Cambridge University Press, 1964.

Akérédolú-Álé, E. O. *The Underdevelopment of Indigenous Entrepreneurship in Nigeria*. Ìbàdàn: Ìbàdàn University Press, 1975.

Akíntóyè, S. A. *Revolution and Power Politics in Yorùbáland, 1840–1893*. London: Oxford University Press, 1971.

Àlùkò, S. A., et al. *Small-scale Industries, Western State of Nigeria*. Ile-Ifè: University of Ifè Press, 1972.

Amin, S., ed. *Modern Migrations in West Africa*. London: Oxford University Press, 1974.

Aronson, D. "Ìjèbu Yorùbá Urban-Rural Relationship and Class." *Canadian Journal of African Studies* 5 (1971).

———. *The City Is Our Farm*. Cambridge, Mass.: Schenkman, 1978.

Ashby Report. *See* Nigeria, Ministry of Education, 1960.

Asiwaju, A. I. "Political Motivation and Oral Historical Traditions in Africa: The Case of Yorùbá Crowns, 1900–1960." *Africa* 46 (1976).

Askari, H., and J. Cummings. *Agricultural Supply Response: A Survey of the Econometric Evidence*. New York: Praeger, 1976.

Àtàndá, J. A. *The New Òyó Empire*. London: Longmans, 1973.

Awè, B. "The Ajélè System: A Study of Ìbàdàn Imperialism in the

Nineteenth Century." *Journal of the Historical Society of Nigeria* 3, 1 (Dec. 1964).

———. "The End of an Experiment: The Collapse of the Ìbàdàn Empire, 1877–1893." *Journal of the Historical Society of Nigeria* 3, 2 (Dec. 1965).

Àyándélé, E. A. *The Missionary Impact in Nigeria.* London: Longmans, 1966.

———. *The Educated Elite in Nigerian Society.* Ìbàdàn: University of Ìbàdàn Press, 1974.

Ayọọla Commission. *Report of the Commission of Inquiry into the Civil Disturbances Which Occurred in Certain Parts of the Western State of Nigeria in the Month of December, 1968.* Ìbàdàn: Government Printer, 1969.

Ayọ̀rínde, Chief J. A. *"Oríkì."* In S. O. Biobaku, ed., *Sources of Yorùbá History.* Oxford: Clarendon Press, 1973.

Baier, S. *An Economic History of Central Niger.* Oxford: Clarendon Press, 1980.

Banaji, J. "Kautsky's *The Agrarian Question.*" *Economy and Society* 5, 1 (1976).

Barber, K. "Oríkì in Òkukù: Relationships between Verbal and Social Structures." Ph.D. diss., University of Ifẹ̀, 1979.

———. "How Man Makes God in West Africa: Yorùbá Attitudes towards the *Òrìṣà.*" *Africa* 51, 5 (1981).

———. "Popular Reactions to the Petro-Naira." Paper presented to the annual meeting of the Canadian African Studies Association, 1982.

Barnes, S. "Social Involvement of Migrants in Lagos, Nigeria." In R. Adepoju, ed. (1976).

Bascom, W. "The Principle of Seniority in the Social Structure of the Yorùbá." *American Anthropologist* 44, 1 (1942).

———. "Social Status, Wealth and Individual Differences among the Yorùbá." *American Anthropologist* 43, 4 (1951).

Bateman, M. J. "Supply Relations for Perennial Crops in the Less-Developed Areas." In C. Wharton, ed., *Subsistence Agriculture and Economic Development.* Chicago: Aldine, 1969.

Bates, R., and M. Lofchie, eds. *Agricultural Development in Africa.* New York: Praeger, 1980.

Bauer, P. T. *West African Trade.* London: Routledge and Kegan Paul, 1963.

Beckett, P., and J. O'Connell. *Education and Power in Nigeria.* New York: Africana, 1978.

Beer, C. E. F. *The Politics of Peasant Groups in Western Nigeria.* Ìbàdàn: University of Ìbàdàn Press, 1976.

Beer, C. E. F., and G. Williams. "The Politics of the Ìbàdàn Peasantry." *African Review* 5, (1975).

Bender, D. R. "Agnatic or Cognatic? A Re-evaluation of Òndó Descent." *Man*, n.s. 5, 1 (1970).

———. "De Facto Families and de Jure Households in Òndó." *American Anthropologist* 73 (1972).

Berghe, P. L. van den. *Power and Privilege in an African University.* Cambridge, Mass.: Schenkman, 1973.

Berman, B., and J. Lonsdale. "Crises of Accumulation, Coercion and the Colonial State: The Development of the Labor Control System in Kenya, 1919–1929." *Canadian Journal of African Studies* 14, 1 (1980).

Berry, S. S. *Cocoa, Custom and Socio-Economic Change in Rural Western Nigeria.* Oxford: Clarendon Press, 1975a.

———. "Export Growth and Rural Class Formation in Western Nigeria." In R. J. Dumett and L. Brainerd, eds., *Problems of Rural Modernization.* Leiden: E. J. Brill, 1975b.

———. "Supply Response Reconsidered: The Case of Cocoa in Western Nigeria." *Journal of Development Studies* 13, 1 (Oct. 1976).

———. "Risk and the Poor Farmer." Paper prepared for Economic Sector Planning, Technical Assistance Bureau, United States Agency for International Development. Washington, D.C., 1977.

———. "Risk Aversion and Rural Class Formation in West Africa," in R. Bates and M. Lofchie, ed., *Agricultural Development in Africa.* New York: Praeger, 1980.

———. "Work, Migration and Class in Western Nigeria: A Reinterpretation." In F. Cooper, ed., *Struggle for the City.* Beverly Hills, Calif.: Sage, 1983.

Bienen, H., and V. Diejomaoh, eds. *The Political Economy of Income Distribution in Nigeria.* New York: Holmes and Meier, 1981.

Caldwell, J. C., ed. *Population Growth and Socio-economic Change in West Africa.* New York: Columbia University Press, 1978.

Callaway, A. *Nigerian Enterprise and the Employment of Youth.* Ìbàdàn: Nigerian Institute of Social and Economic Research, 1973.

Central Bank of Nigeria. *Annual Report* (1977).

———. *Economic and Financial Review.*

Clapperton, H. *Journal of a Second Expedition into the Interior of Africa.* London, 1829.

Clarke, R. J. M. *Agricultural Production in a Rural Yorùbá Community.* Ph.D. diss., University of London, 1978.

———. "Peasantization and Landholding: A Nigerian Case Study." In M. Klein, ed., *Peasants in Africa.* Beverly Hills, Calif.: Sage, 1980.

Clignet, R. P., and P. Foster. *The Fortunate Few: A Study of Secondary*

Schools and Students in the Ivory Coast. Chicago: Northwestern University Press, 1966.

Cocoa Research Institute of Nigeria. *Annual Report, 1962–1969.*

Cohen, A. "Politics of the Kola Trade." *Africa* 36, 1 (Jan. 1966).

——. *Custom and Politics in Urban Africa.* Berkeley and Los Angeles: University of California Press, 1969.

Cohen, R., and R. Sandbrook, eds. *The Development of an African Working Class.* London: Longmans, 1975.

Cole, P. *Modern and Traditional Elites in the Politics of Lagos.* Cambridge: Cambridge University Press, 1975.

Coleman, J. S. *Nigeria: Background to Nationalism.* Berkeley and Los Angeles: University of California Press, 1965.

Collier, P. "Oil and Inequality in Rural Nigeria." ILO World Employment Programme Research Working Paper, WEP 10–6/WP44. Geneva, 1981. Mimeographed.

Cooper, F. *From Slaves to Squatters.* New Haven: Yale University Press, 1979.

——. "Peasants, Capitalists and Historians." *Journal of Southern African Studies* 6 (1981*a*).

——. "Africa in the World Economy." *African Studies Review* (1981*b*).

Cowen, M. "Commodity Production in Kenya's Central Province." In J. Heyer, P. Roberts, and G. Williams, eds., *Rural Development in Tropical Africa.* New York: St. Martin's, 1981.

——. "The Commercialization of Food Production in Kenya after 1945." In R. Rotberg, ed., *Imperialism, Colonialism and Hunger: East and Central Africa.* Lexington, Mass.: D. C. Heath, 1983.

Crowder, M., and O. Ikime, eds. *West African Chiefs.* New York: Africana, 1970.

Curtin, P. D. *Economic Change in Precolonial Africa.* Madison: University of Wisconsin Press, 1975.

Dalton, G. "Theoretical Issues in Economic Anthropology." *Current Anthropology* 10 (1969).

De Janvry, A. *The Agrarian Question and Reformism in Latin America.* Baltimore: Johns Hopkins University Press, 1982.

De Wilde, J. "Price Incentives and African Agricultural Development." In R. Bates and M. Lofchie, eds., *Agricultural Development in Africa.* New York: Praeger, 1980.

Dunn, J., ed. *West African States: Failure and Promise.* Cambridge: Cambridge University Press, 1978.

Eades, J. S. "The Growth of a Migrant Community: The Yorùbá in Northern Ghana." In J. Goody, ed., *Changing Social Structures in Ghana.* London: International African Institute, 1975.

————. "Kinship and Entrepreneurship among Yorùbá in Northern Ghana." In W. Shack and E. P. Skinner, eds., *Strangers in Africa.* Berkeley, Los Angeles, London: University of California Press, 1979.

————. *The Yorùbá Today.* Cambridge: Cambridge University Press, 1980.

Ẹkúndáre, R. O. *An Economic History of Nigeria, 1860–1960.* New York: Africana, 1973.

Elias, T. O. *Nigerian Land Law and Custom.* London: Routledge and Kegan Paul, 1953.

Epstein, A. L. *Politics in an Urban African Community.* Manchester: Manchester University Press, 1958.

Essang, S. M. *The Distribution of Earnings in the Cocoa Economy of Western Nigeria.* Ph.D. diss., Michigan State University, 1970.

————. "Investment Patterns of Licensed Buying Agents in Nigeria." *Nigerian Journal of Economic and Social Studies* 16, 3 (Nov. 1974).

Essang, S. M., and A. Mabawonku. "Determinants and Impact of Rural-Urban Migration: A Case Study of Selected Communities in Western Nigeria." African Rural Employment Paper no. 10. East Lansing, Mich.: Department of Agricultural Economics, Michigan State University, 1974.

Ezera, K. *Constitutional Development of Nigeria.* Cambridge: Cambridge University Press, 1964.

Fádípẹ̀, N. A. *The Sociology of the Yorùbá.* Ed. F. O. Okediji and O. O. Okediji. Ìbàdàn: Ìbàdàn University Press, 1970.

Fájánà, A. "The Nigeria Union of Teachers: A Decade of Growth, 1931–1940." *West African Journal of Education* 17, 3 (Oct. 1973).

Farmer, B. H., ed. *Green Revolution? Technology and Change in Rice-Growing Areas of Tamil Nadu and Sri Lanka.* Boulder, Colo.: Westview Press, 1977.

Forde, C. D., and R. Scott. *The Native Economies of Nigeria.* Vol. I of M. Perham, ed., *The Economics of a Tropical Dependency.* London: Faber and Faber, 1946.

Foster, P. *Education and Social Change in Ghana.* Chicago: University of Chicago Press, 1965.

————. "Education and Social Differentiation in Africa: What We Think We Know and What We Ought to Know." Paper prepared for a Social Science Research Council conference on inequality in Africa, 1976.

Foster-Carter, A. "The Modes of Production Controversy." *New Left Review* 107 (1978).

Francis, P. "Power and Order: A Study of Litigation in a Yorùbá

Community." Ph.D. diss., University of Liverpool, 1981.

Freund, B. *Capital and Labour in the Nigerian Tin Mines.* Atlantic Highlands, N. J.: Humanities Press, 1981.

Galletti, R., K. D. S. Baldwin, and I. O. Dina. *Nigerian Cocoa Farmers.* London: Oxford University Press, 1956.

Gbàdàmọ́sí, T. G. O. *The Growth of Islam among the Yorùbá, 1841—1908.* London: Longmans, 1978.

Great Britain. Colonial Office. "Correspondence Concerning Palm Oil Grants in West Africa." Confidential Print, African no. 1023. London: HMSO, 1914.

Green, R. H., and S. Hymer. "Cocoa in the Gold Coast: A Study of the Relations between African Farmers and Agricultural Experts." *Journal of Economic History* 26, 3 (Sept. 1966).

Gutkind, P. C. W. "From the Anger of Despair to the Energy of Despair: Social Organization of the Unemployed in Two African Cities." *Civilisations* 17, 3 and 4 (1967).

Guyer, J. "The Organizational Plan of Traditional Farming: Idèrè, Western Nigeria." Ph.D. diss., University of Rochester, 1972.

Hancock, W. K. *A Survey of Commonwealth Affairs.* Vol. II, Part 2. London: Oxford University Press, 1942.

Hargreaves, J. D. *The End of Colonial Rule in West Africa.* London: Macmillan, 1979.

Harris, J. R. "Nigerian Enterprise in the Printing Industry." *Nigerian Journal of Economic and Social Studies* 10, 2 (July 1968).

————. In P. Kilby, ed., *Entrepreneurship and Economic Development.* New York: Free Press, 1971.

Harris, J. R., and M. P. Rowe. "Entrepreneurial Patterns in the Nigerian Sawmilling Industry." *Nigerian Journal of Economic and Social Studies* 8, 1 (March 1966).

Hawkins, E. K. *Road Transport in Nigeria.* London: Oxford University Press, 1958.

Helleiner, G. K. "The Fiscal Role of the Marketing Boards in Nigerian Economic Development, 1947—1961." *Economic Journal* 74, 295 (Sept. 1964).

————. *Peasant Agriculture, Government and Economic Growth in Nigeria.* Homewood, Ill.: R. D. Irwin, 1966.

————. "Small-Holder Decision-Making in Tropical Africa." In L. G. Reynolds, ed., *Agriculture and Development Theory.* New Haven: Yale University Press, 1975.

Heyer, J., et al. *Agricultural Development in Kenya.* Nairobi: Oxford University Press, 1976.

Heyer, J., P. Roberts, and G. Williams, eds. *Rural Development in Tropical Africa.* New York: St. Martin's Press, 1981.

Hill, P. *Migrant Cocoa Farmers of Southern Ghana.* Cambridge: Cambridge University Press, 1963.

Hirschman, A. O. *The Strategy of Economic Development.* New Haven: Yale University Press, 1958.

Hogendorn, J. S. "Economic Initiative and African Cash Farming: Pre-colonial Origins and Early Colonial Developments." In P. Duignan and L. H. Gann, eds. (1975).

Hopkins, A. C. "The Lagos Strike of 1897." *Past and Present* 35 (1966*a*).

————. "Economic Aspects of Political Movements in Nigeria and the Gold Coast, 1918–1939." *Journal of African History* 7 (1966*b*).

————. *An Economic History of West Africa.* London: Longmans, 1973.

Hündsalz, M. "Die wanderung der Yorùbá nach Ghana and ihre Ruckkehr nach Nigeria." *Erdkunde* 26 (1972).

Imoagene, O. *Social Mobility in Emergent Society: A Study of the New Elite in Western Nigeria.* Changing African Family Project Series no. 2. Canberra: Australian National University Press, 1976.

International Labor Organization. *Employment, Incomes and Equality in Kenya.* Geneva: ILO, 1972.

Johnson, S. O. *History of the Yorùbás.* Lagos: Church Missionary Society, 1921.

Joseph, R. "Affluence and Underdevelopment: The Nigerian Experience." *Journal of Modern African Studies* 16, 2 (1978).

Kilby, P. *African Enterprise: The Nigerian Bread Industry.* Stanford: Hoover Institute, 1965.

————. *Industrialization in an Open Economy: Nigeria, 1946–66.* Cambridge: Cambridge University Press, 1969.

————. "Industrial Relations and Wage Determination: Failure of the Anglo-Saxon Model." *Journal of Developing Areas* 1, 4 (July 1967); "Reply to John Weeks," ibid. 3, 1 (Oct. 1968); "Further Comment," ibid. 5, 2 (Jan. 1971).

Kirk-Greene, A., and D. Rimmer. *Nigeria since 1970: A Political and Economic Outline.* London: Hodder and Stoughton, 1981.

Kitching, G. *Class and Economic Change in Kenya.* New Haven: Yale University Press, 1980.

Klein, M., ed. *Peasants in Africa.* Beverly Hills, Calif.: Sage, 1980.

Köll, M. *Crafts and Cooperation in Western Nigeria.* Freiburg: Bertelsman Universitätsverl, 1969.

Law, R. C. C. *The Òyó Empire, c. 1600-c. 1836: A West African Imperialism in the Era of the Atlantic Slave Trade.* Oxford: Clarendon Press, 1977.

Leighton, N. S. "The Political Economy of a Stranger Population." In William A. Shack and Elliott P. Skinner, eds. *Strangers in African Society.* Berkeley, Los Angeles, London: University of California Press, 1979.

Lenin, V. I. *The Development of Capitalism in Russia: Vol. III of Collected Works*. Moscow: Progress Publishers, 1960.

Liedholm, C., and E. Chuta. "The Economics of Rural and Urban Small-Scale Industries in Sierra Leone." African Rural Economy Paper no. 14. East Lansing: Michigan State University, 1976.

Lipton, M. "The 'Optimising Peasant.' " *Journal of Development Studies* 4 (1968).

Lloyd, P. C. "The Traditional Political System of the Yorùbá." *Southwestern Journal of Anthropology* 10, 4 (1954).

————. *Yorùbá Land Law*. London: Oxford University Press, 1962.

————. *The Political Development of the Yorùbá Kingdoms in the 18th and 19th Centuries*. London: Royal Anthropological Institute, 1971.

————. *Power and Independence: Urban Africans' Perception of Social Inequality*. London: Routledge and Kegan Paul, 1974.

Lloyd, P. C., A. L. Mábògùnjẹ́, and B. Awẹ́, eds. *The City of Ìbàdàn*. Cambridge: Cambridge University Press, 1967.

Lofchie, M., ed. *The State of the Nations*. Berkeley, Los Angeles, London: University of California Press, 1971.

Lonsdale, J. and B. Berman. "Coping with the Contradictions: The Development of the Colonial State in Kenya, 1895–1914." *Journal of African History* 20 (1979).

Lovejoy, P. *Caravans of Kola*. Zaria: Ahmadu Bello University Press, 1980.

Mábògùnjẹ́, A. L. *Regional Mobility and Resource Development in West Africa*. Montreal: Center for Developing Area Studies, McGill University, 1972.

Mábògùnjẹ́, A. L., and J. D. Omer Cooper. *Òwu in Yorùbá History*. Ìbàdàn: Ìbàdàn University Press, 1971.

Mackintosh, J. *Nigerian Government and Politics*. (London: Allen and Unwin, 1966).

McPhee, A. *The Economic Revolution in British West Africa*. London: George Routledge, 1926.

Margolis, A. M. *Nigeria: A Study of the Educational System of Nigeria and a Guide to the Academic Placement of Students in Educational Institutions of the United States*. American Association of Collegiate Registrars and Admissions Officers, 1977.

Marris, P. and A. Somerset. *African Businessmen: A Study of Entrepreneurship and Development in Kenya*. London, 1971.

Meillassoux, C. "From Reproduction to Production." *Economy and Society* 1, 1 (1972).

Melson, R., and H. Wolpe. *Nigeria: Modernization and the Politics of Communalism*. East Lansing: Michigan State University Press, 1971.

Morton-Williams, P. "The Ọyọ́ Yorùbá and the Atlantic Slave Trade."

Journal of the Historical Society of Nigeria 3, 1 (1964).

Nafziger, W. *African Capitalism: A Case Study in Nigerian Entrepreneurship.* Stanford: Hoover Institute, 1977.

Nigeria. Ministry of Education. *Statistics of Education.*

————. *Investment in Education: Report of the Commission on Post-School Certificate and Higher Education in Nigeria.* Lagos, 1960. Cited herein as Ashby Report.

————. Ministry of Economic Development and Planning. *Third Development Plan, 1975–1980.*

Nigeria. Ministry of Information. *Report of the Coker Commission of Inquiry into the Affairs of Certain Statutory Corporations in Western Nigeria, 1962.* Lagos. Cited herein as Coker Commission.

Nigerian Baptist Convention. *Annual Report.* 1976.

Ọdẹtọlá, T. O. *Military Politics in Nigeria.* New Brunswick, N. J.: Transaction Books, 1978.

Ofonagoro, W. I. *Trade and Imperialism in Southern Nigeria, 1881–1929.* New York: Nok, 1979.

Okonjo, I. M. *British Administration in Nigeria, 1900–1950: A Nigerian View.* New York: Nok, 1974.

Ọlátúnbọsún, D. *Nigeria's Neglected Rural Majority.* Ìbàdàn: Oxford University Press, 1975.

Olúsànyà, P. O. *Socio-Economic Aspects of Rural-Urban Migration in Western Nigeria.* Ìbàdàn: Nigerian Institute of Social and Economic Research, 1969.

Olúsànyà, P. O., S. A. Agboọla, and C. O. Ilori. *Migrant Farmers of the Eastern Cocoa Zone of Southwestern Nigeria: A Study in Forest-Savannah Relationships.* Ile-Ifẹ̀: Department of Demography, University of Ifẹ̀, 1978.

Omíládé, E. A. *Ìtàn bí Ìgbàgbọ́ ti Ṣe Wo Ilè Ìreé Pèlú Àwọn Ìsòro ti o Dojúkò o Àti Àwọn Ìdáṣílè Láàrin Àsìkò Ná.* Ìreé: Adewumi Press, 1967.

Oni, O. "An Econometric Analysis of the Provincial and Aggregate Supply Response among Western Nigerian Cocoa Farmers." Ph.D. diss., University of Ìbàdàn, 1971.

Onitiri, H. M. A., and D. Ọlátúnbọsún, eds. *The Marketing Board System in Nigeria.* Ìbàdàn: Nigerian Institute of Social and Economic Research, 1974.

Ortiz, S. "What Is Decision Analysis About: The Problem of Formal Representation." In S. Ortiz, ed., *Economic Anthropology: Topics and Theories.* New York: Academic Press. In press.

Ọṣọ̀bà, S. O. "The Nigerian Power Elite, 1952–1965." In P. C. W. Gutkind and P. Waterman, eds. *African Social Studies: A Radical Reader.* London: Heineman, 1977.

Ọṣuntogun, A. "Some Causes and Implications for Socio-Economic

Development of Cityward Migration of Rural Youths: A Western Nigeria Case Study." In R. Adepoju, ed. (1976).

Oyèdiran, O. "Local Influence and Traditional Leadership: The Politics of the Ifè Forest Reserve." *Odù*, n.s. 7 (1972).

————. "The Position of the Ọ̀ọni in the Changing Political System of Ile-Ifè." *Journal of the Historical Society of Nigeria* 6, 4 (1973).

————. "Modákẹ́kẹ́ in Ifè." *Odù*, n.s. 10 (1974).

Oyèdiran, O., ed. *Nigerian Government and Politics under Military Rule.* New York: St. Martin's, 1979.

Oyèmákindé, O. "A History of Indigenous Labour on the Nigerian Railway, 1895–1945." Ph.D. diss., University of Ibadan, 1970.

Ọ̀yọ́ State of Nigeria. *Current Education Statistics.*

Oyovbaire, S. E. "The Politics of Revenue Allocation." In K. Panter-Brick, ed. *Soldiers and Oil.* London: Frank Cass, 1978.

Page, J. "Small Enterprise in African Development: A Survey." World Bank Staff Working Paper no. 363. October 1979.

Panter-Brick, K., ed. *Soldiers and Oil: The Political Transformation of Nigeria.* London: Frank Cass, 1978.

Parkin, D. *Palms, Wine and Witnesses.* San Francisco: Chandler, 1972.

Peace, A. *Choice, Class and Conflict: A Study of Southern Nigerian Factory Workers.* Atlantic Highlands, N. J.: Humanities Press, 1979.

Peel, J. D. Y. "Ọ̀làjú: A Yorùbá Concept of Development." *Journal of Development Studies* 14, 2 (Jan. 1978).

————. "Inequality and Action: The Forms of Ìjẹ̀sà Social Conflict." *Canadian Journal of African Studies* (1980).

————. "Sociology and the Historiography of the Yorùbá." *Journal of the Historical Society of Nigeria.* Forthcoming.

————. *Ijeshas and Nigerians.* Cambridge: Cambridge University Press. In press.

Perham, M. *The Native Administrations of Nigeria.* London: Oxford University Press, 1937.

Peters, P. "Cattlemen, Borehole Syndicates and Privatisation in the Kgatleng District of Botswana." Ph.D. diss., Boston University, 1983.

Plotnicov, L. *Strangers to the City.* Pittsburgh: University of Pittsburgh Press, 1967.

Post, K. W. J. *The Nigerian Federal Elections of 1959.* London: Oxford University Press, 1963.

————. " 'Peasantisation' and Rural Political Movements in West Africa." *Archives européennes de sociologie* 13 (1973).

Post, K. W. J., and G. D. Jenkins. *The Price of Liberty.* Cambridge: Cambridge University Press, 1973.

Post, K. W. J., and M. Vickers. *Structure and Conflict in Nigeria 1960–65*. London: Heinemann, 1973.

Rey, P. P. *Les alliances de classes*. Paris: Maspero, 1973.

———. "Class Contradictions in Lineage Societies." *Critique of Anthropology* 13/14 (1979).

Roberts, P. "The Village Schoolteacher in Ghana." In J. Goody, ed. *Changing Social Structure in Ghana*. London: International African Institute, 1975.

Robinson, J. *Essays on Marxian Economics*. 2d ed. New York: St. Martin's Press, 1966.

Roider, W. *Nigerian Farm Settlement Schemes*. Berlin: Institüt für Ausländische Landwirtschaft an der technischen Universität Berlin, 1968.

Roy, P. "Transition in Agriculture: Empirical Indicators and Results." *Journal of Peasant Studies* (1981).

Sahlins, M. *Stone Age Economics*. Chicago: Aldine, 1972.

Sàndà, A. O. *The Dynamics of Ethnicity among the Yorùbá*. Ph.D. diss., University of California, Los Angeles, 1974.

Schatz, S. P. *Nigerian Capitalism*. Berkeley, Los Angeles, London: University of California Press, 1977.

Schneider, H. D. *Economic Man: The Anthropology of Economics*. New York: Free Press, 1974.

Schwab, W. B. "The Political and Social Organization of an Urban African Community." Ph.D. diss., University of Pennsylvania, 1952.

———. "Kinship and Lineage among the Yorùbá." *Africa* 25, 4 (1955).

Sklar, R. *Nigerian Political Parties*. Princeton: Princeton University Press, 1962.

Smyke, R. J. "A History of the Nigerian Union of Teachers." *West African Journal of Education* 16, 3 (Oct. 1972).

Steel, W. F. *Urban Unemployment and Small-Scale Enterprise in Developing Countries: Evidence from Ghana*. New York: Praeger, 1977.

Sudarkasa, N. *Where Women Work: A Study of Yorùbá Women in the Marketplace and in the Home*. Ann Arbor: Museum of Anthropology, University of Michigan, 1973.

———. "From Stranger to Alien: Socio-Political History of the Nigerian Yorùbá in Ghana." In William A. Shack and Elliott P. Skinner, eds. *Strangers in African Society*. Berkeley, Los Angeles, London: University of California Press, 1979.

Taiwo, D. *Ìtàn Ìlú Ìreé*. N.d.

Teríba, O. "Nigerian Revenue Allocation Experience, 1952–1965." *Nigerian Journal of Economic and Social Studies* 8, 3 (Nov. 1966).

Teríba, O., et al. "Some Aspects of Ownership and Control Structure of Business Enterprise in a Developing Economy: The Nigerian

Case." *Nigerian Journal of Economic and Social Studies* 14, 1 (March 1972).

Turner, T. "Commercial Capitalism and the 1975 Coup." In K. Panter-Brick, ed. *Soldiers and Oil.* London: Frank Cass, 1978.

Van den Driesen, I. H. "Patterns of Land Holding and Land Distribution in the Ifẹ̀ Division of Western Nigeria." *Africa* 41, 1 (Jan. 1971). 1971).

———. "Some Observations on the Family Unit, Religion and the Practice of Polygyny in the Ifẹ̀ Division of Western Nigeria." *Africa* 42, 1 (Jan. 1972).

Weeks, J. F. "A Comment on Peter Kilby." *Journal of Developing Areas* 3, 1 (Oct. 1968); "Further Comment," ibid. 5, 2 (Jan. 1971).

Wells, J. C. *Agricultural Policy and Economic Growth in Nigeria, 1962–1968.* Ìbàdàn: Oxford University Press, 1974.

Western State of Nigeria. *Current Education Statistics.*

———. *Report of the Committee on the Review of the Primary Education System in the Western State of Nigeria.* Ìbàdàn: Government Printer, 1968.

———. *Western State Chieftaincy Declarations.* Ìbàdàn: Government Printer, n.d.

Williams, G., ed. *Nigeria: Economy and Society.* London: Rex Collings, 1976.

———. "Taking the Part of Peasants: Rural Development in Nigeria and Tanzania." In P. C. W. Gutkind and I. Wallerstein, eds., *Political Economy of Contemporary Africa.* Vol. I. Beverly Hills, Calif.: Sage, 1976.

———. "Inequalities in Rural Nigeria." University of East Anglia, Development Studies Occasional Paper no. 16. November 1981.

Williams, G., and T. Turner. "Nigeria." In J. Dunn, ed., *West African States.* Cambridge: Cambridge University Press, 1978.

Wolpe, H. ed. *Articulation of Modes of Production.* London: Routledge and Kegan Paul, 1980.

II. Newspapers

Daily Sketch
West Africa

III. Archives

Ìfẹ́lódùn Local Government Secretariat. File on the Areé of Ìreé.
Ìreé Progressive Union. Minutes Book, 1967–1978.
Ìreé Youth Movement. Papers.
Nigerian National Archives, Ìbàdàn
    Ìlorin Province. Annual Report. 1933.
    "Ìré Progressive Union." Òshun Div. 1/1/804.
    "The Aré of Ìré." Òshun Div. 1/1/1331.
    Òshun Division. Annual Report, 1941.
Òbíṣèsan, J. O. Diary. University of Ìbàdàn Library.
Ogbómọ̀ṣọ́ Baptist Theological Seminary Archives
    1. O. G. Adetunji. "The History of Oke-'sa Baptist Church, Ìreé."
       Paper presented to Dr. O. T. High, 7 May 1975.
    2. G. Green. "Travels and Reports." Typescript.
    3. O. T. High. *Notes on the Expansion of Baptist Work in Nigeria.*
       London: Caxton Press, 1970.

Index